Social theory, social policy and ageing

A critical introduction

Social theory, social policy and ageing

A critical introduction

Carroll L. Estes, Simon Biggs and Chris Phillipson

Open University Press

Open University Press
McGraw-Hill Education
McGraw-Hill House
Shoppenhangers Road
Maidenhead
Berkshire
England
SL6 2QL

email: enquiries@openup.co.uk
world wide web: www.openup.co.uk

First published 2003

Copyright © Carroll Estes, Simon Biggs and Chris Phillipson 2003

A catalogue record of this book is available from the British Library

ISBN 0 335 20906 8 (pb)   0 335 20907 6 (hb)

Library of Congress Cataloging-in-Publication Data
CIP data has been applied for

Typeset by RefineCatch Limited, Bungay, Suffolk
Printed in the UK by Bell & Bain Ltd, Glasgow

Contents

Acknowledgements

Carroll Estes expresses appreciation to Sarah Collins, Tracy Weitz and Mauro Hernandez for bibliographic assistance. She is also grateful to her daughter, Duskie Lynn Estes, and grand-daughters Brydie and Mackenzie, for their love and support throughout the process of writing this volume. She is grateful as well for the assistance of Jean Miles in all things big and small, without whom this project would not have been completed.

Simon Biggs would like to thank Irja Haapala as well as his children Eve and Guy for their encouragement and support.

Chris Phillipson thanks Jane, Isabel and Luke for their immense help over the years.

All three authors would like to record thanks to Sue Humphries for her work in preparing the final draft of the manuscript.

1 An introduction to social theory, social policy and ageing

Approaching age, theory and policy

In this book we attempt to cover the main issues facing the study of ageing in the first decades of the twenty-first century. As such, it should provide the reader with an overview of issues and challenges presented by demographic change for social theory, social policy and the social sciences. We present this challenge from an unashamedly critical perspective.

James Birren (Birren and Bengston 1988) makes the point that the study of ageing, or gerontology as it is called, is 'data rich and theory poor'. What he means by this is that while a significant amount of data has been generated over the years (notably around issues such as health and social needs in old age) this has not been paralleled by an equivalent understanding of the meaning and place of ageing within the structure of contemporary society. One of the influential remedies suggested for gerontology has been presented by Robert Butler (in Moody 1993) in terms of 'a union of science and advocacy'. In other words, progress in the expansion of a knowledge base, largely consisting of physical ageing and its bio-technical remedies, accompanied by a political desire to promote the interests of older adults and combat ageism, will prove to be the best way forward for gerontology and for older people themselves. Butler's proposal draws attention to an important feature of the study of ageing, namely, its multidisciplinary and applied character. In consequence, the relationship between theory and policy has been especially close and can be seen in the different strands within sociology, economics, anthropology, psychology and other disciplines.

Policy and theory are both interpretive. Both go beyond data and 'common-sense' definitions, to formulate answers to the 'why' as well as the 'what' of contemporary ageing. They are affected by and exert an influence upon the politics of ageing and in so doing encounter powerful interests. Both can be seen as attempts to shape perspectives on ageing, drawing attention to certain aspects and ignoring or suppressing others. Policy and theory are not, in this respect, value-neutral.

Recent years have seen a growth of interest in ageing, increased research opportunities and the development of ageing studies as part of the mainstream disciplines within the social sciences. Allied to this has been the expansion of professional activities and concerns around the needs of an ageing population. This increase in concern and attention has not, however, been entirely benign. Different professional groups and interests (or what has been termed the 'ageing enterprise') (Estes 1979a) are able to define questions about growing old to their own advantage. This development itself raises difficult issues for the study of ageing. On the one hand, gerontology has undoubtedly benefited from the resurgence of funding and the need for policy-relevant studies. On the other, it also appears still trapped within a discourse subordinate to biomedical and related concerns.

It is precisely this conflict that has provided the inspiration for writing this book. Over the period of the 1980s and 1990s, critical gerontology emerged as a key intervention challenging traditional theories and perspectives within the study of ageing. Critical gerontology was a response to three major concerns arising from research into old age over this period. First, the need for a clearer understanding of what various researchers identified as the 'social construction of dependency' in old age. This was seen to have resulted from the development of services associated with the welfare state, from the continued financial impoverishment of a large section of the elderly population, and from the systematic stereotyping of older people (or 'ageism' as coined by Robert Butler (1975) in the late 1960s). Second was the critique of the biomedical model, a view that associated growing old with physical and mental deterioration and disease. Third was the individualistic focus of traditional gerontology, and the lack of attention to social structure and economic relationships.

Twenty years on from its initial development, critical gerontology has become a dominant force within social gerontology, with some of its key theoretical and policy contributions brought together in volumes such as those by Estes (1979a), Phillipson (1998), Biggs (1999a), Minkler and Estes (1999), Estes and Associates (2001) and Biggs *et al.* (2003). However, it is also clear that critical perspectives now face a different set of challenges as compared with the late 1970s and 1980s. Critical gerontology has itself broadened out to include the humanities as well as social science-based disciplines. Feminism and perspectives on gender have begun to exert greater influence in studies of ageing (Arber and Ginn 1991; Bernard and Meade 1993; Holstein 1999). Globalization, a process which has had profound influence on mainstream sociology (Beck 2000a), is also being recognized as a factor transforming the lives of older people in the developed world as much as in third world countries.

The above elements have helped to transform critical gerontology and have provided the justification for writing this book. Essentially, our aim is to provide the reader with an introduction to key debates within critical gerontology, covering areas such as social theory and ageing, identity and subjectivity in old age, feminist perspectives, productive ageing, globalization, and the new politics of ageing. In essence our objective is to give the reader an overview of some of the key concerns of what has become an influential area within the study of later life.

Adopting a critical perspective

At various points in this book we refer to the need for 'critical' perspectives on ageing. What do we mean by this term? Essentially, our argument is that a critical approach to theory and policy is one that goes beyond everyday appearances and the unreflective acceptance of established positions. It examines the structural inequalities that shape the everyday experience of growing old. Critical gerontology asks why a particular analogy or metaphor is used to explain adult ageing and how the assumptions contained within theory and policy influence our understanding of the position of older people in society. It further examines areas such as the biomedical and economic forces driving globalization and the peculiarly capitalist vision of productive ageing. It seeks to analyse how and why gender, race, class and other inequalities are so often ignored and places questions about meaning and fulfilment in later life age back on the agenda in the search for solidarity between social groups.

As such a critical gerontology requires a fusion of the study of structural inequalities in society and the personal experience of ageing, because both are essential for social action and progressive change. Closely related to this is a commitment to the voice and interests of older people in alliance with recognition that elders, like any other group, are fractured by competing interests based on class, gender and race. This does not, however, imply an uncritical acceptance of whatever 'older people' might say, rather it suggests that questions have to be asked about whose voice is being heard, in whose interests and to what end. A critical approach, then, sees 'common sense' about age as a starting point, not as an answer in itself. The origin and influences of everyday attitudes and the energy put by powerful interests into maintaining a particular world view of age are its raw material. It is guided by the importance of recognizing and valuing differences between groups of people who are ageing; the possibilities for solidarity based on age, between generations and with social groups with shared interests; and in building dissent and progressive alternatives to established expectations.

Social policy is often portrayed as simply responding to issues and problems, although they are in fact socially constructed. Importantly it allows the release of resources and gives permission for professional intervention. It also has a symbolic function in the creation of social spaces that encourage certain forms of behaviour and sanction others. Contemporary policy on ageing evidences a change of emphasis, from responses to isolated problems such as hypothermia, abuse, self-neglect and social support, to attempts to proscribe what it is to age well and responsibly. In other words social policy defines the parameters of legitimate ageing. There is also a tendency to fit older people into policies designed to solve other problems, just as theories are imported from other parts of the life course or generically assume a standard adult, usually in the first half of life, male and white and western in culture.

These solutions to the 'problem of ageing' are seductive to gerontology, because they seem to promise answers to age prejudice and marginalization. Biomedical 'solutions' address our fears about mental and physical incapacity. Productive ageing provides a response to wider economic concerns about an ageing population. Both generate funding for services and research. They also encourage certain forms of the politics of ageing (bureaucratic and institutional), a focus on age as a question of health and welfare, and a particular interpretation of the effects of globalization (in the uncritical extension of capital and corporate values). A critical analysis of ageing sees these phenomena as indicating particular sites of struggle in which definitions of ageing are to be contested and where possible alternatives can be developed.

The structure of the book

We have attempted in this book to identify key areas for the contemporary study of ageing and the links between them. Where areas are chronically underdeveloped – such as would appear to be the case on issues of race and age – we have attempted to weave them into existing topics addressed by policy and theory. All distinctions are to some extent arbitrary and every issue interlaces with others, so there will inevitably be overlaps and scope for further elaboration. Some of these are identified below as 'linking issues'. In the end we came down on the following topics, each of which has a chapter dedicated to it: an overview of theories of ageing, identity and age; feminist approaches; questions of successful and productive ageing; biomedicine and bioethics; the effects of globalization on later life; and the prospect of a politics of ageing.

Chapter 2 examines the development of social theory and its relationship to the study of adult ageing. Key theories are outlined and placed in their socio-historical context. We develop a critique of theories that reproduce or legitimize functionalist definitions of age and attempt an initial integration of political economy, cultural and humanistic approaches. Particular attention has been given to historical attempts to define old age through activity, disengagement and life course models. In many ways this chapter forms a point of reference for the specific debates that are covered in the rest of the book. Links with other chapters include identifying the need for a combination of structural and personal approaches to adult ageing and the relative absence of critiques based on inequalities, class, gender and race within mainstream gerontology.

Chapter 3 looks at changing perspectives on the relationship between identity and adult ageing. Identity is seen as having both social and personal characteristics. With respect to ageing, stability of identity can act as a source of restriction but also a grounding for social action. That the roles and expectations available to older adults are becoming more flexible, is examined as a source of choice and of fragmented identities. Special attention has been paid to the relationship between bodily and social aspects of ageing. The reader is encouraged to see age identity as negotiated and managed. Links with other chapters include an awareness of inequalities as determinants of lifestyle choice and life chances, the power of active, successful and productive ageing as attempts to shape age identity, and biomedicine and ethics as regulators of intergenerational and professional relations.

Chapter 4 addresses the development of a feminist approach to adult ageing and some implications for social policy. Key points include a critical analysis of the gendered state and the reproduction of patriarchal systems within it. A feminist political economy is suggested in order to critique contemporary social policy. Particular reference is made to the effects of neo-conservative moral 'economies' that attempt to define the relationship between social responsibility and age. Attention has also been paid to the politics of care and affirmation, and the development of different streams within feminist politics and social theory. These are seen to be crucial to the production of social movements, resistance and alternative visions of ageing. Linking issues include the structured relationship between body, social stereotyping and personal experience; biomedicine, globalization and the reproduction of structural inequality; and sex-gender systems, as influences on new social movements and political activity.

Chapter 5 examines attempts to define productive and successful ageing. It also looks at the way older people are increasingly encouraged to adopt strategies of self-surveillance, as an alternative to the external control of an ageing population. Key points include an analysis of active, successful and productive models of ageing as attempts to shape personal and social experience. It is suggested that each has been used institutionally and in terms of policy to define adult ageing and that in the case of productive ageing a state of hegemony is close to existing. Here, economic concern about the effects of an ageing population is intimately related to the construction of models of 'ageing well'. This chapter emphasizes the close relationship between theory, policy and experience. Linking issues include the legitimation of particular age identities, the extension of western definitions of productive ageing to other societies and the possibilities for resistance to economic definitions of age value.

Chapter 6 critically assesses the role of biomedicine and ethics in the social construction of ageing. Key points include the role of anti-ageism, political economy and experience in launching a challenge to biomedical definitions of later life. Biomedicine is examined as a hegemonic force that is often powerful enough to ignore other perspectives on ageing. It is, however, subject to commercial drivers of biomedical advance that are brought into conflict with the health needs of older people. Bioethics is examined as a means of regulating professional relationships with older people that more often than not makes the relationship between health, age and social inequality increasingly obscure. Linking issues include biomedicine as an influence on institutional and theoretical models of ageing; the reproduction of gender inequality through biomedical policy; and the impact of globalization and corporate power on responses to health and illness in later life. Political resistance to biomedical definitions of personal identity and public policy are a final link with other chapters.

Chapter 7 looks at the effects of globalization on adult ageing. This chapter begins by arguing that global challenges to the nation state hold profound implications for policy on ageing both locally and transnationally. The role of intergovernmental organizations is critically examined, given their role in shaping a new order for later life. These developments are seen to change the quality of life of older people living within the structures of existing institutions in the developed world and in terms of transnational ageing, migration and ageing in developing countries. Particular consideration is given to the implications for caring across borders, global care chains and political responses to old age. Linking issues include a movement from local to global theoretical approaches to old age; multiplicity, diversity and stability as factors in age identity; global challenges to social patriarchy and state masculinism; and the effects of cultural imperialism in defining a good old age.

Chapter 8 explores the development of a politics of ageing. Among the key issues addressed is an examination of the possibilities and limitations of old age activism. The chapter begins by critically assessing the role of the state and bureaucratic responses to ageing as it impinges on traditional political institutions. This is then contrasted with social movements and questions of diversity in old age, including the impact of arguments asserting civil rights in old age and the notion of citizenship. Examples are drawn primarily from the USA and Europe, with consideration given to the different avenues open to age politics depending upon local traditions and institutions. Linking issues include changing age identities; self-determination and social development through political action; the gendered state and age/gender issues for social movements; the relationship between policy making, political power, corporate power and global economic pressure; and the possibilities for resistance that are emerging through older activism and intergenerational alliances.

Chapter 9 summarizes the various arguments and identifies some major tasks for a critical gerontology to undertake, identifying in the process new challenges and issues for critical perspectives to address.

Each of the authors has worked previously, with differences in emphasis and style, on the question of how to develop a critical perspective on adult ageing that questions comfortable assumptions and powerful interests. We hope that this book challenges established ideas about old age and goes some way to provoke alternatives.

2 Social theory and ageing

Key points:

- A critical approach to social theory and its relationship to adult ageing.
- Critique of theories that reproduce or legitimate functionalist definitions of age.
- Integration of political economy, cultural and humanistic approaches.
- A review of historical attempts to define old age through activity, disengagement and life course theories.

Introduction

Since its inception in 1945, the field of gerontology has evolved into a formal interdisciplinary science involving biology, clinical medicine, and the behavioural and social sciences. While researchers, practitioners, policy makers and the general public agree that ageing is a part of the life course, there has been substantial disagreement among and within these groups regarding the definition of old age, the perception of what constitutes normal ageing, and the extent and scope of public/private responsibility for optimal, successful or productive ageing. This disparity in perspectives is further reflected in the broad and fragmented body of theory that constitutes the field of gerontology (Estes *et al.* 1992a).

One dimension of this fragmented body of work on ageing stems from the larger social science debate between 'micro' and 'macro' perspectives in which the leading theories of ageing emphasize either the individual actor or the structure of society as the primary object of study. A small number of theoretical strands attempt to link micro and macro perspectives (Marshall 1996; Bengston *et al.* 1997). Newer efforts have attempted also to integrate the meso perspective (Estes 1998). Another classification dimension of different gerontological theories (also consistent with the larger disciplinary social sciences) is the 'normative' versus the 'interpretive' perspective (Hendricks 1992; Marshall 1996). A third classification dimension that may be contrasted with the previous two is the 'critical' or 'radical' perspective (Phillipson 1998).

The aim of this chapter is to examine the development of theoretical perspectives within social gerontology. The discussion will focus around four main elements: first, we consider the place of theory within gerontology, and in particular the struggle to incorporate theory into research on ageing. Second, distinctive phases in the development of social theory as applied to ageing are outlined, with examples of key theories from each phase. Third, some of the major themes of critical perspectives on ageing are reviewed, with particular emphasis on political economy and humanistic perspectives. The chapter concludes with an assessment of the current state of theory within social gerontology.

The need for theory

Concern about the absence of theory within social gerontology has been expressed in a variety of ways. From a British perspective, Marion Crawford (1971) has noted the tendency to treat ageing largely in terms of social welfare policies, a perspective which, focusing as it does on the consequences of social arrangements and *ad hoc* responses to discovered 'needs', tends to discourage systematic theorizing. This point was emphasized by Estes (1979a), who observed that gerontologists have been largely content with describing the activities and lifestyles of older people, rather than considering causal linkages between ageing and the social, economic and political structure. Twenty years later, Bengston and Schaie (1999: 3–4) opened their *Handbook of Theories of Aging* with the following set of questions:

> Are theories of aging important? Or have theories become irrelevant – perhaps archaic – in the broad, increasingly differentiated fields of inquiry that constitute gerontology today? Many researchers in gerontology seem to have abandoned any attempt at building theory. Should we be concerned about this? What are the consequences of discounting theory for future knowledge development in gerontology?

Yet, as these writers suggest, the problem may be less the sheer absence of theory; rather, the key question may concern the extent to which theoretical work is built into the research enterprise. Taking the focus of theory as that of *explanation*, in contrast to empirical generalizations, models of relationships or simulations, Bengston and Schaie (1999: 16) note that

. . . many journal editors and reviewers seem to have little concern for theory or its development. The disenchantment with 'general theories' of aging, and the push for practical solutions to problems of the aged, have led to a devaluation of theory, particularly among gerontological practitioners and policy makers. We [suggest] that applications of knowledge in gerontology – whether in medicine, practice or policy – demand good theory, since it is on the basis of *explanations* about problems that interventions should be made; if not they seem doomed to failure.

The problem of integrating theory has, however, been exacerbated by the way in which gerontology has tended to insulate itself from the dominant social science disciplines – sociology and economics in particular. In contrast to other areas of work (for example around crime and deviance, youth studies or race and ethnicity), studies of ageing have often developed in isolation from major developments in the core disciplines. Lamenting what they saw (following C. Wright Mills) as the absence of a 'gerontological imagination', Estes *et al.* (1992a: 50) argued that

> There is little agreement as to what 'gerontology' is, what a gerontologist should know, or, for that matter, what a 'gerontologist' is. Therefore, there is no common thread or tie to a common core of disciplinary knowledge to unify the field. While this was historically, and should continue to be, a strength, we suggest that in the current environment it is often a weakness resulting in the tokenization of gerontology within traditional disciplines such as sociology, psychology, public health, anthropology and social work, and the Balkanization of specialized gerontology programmes *vis-à-vis* other established disciplines.

These characteristics provide an indication of the way in which research into social aspects of ageing has been squeezed between the natural sciences and biomedicine on the one side, and studies on the development of welfare states on the other. In the case of the former, this reflected the way in which interest in gerontology had emerged (from the mid-1940s) in the context of a dramatic expansion of the natural sciences. Andrew Achenbaum (1995) suggests that gerontology developed at a point in time when countries such as the USA were, as he puts it, 'awestruck' by the power of science to facilitate material progress. Science – and most especially biomedicine – was viewed as the most influential source for tackling many of the problems and challenges associated with ageing (see also Katz 1996). Estes and Binney (1989) were to describe this development as representing the 'biomedicalization of ageing', this having two central features: '(1) the social construction of ageing as a medical problem (thinking of ageing as a medical problem), and (2) the praxis (or practice) of ageing as a medical problem' (Estes and Binney 1989: 587). The perspective of the biomedical model was to view the ageing process as characterized by a process of decline and decay. The approach is one that sees old age as a medical problem that can be alleviated, if not eradicated, through the 'magic bullets' of medical science. The focus is on individual organic pathology and medical interventions, with physicians placed in charge of the definition and treatment of old age as a disease.

The influence of biomedicine was further reinforced by the role of the welfare state and social security in constructing a distinctive vision for old age. From the late 1940s onwards, emphasis was placed upon a new identity for older people built around the rights of citizenship associated with the institutional developments that accompanied the rise of the welfare state. In the case of Britain, Peter Hennessy (1993) sees the welfare state as '*the* talisman of a better postwar [society]'. For T.H. Marshall (1949), the welfare state added a third dimension to the historical evolution of citizenship (following on from the development of civil and political rights), with social rights in the form of pensions, health and education.

Of course, in most welfare states during the 1950s and 1960s, older people clustered on or below the poverty line. But the idea of social inclusion remained fundamental at this time. In the case of the Beveridge Plan, this was seen to be '. . . not a system for the poor but for the whole of society' (Batley *et al.* 1997). Older people had become 'citizens', assured of a minimum amount of income to achieve a decent level of subsistence (Myles 1996). As Timmins (1996: 163) argues, this reflected the aim of the welfare state in 'shifting resources between generations at key moments in life'. He summarizes this aspect as follows:

> People paid in taxes in middle life when in work, and in return were helped with their children's upbringing and education, were guaranteed help when sick, and were assisted in old age when earnings ceased. There was therefore and remained a widespread interest – or to put it more kindly, mutual interest – in the welfare state, on top of the 'never again' revulsion felt over the effects of the 1930s depression.

The twin (and in some respects overlapping) influences of biomedicine and the welfare state were to constrain for some time the 'social' dimensions of the study of ageing. This point was clearly made by Peter Townsend (1981: 5–7), in an article for the first issue of *Ageing and Society*, where he emphasized the need for a 'better sociology of ageing and the aged'. He argued:

> For many years after the Second World War scientific research into old age was extraordinarily restricted, and only latterly has fundamental

enquiry begun to assume a critical and wide-ranging and hence more constructive cohesion. The physical, mental and social features of ageing were seen as natural, or as largely inevitable. [Scientists failed to ask] what brought about the modern phenomenon of retirement and accentuated social dependency and the chances of isolation and extreme deprivation in old age, or what explained the mainly custodial and impersonal forms of institutional care for the elderly and the large-scale use to which they were put . . . [Instead,] the inexorable process by which the status of older people has been lowered, or rather, defined at a lowly level in the course of the development of industrial societies, has been largely ignored. The evolution of the economy, the state and social inequality has been taken for granted, and the implications of the trends for people as they become older neglected.

But, while accurate in broad terms, Townsend's argument somewhat overstates the case. For most of the time since the 1950s, while the trend has been to focus upon individual aspects of ageing, work exploring the impact of social structure on ageing has also been apparent. Indeed, in terms of the relationship between social theory and gerontology, it would be accurate to view the past 50 years as one of competition and struggle between paradigms: the welfare–biomedical axis dominant for long periods, but with sociological–critical perspectives also growing in influence. To review this aspect, we now turn to review some of the key social theories of ageing, placing these in the context of distinct phases in their development.

Developing social theory: activity and disengagement theory

A number of authors have charted the growth of theories applied to the field of ageing. Hendricks and Achenbaum (1999) provide an historical account, highlighting pioneers such as I.L. Nascher (who published the first textbook covering the field of geriatrics), the psychologist G. Stanley Hall (whose treatise on old age, *Senescence: The Second Half of Life*, was published in 1922), and the anatomist E.V. Cowdry, whose handbook, *Problems of Ageing*, published in 1939, is regarded as heralding the emergence of gerontology as a field of scientific enquiry in the USA (Achenbaum 1995).

Lynott and Lynott (1996) examine the development of sociological theories of ageing, from disengagement theory in the late 1950s (viewed as the first formal approach to theorizing), to the rise of critical and feminist perspectives in the 1980s and 1990s. Estes *et al.* (1992a) chart the impact on theory of distinctive periods which shaped the 'gerontological imagination', from the focus on individual adaptation to ageing in the 1940s and 1950s to the struggle to develop neo-Marxist and related perspectives from the late 1970s onwards. Victor Marshall (1996, see also 1999) has provided a classification of the main types of social science theories in the field of ageing, identifying normative (e.g. role theory) versus interpretive theories (e.g. symbolic interactionism) on the one hand, and macro (political economy) and micro (continuity theory) on the other.

These different frameworks will be drawn upon for illustrating key social theories in gerontology, starting with the first phase of development in the late 1940s and early 1950s. This period may be regarded as one in which social gerontology started to develop what Anton Amann (1984: 7) refers to as its 'historical identity'. Essentially this was driven by the emergence of research institutes and surveys of older people in the USA and across most European countries (Amann 1984; Katz 1996). The context for this work was the perception, in demographic, economic and medical research, that old age represented a major social problem that would demand new initiatives in areas such as employment, income support and health and social care. For social scientists the dominant theoretical framework at the time (drawn from the USA) was the structural–functionalist paradigm as developed by Talcott Parsons (1942) and others. This theoretical model proved complementary to biomedical approaches given its focus on individual adjustment and its concern with the contribution of the social roles and norms of older individuals and institutions to the functioning of the social system.

The combination of a social problems perspective with the functionalist paradigm produced an emphasis on exploring how older people could achieve integration and adaptation, in the context both of their own changing needs and that of society. Activity theory in the form developed by Ruth Cavan *et al.* (1949) and Havighurst and Albrecht (1953) addressed this question by arguing that psychological and social well-being could be enhanced by involvement in social roles and activities. Lynott and Lynott (1996) suggest that this approach was pre-theoretical in the sense that it was never codified into a formal set of testable propositions. Essentially, it reflected a set of assumptions about appropriate behaviour in later life, faithfully reproduced in research findings. Lynott and Lynott (1996: 750) conclude that

> From Cavan to Havighurst, among others in this period, researchers were writing about ageing as an individual social problem. The implicit sentiments of the researchers dealing with individual membership in the social order, embracing the moral obligation of self-realization through hard work, reveals, in the data, its mirror image. What these researchers discover to be the nature of ageing – individual and life satisfaction in readjustment – has its source in the implicit 'theory' of the nature of growing old. Their work and data

> reproduce the vision. What is characteristic of this period [i.e. the 1950s] is that there is little or no clue that these researchers are aware of this connection . . .

The relationship between activity and life satisfaction was pursued in a variety of ways over the next two decades (see below), but for a time the theoretical debate was taken over by the publication (in 1961) of Cumming and Henry's *Growing Old: The Process of Disengagment.* As with activity theory, this perspective drew inspiration from the functionalist paradigm, focusing on the way in which social institutions promote disengagement, for the benefit of the individual and the social system. Disengagement theory posits that old age is a period in which the ageing individual and society both simultaneously engage in mutual separation (e.g. retirement and disengagement from the workforce). A key assumption made in the theory is that 'ego energy' declines with age and that, as the ageing process develops, individuals become increasingly self-absorbed and less responsive to normative controls. It is further argued that disengagement or withdrawal from social relationships will lead to the individual maintaining higher morale in old age – higher, that is, than if he or she attempted to keep involved in a range of social affairs and activities. Thus, disengagement is viewed as both a natural and desirable outcome, one leading to a stronger sense of psychological well-being. Finally, this feature of ageing is suggested to be a universal phenomenon, associated with ageing in all cultures.

The value of disengagement theory has over the years come to be seen less in terms of its underlying arguments (which have received little if any support), more in its role in 'spurring debate and resistance' (Daatland 2002: 4) within gerontology. Lynott and Lynott (1996: 751) view its importance in terms of making 'the field aware of theory'. Daatland (2002: 4) suggests that disengagement theory served the role of attempting to establish gerontology as a scientific discipline, in a variety of ways:

1   it was a global theory on the ageing process,
2   it included at least two disciplines – psychology and sociology, and
3   it presented old age as a qualitatively distinct phase of life and as a distinct piece of reality that needed a special theoretical and methodological approach, namely, gerontology.

Through the 1960s and for a period in the 1970s, activity and disengagement theory set the parameters of theoretical debates within social gerontology. Activity theory stimulated the development of several social psychological theories of ageing including continuity theory (Costa and McCrae 1980; Atchley 1999) and successful ageing (Rowe and Kahn 1987; Baltes and Baltes 1990; Abeles *et al.* 1994). Drawn from developmental or life cycle theory (Neugarten

1964; Lowenthal 1975), continuity theory asserts that ageing persons have the need and the tendency to maintain the same personalities, habits and perspectives that they developed over their life course. An individual who is successfully ageing maintains a mature integrated personality, which also is the basis of life satisfaction (Neugarten *et al.* 1968; see also Chapter 3). As such, decreases in activity or social interaction are viewed as related more to changes in health and physical function than to an inherent need for a shift in or relinquishment of previous roles.

Increasingly, however, through the 1970s, concern came to be expressed about what Townsend (1981) was to term the 'acquiescent functionalism' of prevailing theories, i.e. their tendency to attribute problems of ageing to individual adjustment rather than to structured inequalities. By the 1970s new theoretical perspectives were beginning to penetrate discussions within gerontology and it is to a review of these that we now turn.

Social theory and ageing: beyond disengagment theory

From the mid-1970s onwards a range of new theories were introduced into gerontology, drawn from diverse sources including human development theory, symbolic interactionism, revisions to existing approaches (such as activity and role theory) and early contributions from neo-Marxist, neo-Weberian and neo-Frankfurt School perspectives. Increasingly, attempts are made to move beyond an individual-level focus with the development of macro-level approaches, life course perspectives and theories influenced by social constructionism.

Two macro-level gerontological theories developed from Matilda Riley's work on age stratification (Riley *et al.* 1972) and its successor the ageing and society paradigm (Riley *et al.* 1999). *Age stratification* attends to the role and influence of social structures on the process of individual ageing and the stratification of age in society (Riley and Riley 1994b, 1994c; Riley 1998). One dimension of this theory is the concept of structural lag, which denotes that social structures (e.g. policies of retirement at age 65) do not keep pace with changes in population dynamic and individual lives (such as increasing life expectancy). A criticism of this approach is its relative inattention to issues of power and social class relationships, especially insofar as these influence the social structure and the policies constituted by it, and ultimately the experience of ageing (Estes 1986). Quadagno and Reid (1999: 47) also suggest that age stratification has '... relied on an inherently static concept of social structure, that it neglected political processes inherent in the creation of inequality, and that it ignored institutionalized patterns of inequality'.

In developing the 'Aging and society paradigm', Matilda Riley and her colleagues (1999: 333) address the 'unintentionally static overtones of age stratification' by introducing 'two dynamisms – changing lives and changing structures – as interdependent but distinct sets of processes'. They assert that

> The aging and society . . . paradigm is a conceptual framework, or approach, for designing and interpreting studies of age and illuminating the place of age in both lives (as people age) and the surrounding social structures. Its central theme is that, against the backdrop of history, changes in people's lives influence and are influenced by changes in social structures and institutions. These reciprocal changes are linked to the meanings of age, which vary over time.
>
> (Riley *et al.* 1999: 327)

Passuth and Bengston (1996) see the importance of the age stratification approach in terms of the way in which it placed social gerontological theorizing within mainstream sociology (for which the dominant theory is functionalism with its emphasis on social order via social roles and norms rather than conflict via social inequalities). They further argue that

> . . . the model emphasizes that there are significant variations in older people depending on the characteristics of their birth cohort; this suggests the need for a more explicit analysis of historical and social factors in aging. [Moreover] age stratification's emphasis on the relations of cohorts within the age structure of society offers a useful analytic framework for distinguishing between developmental changes and cohort age differences.
>
> (Passuth and Bengston 1996: 17)

But the limitations of the theory are also important, with three issues identified in the literature: first, the way that it exaggerates the role of age status in the distribution of economic and social rewards; second, the lack of attention to differences within birth cohorts; third, the retention of functionalist assumptions regarding consensus (as opposed to power struggles and conflict) in determining the structure and operation of social systems and institutions (including social policy).

Another important approach which moved beyond individual adjustment to ageing, and which was also influenced by the age stratification model, has been the *life course perspective* (Elder 1974; Neugarten and Hagestad 1976). Here ageing individuals and cohorts are examined as one phase of the entire lifetime and seen as shaped by historical, social, economic and environmental factors that occur at earlier ages (George 1993; Hagestad and Dannefer 2002). In the work of George (1990) and others, life course theory bridges macro–micro levels of analysis by considering the relationships between social structure, social processes and social psychological states. Passuth and Bengston (1996: 17) suggest that key elements of the approach are that: (1) ageing occurs from birth to death (thereby distinguishing this theory from those that focus exclusively on the elderly); (2) ageing involves social, psychological and biological processes; and (3) ageing experiences are shaped by cohort-historical factors.

Despite these wider concerns, the primary focus remains on the micro, with an emphasis on how macro-level phenomena influence the lives of *individuals in* their journey through the life course. In a recent review of these theories, Dannefer and Uhlenberg (1999: 309) point to three significant intellectual problems in theorizing about the life course: (a) a tendency to equate the significance of social forces with social change; (b) a neglect of intra-cohort variability; and (c) an unwarranted affirmation of choice as an unproblematized determinant of the life course.

Finally in this section, the idea that the lives and problems of older people may be seen as 'socially constructed' was an important theme developed in research from the late 1970s onwards (Estes 1979a; Phillipson 1982; Gubrium 1986). In the earliest development of a political economy theory of ageing, Estes (1979a: 1) begins with the proposition that

> The major problems faced by the elderly in the United States are, in large measure, ones that are socially constructed as a result of our conceptions of aging and the aged. What is done for and about the elderly, as well as what we know about them, including knowledge gained from research, are products of our conceptions of aging. In an important sense, then, the major problems faced by the elderly are the ones we create for them.

Similarly, national and global crises are socially constructed in relation to:

a   the capacity and power of strategically located agents and interests to define 'the problem' and to press their views into public consciousness and law; and
b   the objective facts of the situation (Estes 1979a).

The constructionist perspective posits that 'facts' are highly contested and are not determinative alone of how problems are defined and treated in society.

The processes of social construction occur at all levels – the macro and micro levels as well as the meso level of organizations that operate between the micro and the macro. The state and economy (macro level) influence the experience and condition of ageing, while individuals also actively construct their worlds through personal interactions (micro level) and through organizational and institutional structures and processes (meso level) that constitute their daily social worlds and society.

At the micro and meso levels, a major focus is understanding the constructions of personal meaning in the lives of older people and the settings in which these meanings emerge and evolve. Jaber Gubrium (1993, 1996), for example, has focused on the issue of Alzheimer's disease, examining the way in which the meaning of the illness is derived and communicated. He uses the example of support groups for people with Alzheimer's to show the way in which these can provide a basis for speaking about and interpreting the caregiving experience. For Gubrium the 'local cultures' of residential settings, day centres and support groups provide important contexts for working through and assigning meanings to particular experiences. In this approach, language is seen to play a crucial role in the construction of reality. Lynott and Lynott (1996: 754) summarize this approach as follows:

> Instead of asking how things like age cohorts, life stages, or system needs organise and determine one's experience, [the question asked instead is] how persons (professional and lay alike) make use of age-related explanations and justifications in their treatment and interaction with one another . . . Facts virtually come to life in their assertion, invocation, realization and utility. From this point of view, language is not just a vehicle for symbolically representing realities; its usage, in the practical realities of everyday life, is concretely productive of the realities.

The social construction of reality perspective, which builds upon the original theory of Peter Berger and Thomas Luckmann (1966) and the labelling theories contributed by symbolic interactionists such as Howard Becker (1963) and David Matza (1969), offers several insights for gerontology:

> The experience of old age is dependent in large part upon how others react to the aged; that is social context and cultural meanings are important. Meanings are crucial in influencing how growing old is experienced by the aging in any given society; these meanings are shaped through interaction of the aged with the individuals, organizations, and institutions that comprise the social context. Social context, however, incorporates not only situational events and interactional opportunities but also structural constraints that limit the range of possible interaction and the degree of understanding, reinforcing certain lines of action while barring others.
>
> (Estes 1981: 400)

At the macro level, portrayals of the threatened bankruptcy of public treasuries to support the retirement of the elderly and the 'appropriate' policy response (such as the proposed privatization of social security) are crisis constructions embedded in intense power struggles that are momentous in their social, political and economic consequences, including the sacrifices that are demanded. As Murray Edelman points out, 'the burdens of almost all crises fall disproportionately on the poor, while the influential and the affluent often benefit from them' (1977: 44). This situation reflects 'the divergence between the symbolic import of crises and their [hidden] material impact [which] is basic to their popular acceptance' (Edelman 1977: 46).

Ideology is a key element in the dominant and successful constructions of reality about the problems of ageing. As 'an organized set of convictions . . . which enforces inevitable value judgments' (Bailey 1975: 32), ideologies are partial perspectives that reflect the social position and the values of their beholders. Estes (1979a: 4) takes the view that 'As belief systems, ideologies are world views competing for definition; and they hold major implications for power relations, for in enforcing certain definitions of the situation, they have the power to compel certain types of action while limiting others.'

Gramsci's insights are that ideas have the weight of material force (i.e. power is not just about economics) and that society (e.g. civil culture) and the state are key sites in which struggles for ideological hegemony take place. All political and economic regimes use ideology as the discourse with which to communicate and impose a reflection of the dominant social relations. In the Gramscian sense, ideological hegemony 'binds society together without the use of force' (Sardar and Van Loon 1997: 49).

The variety of constraints affecting the lives of older people (what Townsend (1981) referred to as the problem of 'structured dependency') became a focus of concern for gerontologists from the 1980s onwards. In the next section, one important strand is summarized – critical gerontology – which is then elaborated in more detail in subsequent chapters of this book.

The development of critical gerontology

Critical approaches to ageing build upon an array of intellectual traditions, including the works of Karl Marx, Max Weber, Antonio Gramsci, the Frankfurt School (latterly through the work of Jurgen Habermas), state theorists such as Claus Offe and James O'Connor, psychoanalytic perspectives, conflict theory and structuration theory as developed by Anthony Giddens (1984). Feminist theories (Dressel 1988; Estes 1991a, 1999; Calasanti 1993; Ginn and Arber 1995; Estes and Associates 2001: Chapters 1 and 6. See also Chapter 3 in this volume) and theories of racial inequality (Omi and Winant 1994; Williams 1996) have also been incorporated into critical perspectives on ageing. Utilizing this theoretical seedbed, a field of critical gerontology has emerged and coalesced over the past decade with work in the USA and Europe. The more general aims of critical perspectives in social theory are described by Bottomore as (1983: 183)

> . . . designed with a practical intent to criticize and subvert domination in all its forms . . . It is . . . preoccupied by a critique of ideology – of systematically distorted accounts of reality which attempt to conceal and legitimate asymmetrical power relations . . . [and how] social interests, conflicts and contradictions are expressed in thought, and how they are produced and reproduced in systems of domination.

The political economy perspective is one of the most important strands within the critical tradition. This approach attempts to understand the condition and experience of ageing drawing upon multiple theories and levels of analysis. Beginning in the late 1970s and early 1980s with the work of Estes (1979a), Guillemard (1980), Phillipson (1982) and Walker (1981), these theorists initiated the task of describing the respective roles of capitalism and the state in contributing to systems of domination and marginalization of the aged. Based on the continuing work of these and other authors developing a critical perspective on theories of ageing (Marshall and Tindale 1978) and theories of the welfare state (Myles 1984; Quadagno 1988), the political economy perspective has become one of the major theories in social gerontology (Hendricks and Leedham 1991; Marshall 1996; Bengtson *et al.* 1997; Phillipson 1998; Bengtson and Schaie 1999; Walker 1999).

The political economy perspective is distinguished from the dominant liberal–pluralist theory in political science and sociology in that political economists focus on the role of economic and political systems and other social structures and social forces in shaping and reproducing the prevailing power arrangements and inequalities in society. In the political economy perspective, social policies pertaining to retirement income, health, and social service benefits and entitlements are examined as products of economic, political, and socio-cultural processes, and institutional and individual forces that coalesce in any given socio-historical period (Estes 1991a). Social policy is an outcome of the social struggles, conflicts and the dominant power relations of the period. Policy reflects the structure and culture of advantage and disadvantage as enacted through class, race/ethnicity, gender and age relations. Concurrently, social policy stimulates power struggles along these structural lines of class, race/ethnicity, gender and age. Social policy is itself a powerful determinant of the life chances and conditions of individuals and population groups such as the elderly.

A central assumption of the political economy perspective is that the phenomena of ageing and old age are directly related to the nature of the larger society in which they are situated and, therefore, cannot be considered or analysed in isolation from other societal forces and phenomena. The relative power of the state, business, labour and other social groups and the role of the economy and polity are central concerns. Explicitly recognized in this framework are the structural influences on the ageing experience including social relations and societal institutions such as capital, the state and the sex/gender system, as we seek to understand how ageing and old age are defined and treated in society and the role of ideology in shaping those definitions and the policy outcomes (Estes 1979a). In this respect, a central dynamic is the examination of the contradictions between the social needs of persons throughout the life course and how the organization of work (capitalist modes of production, their transformations and struggles around them) and state actions around them interact and affect these social needs. Political economy scholars have shown that the state reproduces structures of gender and racial domination (Acker 1988; Quadagno 1994; Sainsbury 1996; Williams 1996). For gerontology there is interest in how the state regulates and reproduces different life chances throughout the life course and how that ultimately shapes the economic and health vulnerabilities and inequalities of different subgroups of the ageing (Estes *et al.* 2000b).

Another important element within critical gerontology is the development of cultural and humanistic gerontology, sometimes referred to as moral economy or more broadly as *cultural gerontology* (Cole *et al.* 1992, 1993; Andersson 2003). This approach has gained popularity, as the classical theoretical opposition of structure *versus* agency and culture *versus* structure has given way to an appreciation of the interplay and 'recursive' relationships of culture, structure and agency (Giddens 1991; Estes 1999). Cultural gerontology is part of the trend toward theories that reject the sole determinacy of economics in explaining social institutions such as the state and old age policy. The approach provides a reformulation of the unidirectional causality implied in the classical 'base-superstructure' model of Marxism. What has followed is an intensified focus on questions of meaning and experience. (For more on the developments and fusion of a cultural and political economic perspective, see the chapters on Identity and Productive Ageing in this volume).

In the USA, theories of moral economy have developed largely as part of the political economy of ageing (Minkler and Cole 1991, 1999; Minkler and Estes 1991, 1999). Building on the work of E.P. Thompson (1963), Martin Kohli (1987), Minkler and Cole (1991) and others, those working from a moral economy perspective in gerontology have brought attention to social norms and reciprocal obligations and relations in society and their role in the social integration and social control of the elderly and the workforce. US proponents of this perspective are Moody (1988b, 2002), Hendricks and Leedham (1991), Minkler and Cole (1991, 1999), Robertson (1999) and others. The concept of moral economy reflects 'popular consensus concerning the legitimacy of certain practices based on shared views of social norms and obligations' (Robertson 1999: 39). Scholars working from the moral economy perspectives attend to issues of distributive and economic justice and norms such as reciprocity and generational equity.

Humanistic gerontology adds still another dimension to critical approaches to ageing, by seeking both to critique existing theories and to construct new positive models of ageing based on research by historians, ethicists and other social scientists (Cole *et al.* 1993). Moody (1993) identifies several goals for the critical humanistic perspective in gerontology, including:

- developing theories that emphasize and reveal the subjective and interpretive dimensions of ageing;
- commitment to praxis and social change; and
- the production of emancipatory knowledge.

Consistent with and complementary to both the political economy and feminist theories, this approach draws upon the concepts and relations of power, social action and social meanings as they pertain to ageing. At its core, this approach is concerned with the absence of meaning affecting older people, and the sense of doubt and uncertainty that is thought to permeate and influence their day-to-day lives and social relations (Moody 1988a, 1988b, 1997).

In the mid- to late 1990s, the focus outside gerontology shifted to a critique that underscores the heterogeneity of meanings, experiences and 'knowledges' according to different social and ethnic identities and interests. This reflects two intellectual trends: first, the rise of identity politics and theorization of social movements, wherein the fundamental injustice is defined as cultural domination rather than exploitation or social class divisions; and second, the critique of the 'essentialism' that is said to be incorporated in all areas of representation and social analysis including work (particularly of ethnocentrically biased white scholars) from the standpoint of feminist and race theory. The critique is that much of this work homogenizes and suppresses (obfuscates) crucial differences both within and between social identities and groups (Fraser 1997: 5, 11). These developments reflect the postmodernist tension between those who theorize the diminishing importance (or irrelevance) of social class as compared with culture. Theorists from the Left such as John O'Kane are rethinking the link between 'capital, culture, and socioeconomic justice' (O'Kane 2002: 1) through the

> potential integration of recognition and redistribution . . . connecting the separate 'political problematics' attached to each strain of injustice: one rooted in the political-economic structure of society,

and the other in the social patterns of representation, interpretation, and communication.

(O'Kane 2002: 2)

Conclusion: the future of social gerontological theory

Social theory in gerontology is at present influenced by a variety of cross-cutting trends. In the early 1990s, Estes *et al.* (1992a) argued that the rise of neo-liberalism had led to the entropy of critical and neo-Marxist perspectives. With respect to sociology, they suggested that the prevailing environment was producing disincentives to develop the sociology of ageing, especially as regards furthering an understanding of macro-structural forces. In similar vein, Hagestad and Dannefer (2002: 4) refer to what they view as a 'persistent tendency towards microfication in social science approaches to aging'. They argue that:

> Microfication refers to a trend in the substantive issues and analytic foci, what we might call the ontology of social research in aging. Increasingly, attention has been concentrated on psycho-social characteristics of individuals in microinteractions, to the neglect of the macrolevel. Apart from the population characteristics, macrolevel phenomena of central interest to social scientists, such as social institutions, cohesion and conflict, norms and values, have slipped out of focus.

Clearly, as the authors themselves note, approaches such as those drawn from political economy have provided a powerful critique of microfication. Nonetheless, the fact that micro approaches focused on individual ageing remain dominant within gerontology is a reminder of the work that still needs to be done. Hagestad and Dannefer attribute their influence to factors such as

- the emphasis in late modern society on 'individual agency';
- the role played by the continuing 'medicalization of old age' (see above and Chapter 6);
- the enduring power of the 'social problem' perspective on old age, inherited from the late nineteenth century but which has resurfaced in the 'crisis construction of old age'; and
- the priorities of research funders and the emphasis given to bio-medical and social pathology perspectives on ageing.

Yet, despite these factors, there are some grounds for believing that a resurgence in social science of reflexive perspectives on understanding ageing might be underway. In the first place, many social gerontologists are now more aware of mainstream and critical sociological and psychological theories and appear to be prepared to integrate these into their work. Indeed, one of the reasons for writing this book was to demonstrate how this could be done within the context of a critical gerontology. Subsequent chapters take up this challenge by exploring themes relating to a critical gerontology of identity, feminist perspectives, the debate about productive ageing, globalization and the politics of ageing. Second, it is clear that central theories within gerontology are themselves being adapted in the light of theoretical developments in broader disciplines such as sociology, of which Dannefer's (2002) reconstruction of life course theory in the context of globalization is a significant example. Third, at a professional level, the importance of developing a strong social gerontological presence within the core disciplinary bodies is increasingly recognized. The 'Ageing and the Life Course' section of the American Sociological Association is one notable illustration. In Germany there has been the foundation of a special 'Ageing and Society' (Altern and Gesellschaft) section within the German Sociological Association. In Britain, conferences of the British Sociological Association are starting to become an important forum for presenting the work of gerontologists.

The relationship between social science and social gerontology will remain complex and dynamic, especially given the continuing strength of biomedical and welfare perspectives in the study of later life. In addition, there are major epistemological questions about our science, the different modes of knowing, the critiques of positivism and masculinist methodological approaches, and how we know what we know. Although these issues are not tackled in detail here, they will require the serious attention of those working in critical gerontology. Nonetheless, subsequent chapters will seek to demonstrate the relevance and power of social theory and the importance of securing its close integration into understanding the lives of older people.

3 Age and identity

Key points:

- Stability and fluidity in ageing identities.
- Sources of choice, grounding and fragmentation.
- The relationship between bodily and social aspects of ageing.
- Age identity as negotiated and managed.

Introduction

The previous chapter established the broad characteristics of social theory in gerontology. The next two chapters narrow the focus somewhat, starting first of all with studies concerning the changing nature of identity in old age. Debates about age and identity are often arguments for or against taking a particular stance toward the personal and social experience of growing older. The contested nature of ageing as a social phenomenon is in part a consequence of identity as a meeting point for various attributes that are, more often than not, taken to be bipolar and mutually exclusive. The list extends beyond personal and social factors to include phenomenal and structural ones, the distinction between internal and external worlds, and agency versus determinism. The concept of identity, of selfhood as experienced reflexively by the self and observed by others, stands at the crossroads of these different perspectives. It also crosses disciplinary boundaries, most notably between social and developmental psychology and sociology, but also extending to include biology and medicine. It tells us who we are as we age and what we can expect from life. As such, it is perhaps unsurprising that ageing identities, both as a medium for active subjectivity and as subject to institutional control, have also been the object of considerable political and policy interest (Phillipson 1998; Biggs 2001; Estes *et al.* 2001b).

The purpose of this chapter is to begin to analyse some of the social theories that have been used to explain the process of ageing and its impact on identity. In an attempt to address how various approaches have solved the problem of ageing identities, the issue has been cast in terms of a continuum from stability to fluidity. By stability is meant the degree to which identities are set as being fixed and unchanging. This may take the form of claiming ageing to be a natural process with a series of age-specific roles and identities that have to be worked through. It might equally be based on a reliance on particular social structures or economic relations that restrict human potential to certain predetermined categories. In each case an attempt has been made to increase the certainty of what it means to become old, for good or bad. Fluidity here refers to the degree to which identity is changeable, a subject of choice and desire but also of uncertainty and risk. It is in this respect unrooted. Identity is imagined as a series of 'off-the-peg' options, autonomous self-creations in an attempt to explore alternative possibilities of ageing. It may also deny older people firm ground on which to stand, and may lead to a fragmenting of personal and collective identities.

A degree of both stability and fluidity is necessary for the creation of identities that ageing adults can comfortably inhabit. If there is a perceived excess of fixedness, people feel entrapped, but if there is an absence, people experience the world as frighteningly unstable. If there is an excess of fluidity, life becomes unpredictable and identities fragmented. However, if there is too little, creativity and the ability to adapt to changing circumstances become threatened.

Concern with social inequality, the ageing body and ageist attitudes, perhaps the three most common sources of debate about ageing, each pose the question of degrees of fixedness and change that age allows, although the implications for each vary considerably. For age and identity the question is cast in terms of freedom to manoeuvre, often against a background of personal and structural limitation. An ageing identity is inevitably a negotiated identity, that requires protection against social risks as well as spaces for self-expression. The possibility of finding such spaces is shaped by theory and policy, not only through the supply of ideas and resources, but also because they provide the raw material for construction of the ageing self.

Theories about ageing are important here for a number of reasons. First, as Gubrium and Wallace (1991) have demonstrated, there is a close correspondence between constructions of ageing that are used in everyday life and the formal explanations found in the gerontological literature. Second, older people may actively draw on these and other sources in the creation of their own life narratives (Holstein and Gubrium 2000). Third, age is increasingly seen as a key factor in identity building, which interacts with and in certain circumstances becomes the determining factor in how people perceive themselves and others (Westerhof et al. 2001). Fourth, politicians, policy makers and helping professionals actively use certain models of ageing to influence the behaviour of and social attitudes toward older people (Biggs and Powell 2001). In each case the theories available to us, and the stances taken with regard to degrees of flexibility, reflexively influence the identity choices available to older people themselves.

Identity, gerontology and modernity

Contemporary debate on identity hinges on whether society has undergone a profound change, from a state of modernity to something else, variously referred to as post- or high modernity. Modernity is characterized by an emphasis upon scientific progress, grand, all-explaining narratives and mass social identifications, but also a critical antimony between surface appearances and underlying truths. Postmodernity eschews linear and temporal progression, prefers contextual explanations that are multiple and varied, while celebrating personal choice. Both problematize the grounding of ageing identity in existing structures, the nature of personal autonomy and the degree to which the human body and social expectation set limits to social and personal expression.

This change in the nature of identity has been put succinctly by Zugmunt Bauman (1995):

> If the modern 'problem of identity' was how to construct an identity and keep it solid and stable, the postmodern 'problem of identity' is primarily how to avoid fixation and keep the options open. In the case of identity, as in other cases, the catchword of modernity was 'creation'; the catchword of postmodernity is 'recycling'.
>
> (1995: 81)

Bauman's observation has considerable implications for ageing and identity. In the first 'modern' instance it is assumed that the main question for ageing identity concerns how to keep one's personal world relatively stable and predictable. It must be protected from an inhospitable environment and the predations of social change. In the second, factors that may constrain the options open to people as they age are to be avoided. Adopting an identity based on age becomes one of a number of statements which may be used or redesigned depending upon context.

Modern ageing

Capitalism and ageing identity

Contemporary concerns about the foundations of identity draw directly from the dynamic of continual change brought about by industrial capitalism. This dynamic can be seen reflected in the Communist Manifesto (Marx and Engels [1888] 1976), written at the very beginning of the capitalist era. Here Marx and Engels stated that competition between different entrepreneurs, necessary for survival in a market economy, leads to a constant revolution in the way things are produced. This process of continual change directly affects the relationships between different groups in society, whose livelihood depends upon these changing means of production. However, a second implication of the power of production over modern identities is that while things continually change to keep up with the competition, relationships become increasingly unequal and it is in the interest of dominant groups to keep these inequalities relatively fixed. Identities thus depend on relationships of production, and these identities are intimately related to a particular imbalance of power. Marx's famous call for workers to unite recognizes that, while identity depends upon the individual's relationship to how things are produced in society, there is a need to protect oneself from this relationship and in some way free oneself from it. This is necessary in order to achieve a more enhancing and less constraining sense of being human. However, there is a catch. In order to free identity from fixed forms that are ultimately not in one's interests, it is necessary to emphasize those social identities in order to build a base from which to change them.

This question of stability is certainly doubled-edged. On the one hand, when living in a world of considerable flux and uncertainty, there is a desire to find something reliable, something to hold on to and build oneself around. On the other, if this attempt to fix identity is coercive, externally driven and overly restrictive of personal development, it becomes a prison, which can distort and constrain the self. As Frosh (1991), a British psychoanalyst, has pointed out, although human relationships are possible under such circumstances, they are always in danger of being undercut or destroyed. It is important, then, to protect oneself from excessive fluidity.

The need for some form of personal framework has been identified by Taylor as a key element of identity maintenance, such that:

> My identity is defined by the commitments and identification which provide the frame or horizon within which I try to determine from case to case what is good, or valuable, or what ought to be done, or what I endorse or oppose. In other words it is the horizon within which I am capable of making a stand.
>
> (1989: 26)

In so far as older people were allowed a space in which to make their stand, this was located within the traditional welfare state, and most notably under the auspices of health, pensions and social care policy. Use it, or resist it, or do the two together, the welfare state, with all its faults, provided a socially legitimate focus for late life concerns and social identity (Phillipson and Biggs 1998).

Functionalist approaches to ageing such as Cumming and Henry's (1961), which propose that later life is a time of disengagement from society, are typical of social theorizing which is uncritical of conventional thinking about age and production. Here the process of disengagement is presented as functional because it provides a mechanism for replacing one generation of workers with another. Welfare-based identities thereby become the legitimate end-place for the unproductive and aged self. The notion that intergenerational communication can be seen as an exchange (Dowd 1975), with increasingly unequal returns from the older to the younger person, not only seeks to explain social withdrawal uncritically, it does so using a thinly disguised economistic model of human motivation. The falling rate of return encountered by younger people, itself partly based on the perception of older people as 'past-it' and 'a burden' (in other words, as unproductive), is used to legitimize further marginalization. Its legacy can also be detected in work on identity around midlife crisis (Neugarten 1968), which may be interpreted as a short-lived protest against the loss of status and productive work roles, followed by acceptance of a new status quo for identity in later life.

The depiction of later life as a one-way trip to increasing dependency and withdrawal has held true, at least in social policy thinking, in both welfarism and market approaches. It has been criticized by a number of writers, such as Townsend (1981, 1986) in the UK and Minkler and Estes (1998) in the USA, who have viewed the social construction of ageing through the lens of political economy. According to this perspective, dependent identities in later life are not an inevitable and biologically or developmentally determined 'fact of life', but are a social artefact produced by a number of factors such as: the forced expulsion of older people from the workforce; the growth and self-promotion of professional interests; the manipulation of vulnerable older people as if they were commodities in a welfare market; and a marginalization of later life concerns. While emphasis varies from writer to writer, it is argued that various forms of ageist oppression are held together by an economically determined perception of older people as unproductive and a burden on society as a whole. Thus, if education and health services are perceived to be an economic investment in the future or existing workforce, then it is unsurprising that, as a political economy critique would predict, older people are both denied them and stigmatized into the bargain.

Confronting social ageism

The critique of social ageism can be seen as very much a modernist concern in so far as it attempts to free older identity from the oppressive influence of a social structure that casts adult ageing negatively. It is a critique of ways of fixing ageing identity that demean or denigrate the value of personal and social ageing and thereby artificially restrict identity choices. In his book *Why Survive? Being Old in America*, Butler (1975) identified widespread inequalities based on age and the stereotyping of older adults as unproductive and essentially superfluous members of contemporary society. Indeed, Butler's definition of ageism is now generally accepted as a seminal statement on the phenomenon, and reflects the origins of anti-ageist approaches in the civil rights movement of the 1960s and 1970s. Butler described ageism as the 'systematic stereotyping and discrimination against people because they are old, just as racism and sexism accomplish this for skin colour and gender' (1975: 22).

It is argued that ageism becomes manifest in ways that directly affect age-based identities. At an interpersonal level, younger adults are encouraged to see older people as different from themselves, which leads to an absence of identification with their elders as fully human. This absence is closely associated with a fear of personal ageing, which both reinforces and is reinforced by age-based prejudice itself. At a structural level, excluding older people from the workforce is seen, not as a positive opportunity, a promise of retirement, but as a forced removal of older citizens from a source of self-esteem and social value. This itself rests upon the privileging of sources of identity based on production and the value of work. In civil rights terms, as older people are excluded from work, they are not valued and, rather than contributing to society, older people are identified as a drain upon social resources (Kuhn 1977). As such, anti-ageist struggle evidences an unwillingness to break with identity contingent on production and the benefits flowing from this. However, Maggie Kuhn and the Gray Panthers also engage in a more radical critique of production as a means of building a positive identity and, in particular, have based political activity around intergenerational solidarity. It has been argued that ageism should be seen as interactive with other forms of oppression (Bytheway 1994) and manifests differently depending upon context (Moody 1998a).

Ageist critique has, for example, been used to examine the quality of health provision (Age Concern England 2000) with direct impact on health care policy (Department of Health 2001). Critical approaches to ageism are, then, an attempt to increase the social and personal freedoms available to older people. As such they challenge the fixities, the limits imposed by social structure, interpersonal attitudes and internalized self-perceptions. They are perhaps less effective in identifying alternative sources of identity and the issues raised by Taylor (1989) of finding stability as a basis for struggle and for critical gerontology, a grounding from which to respond to dominant identities attributed to old age.

The next sections of this chapter develop the above themes in more detail through an examination of some of the theories and perspectives outlined in the previous chapter.

Desire for continuity

Continuity theory, an important approach within gerontology, outlined in Chapter 2, also has implications for the relationship between ageing and identity. This perspective is again profoundly modern, in so far as an emphasis has been placed upon maintaining continuity of identity in the face of a changing social environment. Atchley (1989, 1999) maintains that continuity of identity supplies a robust framework of ideas that neutralize disadvantage and insulate the self from ageism. Continuity theory 'presumes that most people learn continuously from their life experiences and continue to grow and evolve in directions of their own choosing' (Atchley 1999: vii). Continuity is a 'consistency in *general* patterns of thought, behaviour, relationships, and living circumstances over an extended time period' (author's emphasis) (1999: 148). The logic of continuity of identity as a source of positive value in later life is reflected in therapeutic approaches such as life story and reminiscence (Coleman 1996) and as an aid to coping with transitions, most notably around institutional care (Tobin 1989). Atchley (1999) maintains that adult development and adaptation are relatively continuous and cites empirical findings from a longitudinal study, spanning some 20 years, in support of this conclusion. These findings were, however, collected in a stable 'college town' neighbourhood, 'relatively free of urban problems', and 'with a full range of retirement activities, health and social care programs' (Atchley 1999: xi). This is arguably a population relatively unchallenged by uncertainty and significant socio-economic disruption of chosen life trajectories, which throws some doubt as to how generalizable the findings may be. Continuity is nevertheless presented as both empirically valid and as an effective strategy with which to sustain identity as adults age.

In creating a theoretical position around continuity and adaptation to challenges to that continuity occasioned by growing older, Atchley (1999) is self-consciously embarking on the modernist project of creating a general theory of ageing, while further elaborating a paradigm initiated by Neugarten (1964) three decades earlier. The theory, as its name suggests, emphasizes the enduring nature of identity traits and coping strategies across the life course and therefore explains adult ageing largely in terms of fixity.

Once continuity theory is seen as an attempt to justify stability of identity over time, its relatedness to other models that are often interpreted as alternatives to it becomes clear. One example can be seen in the notion of age identity

as the product of a cohort of people with a common socio-historical experience, such as the 'war generation' or 'baby boomers' travelling through time
together. This view was first theorized by Riley (1971) and has been developed
conceptually by Antonucci (1990) and in a popular idiom by Sheehey (1976,
1996). It is often contrasted to the proposition that age identity is constant and
unchanging. When examined from the perspective of degrees of fixity and
flux, however, cohorts can be seen as a means of carrying one's fixity along as
ageing takes place, maintained by continuities of peer reinforcement. Cohort
and continuity are both models of stability in identity maintenance.

While a mechanism for protecting identity is proposed in continuity theory, it lacks the critical perspective of anti-ageism and political economy. Continuity is essentially an 'investment' model of identity that works by building
up certain continuities of adult identity over time. There appear to be few
crises occasioned by exclusion from production or by existential doubt.
Indeed, it is assumed that identities from the 'productive' part of life can be
unproblematically maintained into old age. Similarly, a common theme can
be seen to emerge between anti-ageism, ageism itself and continuity. In each,
ageing is in some way irrelevant. Older and younger people only differ in terms
of chronological age and difference can be explained by social prejudice on the
one hand and failures of adaptation on the other. There is thus an absence of
consideration of existential questions arising for identity precisely because
ageing processes are taking place (Cole 1992; Biggs 1999a).

Ageing and the modern life course

Structuring identity around production also has consequences for theories
using a life course perspective. If certain periods of the life course are particularly concerned with production, both in terms of work and in terms of rearing
the next generation, then these periods tend to be seen as the most important.
Similarly, other parts of the life course are valued according to the priorities
arising from this dominant discourse. Even the division of human development into segments, distinguished by particular functions, and the perception
of life course as a linear progression, reflect something of the steps involved in
the division of labour itself. One rolls along in life, just like items on the
production line in a manufacturing process.

Once a particular way of constructing the life course is accepted, human
ageing tends to be perceived as conforming to that model. It becomes a way of
seeing that shapes what is seen, as people actively use the model as a guide for
their own development. Such models become accepted by formal communities, professions and policy makers and the collection of evidence and
the formal classification of what is normal and what is deviant follows. They
become, in Foucault's (1976) sense, 'normative judgement', a legitimizing
activity of what to expect and what to classify as unacceptable, and in Berger

and Luckmann's (1966) sense are 'recipes' that are institutionalized as part of the 'collective stock of knowledge' (1966: 67) that reflect some (dominant) variant of truth.

At the beginning of the twentieth century, a model of ageing identity based on decline was more or less uncritically accepted. Thus it was quite acceptable for Freud, the founder of psychoanalysis, to maintain that 'Near or above 50, the elasticity of the mental processes, on which treatment depends, are as a rule lacking; old people are not educable' (Freud [1905] 1953: 264).

The model of identity emerging from psychoanalysis is, when viewed from the perspective of adult ageing, subject to considerable bias. First, it clearly privileges childhood as the most important period for the formation of adult personality. Second, the parents – who are at once formative and restrictive of the child's identity – are cast as the villains of the piece because problems of identity are seen as stemming from traumatic interactions with the older, parental generation. Finally, as the above quotation amply illustrates, it associates adult ageing with personal rigidity and an inability to adapt to changing social circumstances.

Attempts to reform and socialize the psychodynamic modelling of life course identity, such as Erikson's (1950) 'ego psychology', went some way to exploring parts of the life course other than childhood. Erikson extended the classical Freudian stages of development from five to eight. He also drew attention to the degree to which individual development constituted an adaptation to the demands of adult social functioning.

Eriksonian stages and their associated life tasks can, however, be seen as an uncritical reflection of a production model of ageing: one travels through a preparation for adulthood, finding a partner, the core generative period of career and child rearing and finally the post-generative tension between wisdom and despair. Such a model of identity development, expanded by Levinson (1986) and Vaillant (1993), uncritically reflects the assumptions and priorities of the society from which it emerges, in this case 1950's America. They have, however, been deeply influential in the creation of social programmes based upon 'passing on' intergenerational experience.

Lynott and Lynott (1996) have argued that it was typical of theorizing of this period that it uncritically accepted descriptions of what social theorists saw around them as universal facts of ageing. In other words, culturally and historically contingent concepts were taken to create criteria for 'normal ageing' (Dannefer 2002). At least in terms of ageing, it amounts to theory without theorizing.

However, these models of identity within a life stage perspective are not simply reflections of a society based on production. They also intimate attempts to fix or protect parts of the life course, however inexplicitly. Erikson *et al.* (1986), for example, can be found pointing to the wasted human potential and transmission of experience that occurs if rapid social change erodes the achievement of wisdom. The problem is that they fix identity unthinkingly.

Critical reflections on the life course have been marked by attempts to distinguish differences in existential priorities between younger and older adults, a perspective that Eriksonian theorizing avoids by centring on generativity and a life well lived. Cole (1992) has criticized a continuing dualism with respect to ageing, which centres on enduring the privations of age on the one hand and technological solutions to limitation on the other. Ageing is turned into a problem to be solved as part of a 'moral economy' of the life course (Kohli 1989). The promise of medico-technical innovation, diet and exercise turns ageing into a failure to 'remain young'. Avoiding ageing becomes something of a choice and is therefore subject to moral sanction. Cole (1992) and Biggs (1993) have suggested that 'remaining young' is itself a form of age imperialism, whereby the priorities of earlier stages of the life course are extended to eclipse those arising from the ageing process itself. A preoccupation with ageing processes in order to defeat them has led to an avoidance of important existential questions concerning the finite nature of the embodied self. This sense of finitude has been cited by psychotherapists such as Frankel (1969) and Jung ([1932] 1967) as key to understanding identity in life course terms. It becomes a reference point around which all life projects come to circulate in the second half of life. Contemporary society, it is argued, has no space for the consideration of finitude. That life ends, and this affects the priorities of an ageing identity, is only tacitly recognized in so far as it can be packaged as a time to purchase as many leisure pursuits as possible. However, increasing awareness of finitude provokes a radical rethinking of identity, from the infinite possibilities of youth to marking life in terms of 'time left'. A resulting development of parts of the personality that have previously been suppressed through social conformity, and an increased awareness of transcendental concerns (Tornstam 1996), has the potential to undermine identities based on either production or consumption.

Threats to identity arise, then, because the grounding supplied by contemporary society contains the wrong forms of fluidity. From this perspective, the flexibility offered by consumer society simply offers a more sophisticated form of fixity, whereby one stands still by engaging in change for change's sake and by not being grounded in life course priorities. When seen in this light, the critique of life stages and continuities closely resembles Marcuse's (1964) view, that contemporary capitalism attempts to divert identity away from genuine needs and toward manufactured wants.

Postmodern identities and ageing

Identity and consumption

The argument that modern concerns have been usurped by those of post-modernity is largely reflected in a move away from identities being based on relations of production and toward identities constructed around consumption. As 'You are what you do (at work)' has created problems for ageing and identity, it might be anticipated that a 'postmodern turn' offers better opportunities for a flexible, yet grounded, ageing to emerge. Under post-modern conditions, an ageing identity maintains its bouyancy through the purchasing of lifestyles and props to support it. So long as one has an adequate post-retirement income, fuelled by the growth of occupational pensions, and contingent on continued performance of a capitalist economy (Phillipson 1998), one can 'buy into' a variety of lifestyles and escape the constraints associated with disengagement and decline. Such 'choices' are, of course, shaped by education, social class, race and gender. Lifestyle options may include 'sun city' retirement or 'sno-bird' migratory communities of older people (Phillips *et al.* 2001) or the consumption of leisure, fashion or technical innovations to support particular lifestyle statements (Gilleard and Higgs 2000). Gilleard (1996) has argued that a shift toward identities based upon consumption rather than production has profoundly changed the perception of ageing in contemporary society and the possibilities open to older adults. According to this viewpoint, we are faced with a surplus of commodities and images that defy coherent structure, thus forcing a continuous series of choices about identity and age. A heady mixture emerges, associating activity and well-being in old age with leisured consumption in the grey market and result-ing in commercially legitimized means of managing later life (Katz 2000a). The keyword, and promise to ageing identity, is that of almost infinite flexibility. Postmodern theorizing of ageing and identity has therefore centred on two issues: first is the effect of such fluidity on the life course and second is the role of the body as a site where flexibility and limitation come into contention.

The postmodern life course

Contemporary lifestyles of older people are said to allow 'individuals who look after their bodies and adopt a positive attitude toward life . . . to avoid the decline and negative effects of the ageing process and thereby prolong their capacity to enjoy the full benefits of consumer culture' (Featherstone and Hepworth 1983: 87).

Featherstone and Hepworth (1983, 1989) propose that adult ageing no longer consists of a transition from productivity to disengagement. Feather-stone (1991) has gone so far as to suggest that social divisions, such as age categories, are becoming irrelevant. Ageing, it is argued, has become a life course 'plateau' that starts in midlife and extends into deep old age and upon which the self can be repeatedly reinvented. Lifestyle choice has thus contributed to a 'blurring of what appeared previously to be relatively clearly marked stages and the experiences and characteristic behaviour which were associated with those stages' (Featherstone and Hepworth 1989: 144). As part of this process, it is implied that older adulthood is liberated from ageist stereotyping and has ceased to be understandable in terms of a single experience, common to all (Gilleard and Higgs 2000).

If these theorists are correct, then ageing identity is becoming increasingly freed from the life stages and expectations formerly used to structure the process of adult ageing. Observations of popular culture would seem to support this view in so far as

> Popular perceptions of ageing have shifted, from the dark days when the 'aged poor' sat in motionless rows in the workhouse, to a modernising interwar phase when 'the elderly' were expected to don the retirement uniform, to postmodern times when older citizens are encouraged not just to dress 'young' and look youthful, but to exercise, have sex, take holidays, socialise in ways indistinguishable from those of their children's generation.
>
> (Blaikie 1999: 104).

There are no rules now, Blaikie concludes, only choices. Paradoxically, this may be the postmodern twist on earlier functionalist work on 'the roleless role' (Rosow 1967, 1974). Functionalist theorists interpreted this role as a negative and alienating (*a la* Durkheim) by-product of 'modernization' (Cowgill and Holmes 1972).

In the present postmodernist version, however, older adults are expected to generate identities from their own imaginative resources, as the certainties of stage-appropriate codes of behaviour appear to be dissolving in front of their eyes. The trick of identity management under such conditions is to discover techniques whereby options for identity can be negotiated in the absence of binding cultural guidelines.

It is, however, a considerable leap from claiming that older adults now behave like the generation below them, to claiming that the social categorization of adult ageing has been abolished. It is an even more radical leap to claim, as Featherstone and Wernick (1995) have, that biomedical advances allow the ageing body to be 'reshaped, remade, fused with machines' such that ageing can be 'recoded' and simply be one of many identity options. In postmodern times social fixity has been replaced by attempts to manipulate, control and thereby 'fix' an embodied self so as to avoid ageing.

Identity and the body

The question of the body brings the issue of postmodern ageing to crisis point. Rather than being a surface that can be elaborated at the discretion of the individual, as may be the case for younger adults, ageing raises the question of limits to autonomy and choice. The tension between fixity and flux becomes ever more acute and lifestyle options increasingly narrowed.

A number of writers have observed reluctance on behalf of contemporary sociology to come to terms with the ageing body (Turner 1995; Oberg 1996; Tulle-Winton 2000). This has been put down to a deep-seated dualism in western thought that separates the mind from the body, such that notions of self and identity have been associated with mind alone. This dualism seems to affect the self-perception of age as well as the study of gerontology. Kaufman (1986) has observed, for example, that older Americans see themselves as separate from their bodies, in such a way as to reinforce the notion of an 'ageless' identity. In the study of ageing itself, critical gerontologists have made great play of the power of social determination by contrasting it with the popular and medically dominated notion of ageing as a purely biological process (Phillipson and Walker 1986). This has contributed to a paradoxical situation in which, while ageing and bodily change are closely linked in popular culture, the impact of the body on identity has been relatively ignored by social gerontology (Oberg 1996).

Turner (1995) argues that, with the emergence of postmodernity, the body has become a primary site of self-regulation, a phenomenon that he relates to the erosion of traditional social structures and conventions. In the absence of external frameworks, then, individuals attempt to establish a sense of control over their lives through diet, exercise and other regimes aimed at shaping the self. The embodied self has thereby become a project, a trajectory that guides one's passage through time and space. Under such conditions it is impossible, he concludes, to distinguish between body and self-identity. One's body even becomes a record of personal experiences, inscribed upon the physical self, and, as the condition and functioning of a person's body mediates opportunities for social interaction and activity, it becomes core to understanding personal identity.

This is particularly true of old age, where the 'progressive betrayals' of the body accumulate and force themselves onto identity's agenda. Thus, there may be younger selves trapped in ageing bodies (Featherstone and Hepworth 1995); the state of one's body comes to stand for an inner moral condition (Cole 1992); or observed bodies become a source of distance and 'otherness' impeding intergenerational communication (Meador 1998). Tulle-Winton (2000) suggests that, rather than being ignored, embodied ageing has become over-determined, colonized even, to the exclusion of alternative perspectives. She argues that modernist conceptions of old age, dominated by a medical/

technical understanding of ageing as illness, have led to the production of 'unwanted bodies' in later life. The medicalization of bodily old age both eclipses the lived experience of ageing and reduces embodied selves to a biology of terminal stages. Under such conditions it is very difficult to incorporate bodily identity into a positive sense of self. The paradox of age and identity is that the body simultaneously eclipses social and personal experience while itself being ignored by avowedly social understandings of ageing.

Strategies for ageing and identity

The threats and opportunities that have been identified by modern and post-modern approaches to ageing have led to a shift of attention toward how older people manage ageing identities.

Each theory engages with the issues of fixed identities and the room allowed for manoeuvre in a slightly different way, and in terms of the relationship between youth and age, depth and surface, positive and negative evaluation, come to markedly different conclusions. They require that we think of ageing identities in radically different ways and draw different conclusions as to the possibilities for social change. Three positions will be described below: first, the 'mask of ageing'; second, the uses of masquerade; and third, the narrative approach to ageing identities.

The mask of ageing

Tension between an increasingly fixed body and the options arising from consumer culture has led Featherstone and Hepworth (1989, 1995) to the view that ageing can best be explained as a mask. Here, physical processes of ageing, as reflected in outward appearance, are contrasted to a real self which remains young (Hepworth 1991). This theory, which has come to be known as the 'mask of ageing', holds that over time the ageing body becomes a cage from which a younger self-identity cannot escape. The body, while it is malleable, can still provide access to a variety of consumer identities. However, as ageing gathers pace, it becomes increasingly difficult to 'recycle' the failing body, which simultaneously denies access to that world of choice. An endgame emerges with older people being at war with themselves, in a battle between a desire for youthful expression and an ageing body. Ageing, as a mask, becomes a nightmare version of the consumer dream of endless reinvention as identity emerges as a contradiction between the fixedness of the body and the fluidity of social images. Here, positive identity is identified with a youthful self, while the old body colonizes the ageing process and as such the theory has little good to say about age and identity. At some point this young person has become trapped in an old body, but the precise nature and timing of this entrapment is left unclear.

The task for a critical study of ageing is presumably to 'see' the younger (good) identity that is hidden behind the aged (bad) appearance. The 'solution' to the problems of an ageing identity would consist in techniques that release the youthful self. Hence these theorists' interest in bio-technology.

Age and masquerade

Theorists working within a psycho-dynamic framework (Woodward 1991, 1995; Biggs 1993, 1999a) have understood the relationship between appearance and identity in terms of depth and surface and have used a masquerade motif to examine the ageing self. Masquerade is of particular interest because it occurs at the meeting point of both the personal and the social and also surface appearances and the inner worlds of identity. In other words, identity becomes a bridge between the inner and outer logics of adult ageing.

Woodward (1991) suggests that masquerade in later life includes a simultaneous submission to dominant social codes and a resistance to them. So while older people might submit to ageist expectations by attempting to appear young, they resist by knowingly playing with these appearances, thus underlining their artificial nature. In old age, masking both conceals and reveals the marks of age, with a key factor being a recognition that masquerade has to do with concealing something and presenting the very conditions of that concealment. She also argues that a mask may express as well as hide a truth, or multiple truths.

Masking emerges as a technique for managing identity that is both subtle and permeable. There is an element of play involved in creating a convincing ageing identity while the need to conceal hints at possible sanctions that make masquerade necessary.

In Biggs's approach (1997, 1999b), masquerade is presented as a tactical manoeuvre to negotiate the contradiction between social ageism and the increased personal integration that accompanies adult ageing. The distinction between hidden and surface elements of identity is not seen, however, as an inevitable part of the ageing process and under certain conditions the self-integration that comes with maturity should allow a more settled identity, at ease with itself, to come into play.

Masking connects inner psychological and external social logic while affording an element of protection for parts of the self that cannot be easily expressed. It is used to cloak socially unacceptable aspects of ageing in circumstances where an ageing identity is perceived to be threatened. The mask becomes a source of conformity, which nevertheless protects this mature self from external attack and, as such, creates a necessary inner space where one can build a stable identity.

A theoretical consideration of masquerade and ageing allows positive environments to be defined as ones that enhance harmony between internal and external identities, where one can 'be oneself' with minimal resort to artifice or masquerade. In contrast to the bodily 'mask of ageing', surface appearance is largely fluid and performative, while the hidden mature identity is relatively stable. Also the relationship between youth and age is reversed, so that the masquerade of youth covers an internal ageing self. Here, the 'solution' to ageing would be to encourage environments in which this inner identity can be freely expressed.

Narrative ageing

Narrative approaches to ageing and identity draw on the metaphor of 'stories to age by' (Randall and Kenyon 1999; Holstein and Gubrium 2000). These stories may be drawn from existing cultural material or be the product of self-invention. More often than not they are described as using elements of the personal past in conjunction with contemporary imagery to construct what Giddens (1991) has referred to as a 'convincing narrative'. In so doing, the indeterminacy of postmodern culture has been turned to advantage by older adults, in so far as aspects of their own experience can be recombined to suit specific situations. More enduring 'trajectories of the self' may also be developed to negotiate the later life course, given the erosion of traditionally ascribed roles and relationships.

Holstein and Gubrium (2000) present narrative ageing as a solution to the problem posed by Gergen (1991) in his book *The Saturated Self*. According to Gergen, contemporary society is so full of multiple meanings and interpretations that personal identity is in danger of becoming overwhelmed. Any interior space is potentially filled with so many possible alternatives that a sense of distinct identity may be lost entirely. Holstein and Gubrium propose that narrative identities exist in the space between selfhood as a work in progress in the immediate present and pre-existing Foucauldian domains that shape social identities by supplying the raw material from which they are made. Stories of the ageing self arise from an interplay of these two poles of attraction. A narrative approach also incorporates a strong element of the 'here and now' of personal construction, which is common to the wider debate on narrative approaches. Spence (1992), for example, when discussing narrative therapy, states that the validity of a new narrative over an older one depends upon the storyteller's immediate satisfaction with the story that emerges. Historical truth should give way to 'narrative truth' as individuals are expected to 're-author parts of the lifestory' in accordance with whether an account is coherent and allows the client a satisfying existence (McLeod 1997).

The absence of a sense of historical continuity and depth to these trends within the narrative approach has caused Meador (1998) to argue that a narrative understanding of the postmodern self must 'not deny the developmental realities of the life course', and Biggs (1999a) to criticize the way that lived experience is treated as if it is source material for a 'pick and mix' identity, with scant regard for actual personal and historical events. Narrative resolves the ambiguity left by approaches such as continuity theory, between self-construction and externally observed continuities in behaviour, in favour of the retrospective creation of a convincing narrative. The attractiveness of a narrative approach to ageing is very similar to that of masquerade, in so far as it opens a critical distance between who we are and what we do. Both allow a potentially critical stance to be taken toward existing roles and identity statements. It attempts to come to terms with fluidity of identity and blurred traditional reference points, by incorporating them into the personal sphere. A danger is that, as part of this process, structural inequalities and the need to negotiate ageing identity as a social phenomenon are underplayed.

Concluding comments: what hope for a critical gerontology of identity?

The overview of approaches to ageing and identity found above raises a number of issues for the critical study of adult ageing.

First, each of the theoretical positions outlined places a different emphasis on stability and fluidity as they have affected ageing identities. It is probable that both are necessary for a critical gerontology. On the one hand the need for ground on which to make a stand, as identified by Taylor (1989), a stable core or basis from which to argue and build solidarities, suggests that certain forms of stability are essential for social agency around ageing issues. On the other hand, an awareness of oppressive social structures has led modern and postmodern theorists to concentrate on the need for flexibility in the construction of serviceable identities for older people. Ageing through grounded identities that have adequate freedom to manoeuvre is essential for concerted action, by older people themselves and by those who work with them.

Second lies the question of whether it is possible to build an identity which takes into account the special life challenges and circumstances of older adults. From the positions discussed above, it would seem that the majority of social theorists have paid much more attention to restrictions on self-expression in later life than on what grounded or authentic ageing might actually be like. Whether ageing identity is constrained by bodily betrayals, social attitudes or material inequalities, critical studies of ageing should be able to say what is being argued for as well as against. It may not be enough to claim that all identities are socially constructed, or that ageing is simply one of many identity choices and therefore questions of centrality or genuineness are redundant. New fixes are often adopted to establish a degree of control in an uncertain world. A critical approach should demand for what purpose and in whose interests particular stances are made rather than others and how the alternatives might enhance identities that take ageing into account. In other words, we should ask what is special about age, given particular social, cultural and historical circumstances.

Third, the tension between modern and postmodern arguments for or against different forms of stability and fluidity has slowly transformed into a consideration of the strategies that might be used to negotiate ageing identities. The value of studying strategies for ageing identity, such as narrative and masquerade, is that they unpeel descriptions of ageing from the stance that older adults and others might take toward material events. A critical space between performance and intention is opened up. But there is a danger that by focusing on narrative invention, theory and policy might deny the role of past events and memory in the creation of ageing identities.

Fourth, if it is accepted that in complex societies development is often uneven, then it is quite possible that the ageing adult will encounter modern challenges to identity in one context and postmodern ones in another. Modernity to postmodernity can now themselves be seen as different possible trajectories for identity in contemporary society and may inhabit different institutions and progress at different rates. From a narrative perspective they are perhaps different stories by which to understand a life, depending upon the resources and opportunities available to each person or group of people. A major source of uncertainty in later life might arise from the contradictions between different ageing identities demanded by the narratives of ageing adopted within different institutional contexts.

Fifth, it has become clear that attempts to preserve fluidity of identity may paradoxically create new forms of restriction. If, for example, attempts are made to replace the process of ageing with an 'ageless' identity, then the original intention to escape from social and bodily restriction is simply replaced by a second set of demands. Not only is ageing itself denied, but the 'new' bid for freedom turns into an attempt to fix identity at one point in time. Much of postmodern theorizing appears to have tried to do this, and failed when it hit the question of ageing. Further, attempts to abolish ageing, through claims of an explosion of multiplicity, seriously threaten the possibility of common identity or social action based on age, or with groups facing related inequalities. In this sense multiplicity destabilizes and disenfranchises ageing identity while appearing to free people from it, and diversity must be partnered by a sense of collective identity to retain its critical power.

Sixth, and beyond stability and fluidity, much of the writing on identity appears to be genuinely innocent of race, sex and social class, not only as personal characteristics and attributes but also in terms of the effects on identity of their institutional embodiments, for example institutional racism and sexism. A paradox is that amidst the reassertions of the import of culture, especially versus class, that are replete in postmodernist theorizing, there is so little accommodation to the diversity and intersectionality of race, gender and class with identity. There is a lack of connection in this work with the macro considerations of identity that currently dominate much of the sociological discourse on social movements.

A critical study of ageing should engage with questions such as: what is special about ageing identity? How can links be made across uncertain boundaries to other social groups? These questions are almost absent from the current study of identity and age. Ageing identity is not just a site for inequalities, but is itself a catalyst of fixed structures and the creation of unequal relationships. It is the way in which people negotiate age relations, across cultures and over time. At one time old age may be seen as fixed; at another, fluid. There may nevertheless be sources of stability and uncertainty that are part and parcel of ageing. If social actors see things differently at different ages, then it is legitimate to interrogate the age structure of decision making, of research and of the creation of social theory itself, each of which will have an age/power dimension, and will provoke different strategies and narratives and produce different truths. This raises profound epistemological questions and the urgent call for reflexivity in the production of the knowledges that contest for the status of truth. As critical gerontologists it is not enough to interpret; it is also necessary to build a base from which to effect radical change.

4 Feminist perspectives and old age policy

Key points:

- The gendered state and the reproduction of patriarchal systems.
- Feminist political economy and critique of social policy.
- Neo-conservative moral economies and the politics of care and affirmation.
- Social movements, resistance and alternative visions of ageing.

Feminist theorizing is one of the most significant areas of theoretical development in critical approaches to social policy and ageing. Gender itself is a crucial organizing principle in the economic and power relations of societal institutions as well as of social life throughout the life course, playing an important role in the distribution of resources to older men and women (Estes 1991a, 1998; Diamond 1992; Calasanti 1993; Calasanti and Zajicek 1993; Quadagno 1994; Ginn and Arber 1995; McMullin 1995).

A major goal of feminist political economy in regard to ageing is understanding how the state, capital and the sex and gender system conjointly *produce* and *reproduce* the dominant institutions that render older women vulnerable and dependent throughout their life course (Estes 1991a). An important consideration is how state policies define, individualize and commodify the problems of ageing (e.g. as individual problems and personal private responsibility for the purchase of services sold for profit); and how these processes are ideologically and practically consistent with state roles that advance the interests of capital accumulation, a gender ideology, and the legitimation of capitalist and patriarchal social relations (Estes 1979a).

Three premises undergird the theoretical approach adopted in this chapter. The *first premise* is that the experiences and situation of women under public policy in general, and old age policy in particular, are socially produced in accord with how women and men are viewed and treated in society (social position, normative roles, responsibilities and rewards), and the cumulative results of these processes over the life course in a capitalist society and democratic state (and with all the inherent tensions therein).

The *second premise* follows from the first. It is that 'the problems' of older women are structurally conditioned rather than simply a product of individual behaviour and individual 'choices'. In contrast to classical and dominant contemporary economic theory, the 'choices' and 'preferences' (in economists' terms) that are available to women and other structurally disadvantaged groups are largely illusory and more market rhetoric than reality. Instead, the role and influence of the state, the market and the family are pivotal in understanding old age policy and how it is constructed in ways that produce the relatively disadvantaged social, political and economic status for older women, and particularly for older women of colour.

The *third premise* builds on Patricia Hill Collins's work on the complex interlocking systems of oppression as reflected in race, ethnicity, social class and gender across the life course (Collins 1991). These interlocking oppressions are 'interrelated axes of social structure' rather than 'just separate features of existence'. In other words, they are not simply additive; they contribute significantly to the precarious situation of older women and their treatment through public policy (Dressel 1988; Bernard and Meade 1993). Sexuality, age, ethnicity and nation also are part of these intersecting systems of oppression (Collins 2000). The approach here constitutes a critique of essentialist thinking that has characterized mainstream (most often white) feminist writings that simplify or homogenize the diversity and intersectionality of the oppressions of gender, sexuality, race, ethnicity, class, age and nation.

The discussion provides a further strand to the theoretical debates reviewed in the preceding chapters, but with a particular focus on various elements within feminist social theory that may be applied to the lives of women in old age. Some of the arguments are illustrated in more detail in later chapters of the book.

Critical feminist epistemology

Work from a feminist perspective on old age policy requires critical reflexivity in addition to feminist epistemology (Smith 1990; Collins 1991; Harding 1996). Scholars engaged in the gerontological imagination and the production of gerontological knowledge (Estes 1979a, 2001a, b; Estes *et al.* 1992a) must take explicit steps to work outside the frame of 'patriarchal thought' (Lerner 1986: 228). This means 'accepting . . . our [women's] knowledge as valid . . . [and] developing intellectual courage' to push well beyond mainstream and masculinist social science frameworks and methods (Lerner 1986: 228). Sandra Harding notes that feminist standpoint approaches and feminist epistemology 'enable one to appropriate and redefine objectivity' (Harding 1996: 134), which is crucial because

> Culture's best beliefs – what it calls knowledge – are socially situated. The distinctive features of women's situation in a gender stratified society are being used as resources in the new feminist research. It is these distinctive resources, . . . not used by conventional researchers, that enable feminism to produce empirically more accurate descriptions and theoretically richer explanations than does conventional research.
>
> (Harding 1996: 119).

Harding (1996: 128) also expresses the view that 'Women's perspective comes from everyday life . . . The perspective from women's everyday activity is scientifically preferable to the perspective available only from the "ruling" activities of men in the dominant groups.' A critical feminist epistemology is consistent with Dorothy Smith's (1990) critique of male power and 'relations of ruling' that are embedded in objectified and alienated knowledge of social science. Smith's proposal is for 'an alternative sociology, from the standpoint of women, [that] makes the everyday world its problematic' (Smith 1990: 27).

Feminist theory and social policy

Substantial developments have occurred in the past two decades in feminist theoretical and empirical work relevant to social policy (Gold *et al.* 1975; Redclift and Mingione 1985; Dickinson and Russell 1986; Sassoon 1987; Abramovitz 1988; Acker 1988; Quadagno 1994; O'Connor *et al.* 1999). Gender is now recognized as a key structuring element in contemporary society. Work on gender, social policy and the state has been animated by four broad paradigmatic approaches – conservative, liberal, socialist and radical. More recently, three other paradigms have been added – libertarian feminism, welfare feminism and Black and third world feminism (Williams 1996).

Conservative feminism locates women's predicament in nature and biology, which is consistent with the idea that the 'traditional gender arrangements are either inevitable or at least preferable [while it is claimed that] . . . departures from these arrangements . . . impose high costs of social inefficiency and human unhappiness' (Jaggar and Rothenberg 1984: 83). Sex role theory is the sociological version of this perspective developed by structural functionalists (Connell 1983; Demetriou 2001), in which the 'natural' (normative) 'female role' is cast as inevitable and functional for society, the family and the individual, while gender inequality and male dominance and power in these structures and stratification systems are ignored (see also Ferree and Hall 1996).

Liberal feminism deals with inequalities associated with unfair sex discrimination and related attitudes, while the state is seen as a neutral and basically democratic institution. Sex discrimination, sex bias and inequality are thought to be remediable via political participation and changes in the law (Jaggar and Rothenberg 1984; O'Connor 1993). Liberals seek to improve attitudes toward women to assure women's access to positions within the existing system rather than promoting deep structural system changes.

Socialist feminism posits the inseparability of class and gender oppression (Jaggar and Rothenberg 1984) in the structuring of inequality, citing the salience of production in the market for both capitalism and men's patriarchal control of women and reproduction in the private sphere of the family. This dual systems theory emphasizes the interaction of two materially based systems of capitalism and patriarchy (Mutari 2001: 390). Women's unpaid (reproductive) labour advances the interest of capitalism by reproducing and maintaining the workforce, as well as men's oppression of women. The dominant institutions of capitalism and patriarchy must be challenged and changed.

Radical feminism posits that women's oppression is the fundamental oppression, in which patriarchy is seen as the ultimate source of inequality (Firestone 1970, 1979; Jaggar and Rothenberg 1984). It is men's collective control over social institutions such as the state that is seen as imposing hegemonic and oppressive control over women's lives, sexuality and coerced 'choices'. The eradication of patriarchic systems of thought and social organization is the only option.

Libertarian feminism emphasizes 'individual liberty achieved through freedom of the market, rather than through laws of equality and social justice' (Williams 1996: 43). A UK version of this New Right approach, which promotes individualism, neo-liberalism and welfare state retrenchment, employs the slogan 'For Life, Liberty and Property'. State intervention is seen as a problem inhibiting women's liberty because it 'regulates and confines the natural state of motherhood' (Williams 1996: 44).

Welfare feminism seeks reforms to address the needs of mothers, children and wives within the private sphere such as maternal and child benefits of health care and family allowances. This approach 'retains a clear distinction between the public and private spheres of work and family . . . without any challenge to existing relationships between the state and the family, nor the paternalistic organization of welfare provision' (Williams 1996: 51).

Black and third world feminism (Collins 1991, 2000; Mohanty 1991; Williams 1996) critiques white feminism and its treatment of patriarchy, capitalism and the family without reference to racism and 'Black women's struggles against slavery, colonialism, imperialism and racism' (Williams 1996: 70).

Most work on social policy and ageing from a feminist perspective has been engaged either from the liberal feminist or welfare reform perspectives. Aimed at promoting equality under the law, the liberal feminist approach is critiqued for being oblivious to the discourse of the late 1990s on the problems of equality and difference (Sassoon 2001), including the problem that policies that provide 'equality under the law' may not achieve equality (i.e. are not gender-neutral in their outcomes) due to the basic gender, race, ethnic and other differences that continue to operate. The work from welfare feminism perspectives in ageing seeks to address the needs of families, elders and their burdened and unpaid caregivers through reforms that, for example, provide respite care for long-term care provided informally by women.

Another way of organizing different streams of feminist thought that is relevant to women and old age policy is the tripartite division of gender reform feminism, gender resistance feminism and gender rebellion feminism (Lorber 1998). Those working from a *gender reform* perspective seek a change in the content of gender relations in the family and the economy, but not a major restructuring of the social order including the gender order. Feminists working from a *gender resistance* perspective argue that women's oppressions (e.g. violence, sexual control and exploitation) are so pervasive and negative that women should resist rather than cooperate with the gender order. *Gender rebellion* adherents challenge both the structure of the gender order and the unproblematic binary thinking of the division between two sexes or genders. Work on old age policy from a feminist perspective may be categorized as largely reform feminism as described above.

Feminist theories of the state

Joan Acker points out that theories of the state and social class that do not explicitly and adequately address the subordination of women and the 'privileging of men' fail as comprehensive frameworks for understanding social phenomena (Acker 1988). Acker further contends that class is produced through gendered processes, structured by production and distribution. Distribution, in particular, is vitally affected by first, the dominance of market relations as the basis of distribution; and second, the indifference of the economic system to the reproduction of the working class and the demands of working-class daily life (Acker 1988), responsibility for which is borne by women.

Acker asks to what extent the overall institutional structure of the state has 'been formed by and through gender'. A crucial question is: 'How are men's interests and masculinity . . . intertwined in the creation and maintenance of particular institutions, and how have the subordination and exclusion of women been built into ordinary institutional functioning?' (Acker 1992: 568).

Utilizing the concept of 'gendered institutions', Acker contends that

> Gender is a dimension of domination and discrimination [that is] neither obviously discrete nor structurally analogous [to social class and race]. Class relations do not function in the same way as gender relations; race relations are still another matter. All of these come together in cross-cutting ways . . . Gender is present in the processes, practices, images and ideologies and distributions of power in the various sectors of social life.
>
> (Acker 1992: 566–7)

Quadagno (1994) also has faulted class theory for its inattention to the role of state policy in mediating race relations and for its blindness to 'a defining feature of social provision: its organization around gender' (1994: 14).

Acker observes that both the state and the economy, among other social institutions, have been developed and dominated by men; therefore, they have been 'symbolically interpreted from the standpoint of men [and] defined by the absence of women' (Acker 1992: 567). Connell (1987) argues that the power of the state extends beyond the distribution of resources to the formation and reformation of social patterns. The state does more than regulate institutions and relations like marriage and motherhood; it manages them. The state actually *constitutes* 'the social categories of the gender order', as 'patriarchy is both constructed and contested through the state' (Connell 1987).

'State masculinism' is a concept introduced by Wendy Brown (1995), who argues that female subjects are produced by the state first through reproduction and the regulation of pornography, and second, through women's dependence on the state for survival. Brown cites four features of 'state masculinism': first, *juridicial–legislative* – the formal and constitutional rights in which civil society is seen as a masculine right in relation to the natural and pre-political place of women and the family; second, *capitalist* – the defined property rights and the possibilities for active involvement in wealth accumulation; third, *prerogative* – the [state's] legitimate monopoly of force and violence; and fourth, *bureaucratic* – expressed through the institution of the state and its discourse, as discipline, presented as a neutral means of power.

Each of these features of the state has implications for women and old age policy. Reflecting the juridicial–legislative state role, the caregiving role of women is assumed as the natural and pre-political place for females. Under the state's role *vis-à-vis* capitalism, property rights and the ability to accumulate wealth are limited by the impaired ability of women actively to access paid employment as a result of their substantial caregiving responsibilities and sexism in the workplace (Orloff 1993; Ferree and Hall 1996; Phillips *et al.* 2002). In the state's prerogative role, violence, hate crimes against women, and state control of reproductive options each profoundly shape women's opportunities for participation and livelihood in the society. In the state's bureaucratic role, older women, as clients of welfare and other state assistance programmes, may deal with demeaning and assymetrical power relations with state agents of social control.

Patriarchy and the sex/gender system

Carol Pateman (1989) describes 'the patriarchal welfare state' in which 'since the early twentieth century, welfare policies have reached across from public to private, and have helped uphold a patriarchal structure of family life' (Pateman 1989: 183). Theories of patriarchy have been critiqued for giving insufficient attention both to social class and to ideology, and for being too deterministic and functionalist in assuming the state is the modern instrument of patriarchal relations (Lorber 1998). Others contend that the concept of patriarchy is central because of its emphasis on power (Mutari 2001: 384) and human agency (Ortner 1996). Wiegersma (1991: 174) defines patriarchy 'as more than a form of male-dominant family structure. It is also an independent political-economic system of production.'

Supporting this view, Ciscel and Heath assert that 'patriarchy is irrepressible' in that

> a new form of patriarchy has arisen with women primarily performing gendered labor in the service sector of the capitalist marketplace, and the unpaid domestic labor of the home. The face of patriarchy is now that of the virtual male, where patriarchal rules and values are transmitted through the media, at home, at work, and in leisure activities.
>
> (Ciscel and Heath 2001: 407)

Women are left with whatever the market has not usurped as profitable – 'the creation of the web of relationships'. This: '. . . ersatz freedom from the unfettered expansion of markets in reality represents another form of oppression, confining women and their families to lives of market supporting activities' (Ciscel and Heath 2001: 408).

Bonnie Fox (1988: 177) argues that both social structure and 'gendered subjectivity/ideology' are more important than patriarchy in 'explaining women's oppression' (for more on ideology, see later section). Gayle Rubin (1984: 33) proposes an alternative concept, the 'sex/gender system', to denote the 'empirically oppressive ways in which sexual worlds have been organized' and in which the evolution of kinship structures and marriage rituals have established 'the traffic in women'. This 'traffic' occurs without granting women access to the networks of power, money and culture because 'kinship and marriage systems are always parts of total social systems and are always tied to economic and political arrangements' (Rubin 1984: 56). These arrangements form the basis of the 'political economy of sex'.

Social reproduction

As noted at the outset of this chapter, any comprehensive theory of the state and old age policy cannot omit gender; it must articulate not only the relations between the state and the economy, but also the relations with the household (Dickinson and Russell 1986; O'Connor *et al.* 1999). Social reproduction is a concept that embraces the work of both producing the members of society as educated, healthy, knowledgeable and productive human beings and the work of setting up conditions by which such production of individuals and society may continue across generations and time.

As Ginn *et al.* (2001: 20) suggest, a key component of the relationship between the labour market and the household is women's paid and unpaid work. Under capitalism, women's role historically has been in reproduction, which was dubbed the 'complement' or equivalent of man's role in production (Mitchell 1966). Acker (2000: 49) notes that a major lacuna in feminist work is the dearth of conceptual attention to the social and economic contributions of domestic labour. As Brush observes, 'The question of what counts as work is related to who does it (men "labor," women "love") and where (in the formal labor market, in the underground economy, or in the "domestic" realm)' (Brush 2000: 179).

Feminists critique traditional Marxist views of reproduction, which have 'privileged' relations of production that men do through paid work and 'ignore . . . much of the process by which people and their labour power are reproduced' (Himmelweit 1983: 419). This is the reproduction work that women do, which is seen as informal, unpaid, invisible and devalued. Reproduction takes place on two levels: 'The reproduction of labour power both on a daily and generational sense; and human and biological reproduction' (Himmelweit 1983: 419). The blindness toward reproductive work (and its lack of recognition and devaluation by public policy) explains the treatment of women's and men's relations in the family (the division of caregiving and household work) as private and beyond the scope of state intervention (O'Connor *et al.* 1999: 3).

When attention is given to reproductive relations in the context of the two major old age policy arenas of retirement income and long-term care, the gendered division of labour, the lack of women's equal access to the labour market, and the unpaid informal work of women throughout the life course must be squarely placed at the centre of analysis. The vital import of social reproduction in old age is illustrated by the significant unpaid caring labour which, for women, has lifelong cumulative (and negative) consequences. In Britain, Falkingham (1998: 108) observes that 'Unemployment, interrupted earnings histories, time out of the labour force to care for children or dependent adults, part-time work and low pay may all preclude the building up of non-state pension contributions.' Under US social security policy, this refusal to count the contributions of reproductive relations as part of economic activity results in 'zeroes' (zero dollar contributions toward social security) for the years out of the labour market to care for children and elders. The assumption of women's 'free' reproductive relations and its categorization as 'non-work' is a 'care penalty' (Folbre 2001) that explains much about the economic vulnerability of older women in countries such as the USA (Estes and Binney 1990) inasmuch as it is a core assumption of old age policy, as demonstrated by both social security and long-term care policy.

Feminist economics

The developing field of feminist economics offers great potential to contribute to the study of gender and old age policy. Scholars are challenging and reformulating the work of classical 'liberal' economists such as Adam Smith and 'the failure of neo-classical economics to accurately analyze (or even recognize) the role of the market in creating intractable inequalities in power relations within the family' (Ciscel and Heath 2001: 408, citing Bergmann 1995). Gillian Hewitson's *Feminist Economics* (1999) brings feminist poststructuralism to economics in her critique of neoclassical economics (e.g. abstract individualism and theory of individual optimizing behaviour) for distorting the experience of women in its production of gender meanings and sexed bodies.

A number of special issues of the *Review of Radical Political Economics* have developed feminist perspectives on issues relating to capitalism, patriarchy, class, ideology and classical economics. New feminist principles of economics are proposed, in which

- non-market activities and the household are conceptualized as loci of economic activity;
- gender, race and ethnicity are seen as important concepts;
- cooperation and caring (not just competition) are given emphasis;
- power relationships are conceptualized as an important force in the economy; and
- government action is understood as potentially improving (rather than impeding) market outcomes (Schneider and Shackelford 2001).

Nancy Folbre challenges Adam Smith's theory that 'the invisible hand' of the market promotes selfish behaviour that benefits all. Instead, she posits that:

The invisible hand of the market depends upon the invisible heart of care. Markets cannot function effectively outside the framework of families and communities built on values of love, obligation, and reciprocity . . . The invisible hand is about achievement. The invisible heart is about care for others. The hand and the heart are inter-dependent, but they are also in conflict. The only way to balance them successfully is to find fair ways of rewarding those who care for other people. This is not a problem that economists or business people take seriously.

(Folbre 2001: 4)

A woman's dilemma, Folbre states, is that women 'know they can benefit economically by becoming achievers rather than caregivers' (Folbre 2001: 4). This work is squarely relevant to multiple dimensions of the problem of women under old age policy as exemplified in social security and long-term care policy, and that will only be exacerbated by the privatization of core health and social services.

Theories of masculine domination

We are not solely dependent upon feminist theory in order to grasp the signifi-cance of gender issues in social policy. There is a growing body of work on gender relations in the form of theories of masculinity. French sociologist Pierre Bourdieu in *Masculine Domination* (2001) speaks to the social practices of a society that are so dominant that they are hardly perceived. Masculine dom-ination is 'a form of symbolic violence, a kind of gentle invisible pervasive violence that is experienced through the everyday practices of social life'.

Robert Connell advances the concept of *hegemonic masculinity*, referring to the gender practices of everyday life that 'embod[y] the currently accepted answer to the problem of the legitimacy of patriarchy which guarantees (or is taken to guarantee) the dominant position of men and the subordination of women' (Connell 1995: 77). In his threefold model of the structure of gender relations – which he calls 'gender regimes' – he distinguishes between the relations of labour, power and cathexis or emotional attachment (Connell 1987). The *structure of labour* (labour market) is such that men gain material advantage, which he labels the 'patriarchal dividend' (Connell 1996: 161–2). The *structure of power* is one in which men also control the means of insti-tutionalized power – the state and the army. The *structure of cathexis* is con-trolled by men through the institution of the family and male superiority and violence therein, rather than reciprocity and intimacy (Connell 1987, 2000). More recently, Connell has added a fourth category to his earlier work on the structure of gender relations. This is called the *structure of symbolism* which incorporates the idea that 'gender subordination may be reproduced through linguistic practices such as addressing women by titles that define them through their marital relationships to men' (Connell 2000). These different forms of male domination may exert particular forms of control on women in old age, with distinctive forms of ageism and marginalization.

Welfare state regimes

Gosta Esping-Andersen (1990) typologizes different welfare state regimes and their principles of stratification and bases of social rights involving varying arrangements between the state, the market and the family. Under liberal regimes (e.g. the US case), state intervention is subordinated to the market, and there is emphasis on means-testing of income for access to benefits. Universalism, when applied, has an 'equal-opportunity' focus (O'Connor et al. 1999). The approach of liberal regimes is most consistent with liberal feminism and, to some extent, welfare feminism.

An important development in the literature is the focus on the 'contradictory character of welfare states' (O'Connor et al. 1999: 2–3) in which the two faces of the state are highlighted: first, the *woman friendliness* of the state (Hernes 1987), opening political participation, recognizing and improving women's situation, and secondly, the other *less friendly side of the state*: the long-term care system, and pension systems that reward those engaging in paid labour at the expense of those in unpaid caregiving; workplace policies that ignore workers' caregiving work; laws that impede reproductive choice and provide little protection against male violence (Pateman 1989; O'Connor et al. 1999).

O'Connor and her colleagues (1999: 3) argue that the state has promoted an 'agenda for gender equality' and has also served as an instrument 'for reshaping family practices relevant for women's emancipation, while families adapt to changes introduced by women's employment'. This is the legacy of liberal feminism, and one consequence is that 'economically and socially conservative forces' have greatly concerned themselves with gaining control of government and state policy, and have explicitly opposed feminist demands (O'Connor et al. 1999: 3).

O'Connor (1993) notes that theoretical and analytical treatment of gender and the welfare state changed from the 1970s, when attention was directed to assessing the effects of the welfare state on women (welfare feminism), to the 1980s, where the focus was institutional and comparative, with emphasis on social class as a major explanatory factor (socialist feminism). The 1990s brought debate on citizenship and critiques of 'the gender bias' of the apparently 'gender-neutral' conception of the 'universal citizen' (Pateman 1989; Jones 1990; Sassoon 1991; O'Connor 1993).

The typologies of Esping-Andersen are subject to this same critique: that the citizenship concept is rendered unproblematically in terms of gender, as if men and women experience the same citizenship status. An alternative 'feminist pluralistic notion of citizenship' builds upon the 'notion of difference that includes gender as well as race, class, ethnicity, nationality, and sexual orientation [with] interest and ideology as dimensions of political mobilization and participation' (Sarvasy and Siim 1994: 253). As Sarvasy and Siim note, 'Feminist treatments of republican and maternalist notions of citizenship . . . share a focus on how to connect a politics of diversity and of everyday life to a politics of collective common good' (1994: 254). Here we must be reminded of the fallacy of the theoretical 'universal citizen' under social security and other public policies of the state. Equal laws (including what the mainstream in the USA describes as a 'gender neutral' social security policy) produce different outcomes depending on the social circumstances of the citizen (Sassoon 1991). Nevertheless, prominent US economists and other policy makers continue to describe such policies that produce radically divergent outcomes, highly defined by other statuses (e.g. gender and race), as 'gender neutral' and 'race neutral'.

Feminist perspectives on old age and the state

Feminist perspectives on the state and old age policy have addressed:

1 the concepts of the gendered wage and the family wage in producing the economic vulnerability of older women;
2 how the fate of the older woman in the welfare state is predicated upon her marital status and her husband's work history and how social policy is built around the model of the traditional autonomous nuclear family; and
3 the two tiers of social policy that divide women by race and class: means-tested social assistance and social insurance (Harrington Meyer 1990, 1996).

Old age income provisions are gendered in three key ways:

1 retirement income is linked to waged labour, which is itself gendered;
2 non-waged reproductive labour, performed predominantly by women, is not recognized or counted under state policy as labour; and
3 retirement policy is based on a model of family status as married with male breadwinner (and with marital status as permanent rather than transient).

Thus, retirement income programmes produce what Harrington Meyer refers to as a 'gendered distribution of old age income' (Harrington Meyer 1996: 551). Insofar as benefits are higher for married than non-married persons and for dependent spouses than non-dependent spouses and single individuals (who are more likely to be women than men), state policy sustains the subordination of women by imposing a normative and preferential view of a particular family form with a male breadwinner and a dependent wife (Pascall 1986) that is inherently disadvantageous to the majority of older women.

The degree of dependency of older women increases as they move through the life course (Arber and Ginn 1995). This is especially associated with widowhood, divorce, retirement and the associated declines in economic and health status. The potentially negative results of all of these factors pose a serious threat for all women, and particularly for non-whites (both women and men), the less educated and the poor and near-poor. Current policies do little to redress the multiple lifetime jeopardies of gender, race, ethnicity and lower social class. Further, from the 1990s to the present, welfare reform in many advanced industrial societies has added to the burdens of women of all generations including older women. Public policies are often highly punitive and painfully regressive for women – even older women, many of whom now find themselves in a new form of indentured servitude, this time through caregiving for grandchildren, and without cash assistance if the elder is the parent of an adult child with children who also is a welfare recipient, disabled and poor or a substance abuser. Welfare reform has augmented the burdens of women's childbearing and caregiving across the life cycle, extracting an enormous cost across all female generations (young and old), producing multiple deleterious ripple effects.

Dependent relations are sustained by social security and other agencies of the welfare state that *lock women into a spousal wage relationship*. As noted, the state and social policy support this relationship through the labour market and the refusal to pay for the caring work of women. 'The price of such caring work is economic dependence . . . [which] amounts to the exploitation of one kind of dependency to deal with another' (Pascall 1986: 29). Harrington Meyer further explains:

> [The] paradox for women is either to live without a male wage and risk impoverishment or to live with a male's wages and risk dependency. Policies that deny the realities of women's lives by assuming or forcing economic independence ignore the economic dependency associated with reproductive labor under the current system. Yet policies that recognize women's economic dependency also sustain that dependency . . . The gendered structure of waged labor, the gendered definition of work, and the conceptualization of family status as

permanent rather than transient all intersect to impoverish old women.

(Harrington Meyer 1990: 560–1)

Thus, the gendered status of working and retirement wages has resulted in women's continuing dependency on the 'family wage' of a male breadwinner or, alternatively, vulnerability to poverty. Although 'supposedly designed to provide economic security to dependent wives, [the family wage] has historically served to increase men's status in both the labor market and the family'. Further, 'in the eyes of the state, it does not belong to [women] . . . in the case of marital dissolution' (Harrington Meyer 1990: 559). This is a particularly crucial historic and contemporary element in understanding why the privatization of social security in the USA (a form of individualization of investment – and ownership – by the breadwinner) is disadvantageous to women.

Ideology

Ideology is used by all political regimes to justify their position and impose their political will on others. The contest for ideological hegemony is about achieving and maintaining power through the means of the production and control of ideas. In the feminist political economy perspective, 'the value systems, normative orientations, moral codes, and belief systems of . . . society . . . are . . . connected [both] to the larger process of class rule and domination' (Knuttila 1996: 164), as well as the processes of gender rule and domination (Connell 1996, 2000; Bourdieu 2001).

The strength of the New Right's ideological political assault on all domestic government programmes and especially entitlements is the most successful and enduring element of the Reagan and Thatcher legacy in the USA and Britain (Estes 1991b; Phillipson 1998). The twin ideologies of neo-liberalism and neo-conservatism have been deployed in the political struggles to transform radically the social security and Medicare programmes in the USA from government-defined benefits to market-dependent programmes. The policy shift to privatization is generally treated by politicians and the media as gender neutral, but the outcomes of privatization would decidedly *not* be gender neutral. The *gender ideology* and the ideology of familism and separate public and private spheres remain powerful forces bolstering both ideologies of neo-liberalism and neo-conservatism.

Neo-liberal ideology argues for a 'minimalist state' and is hostile to anything that may impede the 'natural superiority' of the market (Levitas 1986). In advanced capitalist societies, the sanctity of the market over the state including the 'imperatives of international markets (i.e. globalization), and the inevitable need to align domestic wages and public policies with the terms of those markets' (Piven and Cloward 1997: 34) has become the dominant ideology. This view of 'markets over politics' is an ideology that has been successfully employed to achieve larger political and economic goals of welfare reform, and now provides the impetus for the attempts to privatize public programmes, entitlements and social insurance.

Neo-conservative ideology, which has been an invaluable tool in rekindling a gender war, has the base for increased pressures for family responsibility. As corporate capital and the state grow, Habermas argues that traditional and religious values are undermined and 'motivation deficits' (Habermas 1975) occur as the reach of the state political administrative system is extended to more and more problems of capitalist society (Estes and Alford 1990) and of the family. The central importance of the family is accepted, and a 'crisis of the family' justifies the adoption of new policies that seek to reinforce traditional family structures and norms. Understood from the feminist critical lens of the sex/gender system, the neo-conservative ideological current posits that the 'independence' of women from the traditional (male-dominated) nuclear family is the cause of a crisis in the family and the loss of family values. The goal therefore is the reinstatement of (patriarchal) male dominance and the traditional subjugation of women through *more reproductive work* without recognition of its economic contribution. This occurs through attacks on reproductive 'choice' and state policies like welfare that permit women to live (and even procreate) independent of the traditional and legal nuclear family, but nevertheless severely penalize and control women if they live outside the holy state of matrimony.

An important function of ideologies is that they structure beliefs and limit a vision of possible alternatives to those proposed by people in the position to manufacture the reigning ideology concerning problems and their solutions (Therborn 1978). A necessary condition of acquiescence and resignation to policy 'choices' that economic and policy elites proffer (e.g. the privatization of public entitlements such as social security) is whether or not alternative regimes or strategies are even conceivable. The most successful ideologies are distinguished by their remarkable capacity to shape public consciousness. Successful neo-liberalist ideology thus limits the vision of the 'possible' to inherently pro-market solutions, and neo-conservative ideology limits solutions to those that impose benefits according to the market and the traditional (patriarchal) family structure, accompanied by a 'profoundly pessimistic view of the possibilities of change' (Therborn 1980: 98).

The 'welfare state cleansing' from the 1990s to the present through welfare reform and privatization advanced in the USA and Britain, directly and personally, is likely to generate substantial and negative effects across the lifespan of women. *One significant limitation on old age policy is that the dominant power group comprised of white males does not equally share with women the benefits of the longevity revolution.*

There is a very limited public discourse about the existence and the positive elements of intergenerational relationships and the significant exchanges (monetary and non-monetary) that occur across gender, time and the generations. This should be surprising, given the stability in the positive opinion polling concerning support for older people. However, a distinctly male perspective is reflected among the proponents of 'generational accounting' that ignore caregiving within and across the generations and all non-economic exchanges as well as monetary exchanges that exist between generations that are outside the labour market.

Gender and social movements

The enormous gender stakes in the struggle over welfare reform and in other key old age policy arenas such as long-term care highlight the importance of research on gender and social movements and in understanding the factors that constrain or promote insurgency (Kuumba 2001: 140). Scholarly efforts are contributing to a 'systematic theory of gender and social movements' (Taylor 1999), including work on:

- the creation of gender hierarchies in organizational practices;
- the role of gender stratification in the emergence of social movements;
- the collective identities within which gender is fused; and
- the processes of resistance and challenge to oppressive gender relations.

Work is developing on the macro, meso and micro levels.

- On the *macro level*, attention is given to structural conditions and how they open different paths to social movement mobilization based on gender.
- On the *meso level*, the focus is on gender-different social networks that may place individuals within what are called 'gender separate', 'gender parallel' and 'gender integrated' movement structures or with distinct roles in social movement organizations (SMOs) (Rodriguez 1994; Nauright 1996; Robnett 1996, 1997). Informal and community-based networks (church and kinship) are also examined as avenues for women movement mobilization.
- On the *micro level*, work addresses individual-level 'consciousness and perception of the situation that varies with different social positioning. Class/race/ethnicity/cultural factors intersect with gender to configure paths and levels of mobilization, hierarchies and power

dynamics within mobilizing structures and stimulus for action'
(Kuumba 2001: 93).

Finally, a synthesis is proposed of 'old competing theoretical dichotomies –
objective/structural *versus* subjective/ideological factors to recognize dialectical relations between these levels of social struggle' (Kuumba 2001: 93).
Interestingly, Kuumba argues that women are 'more often willing to take a
radical stance and to push further in demands, since they . . . had more to gain
and less to lose from capitulating to the power structures' (Kuumba 2001: 81).
    A crucial issue concerns whether 'women and men have different com-
plaints or interpretations of a given situation [and] how . . . grievances that
motivate individuals to join resistance struggles differ by gender' (Kuumba
2001: 81). In both cases of the struggles around privatization and women's
unpaid labour and burden in long-term care, women's complaints should be
fertile ground for social movement development. Understanding why this has
not been the case will be informative for the development of the field of study
of women and old age movements.

Conclusion: feminist transformation and old age policy

Julie Matthaei (2001) proposes three 'semihistorical' and overlapping (wave-
like, emerging and receding) stages of 'feminist economic transformation' in
Healing Ourselves, Healing our Economy. Stage 1 (mid-1880s to 1960s) is gender
polarization; Stage 2 (1970s to the present) is gender freedom; and Stage 3 (the
next stage emerging since the 1970s) is gender integration (Matthaei 2001:
463). Each stage portrays a 'way of organizing work' by sex and a 'set of generally accepted beliefs' (2001: 464).
    In Stage 1 there is a rigid division of labour, separate sexual spheres and a
definition of women's work as 'homemaking' in a 'cult of domesticity' focused
on immediate, direct and personal caring for the family. Stage 2 involves the
breakdown of the sexual division of labour and 'equal-opportunity' feminism
with a dramatic increase in women's labour force participation and 'competitive consumerism, competitive careerism, and the oppression of the home-
maker' (Matthaei 2001: 469).

> The Stage 3 solution to the feminist dilemma is both for women and
> men to become more alike and for femininity to be revalued, through
> an integrative feminism movement-through which individuals of
> both sexes begin to combine and redefine femininity and masculin-
> ity, while restructuring economic and familial institutions and
> practices.
>
> (Matthaei 2001: 476)

Stage 3 feminism moves to socially responsible individualism and the combination and rebalancing of paid and unpaid work. This

> begin[s] to transcend the negative masculine struggle to dominate and control others, and the negative feminine quality of self-subordination and sacrifice, creating a new kind of masculine-with-feminine self that develops and expresses itself (positive masculine) in ways that integrate caring and concern for others (positive feminine).
> (Matthaei 2001: 463).

In terms of old age policy, Stage 3 feminism would open up space for the recognition and valuing of women's caregiving roles through state policy and the replacement of the division of labour between the sexes, rebalancing the current gender-biased policy schemes of private–public responsibility for long-term care. Matthaei's Stage 3, gender integration, would be part of the valuing of the feminine and an integration of 'caring into the economy (stripped of their negative, subordinated qualities)' (Matthaei 2001: 465).

Stage 3 feminism is expressed in a 'new type of movement' that may be labelled the 'care movement', which Deborah Stone contends is developing around three rights: (1) the right of families to care for and be helped to care for their members; (2) the right of paid caregivers to give humane, high-quality care without compromising their own well-being; and (3) the right for people who need care to get it (Stone 2000 as quoted in Matthaei 2001: 483). In Matthaei's words, such a movement would reaffirm care as a value 'while striving to distance it from the negative feminine self-subordination and dependency . . . and revaluing unpaid caring work as an activity for both sexes, as combined with independence and self-actualization', while also transforming 'the paid workplace so that it allows individuals time to care for themselves and their loved ones' (Matthaei 2001: 483).

As this chapter illustrates, insightful and influential feminist scholarship is growing in disciplines such as economics, sociology, philosophy and political science. Voice is being given to erudite and blistering intellectual critiques. These critiques are often accompanied by calls for profound social change; yet they are presented amid the reality of little state old age policy action relevant to the critiques levelled and virtually no visible grass roots feminist social movement activity in this arena. Estes (2001d) calls this 'the missing feminist revolution in long-term care'.

This perplexing circumstance underscores the import of engaging the study of gender and social movements along the lines proposed by Kuumba (2001) (see above). From a critical theoretical perspective, some of the key questions must address differences from the vantage point of structural power: who has material resources? Who has autonomy to enter the labour market? And who has the power to set the terms of pay or no-pay for the labour provided? This work necessitates a feminist epistemology that considers the social construction of 'knowledges' and consciousness that shape the current gendered old age policy and the likelihood of feminist social movement responses in opposition to it or in support of it.

5 Productive ageing, self-surveillance and social policy

Key points:

- Active, successful and productive ageing as attempts to shape experience.
- The relationship between hegemony and self-surveillance.
- Economic attitudes to ageing populations and the construction of 'ageing well'.
- Theory, policy and experience.

Introduction

In a previous discussion (see Chapter 2) we highlighted the idea of 'successful ageing' as an important strand in the development of social theory in gerontology. This chapter examines this tradition in more detail, separating the various contributions relating to 'active', 'successful' and 'productive' ageing. The question of defining successful and unsuccessful ageing is approached through theoretical positions arising from the work of Antonio Gramsci and Michel Foucault. Examples of the use of theory to expand our critical understanding of what it means to grow old are explored at different points in the chapter.

Public policy is often presented as solving social problems that are visited upon us like the weather or a natural disaster. However, the problems of ageing and their solutions are socially constructed, interpreted and internalized using mechanisms that frequently obscure the power relations that determine them. The close connection between dominant discourses on ageing, policy, and their adoption by older adults as part of their own identity is explored below.

From control to self-control

Antonio Gramsci (1971) has pointed out that in different historical circumstances the balance between consent and coercion changes as the means by
which dominant groups in society maintain control over subordinate groups.
When a dominant group has achieved widespread support for its priorities, its
world view is said to have gained hegemony (Sassoon 2001). Coercion occurs
when consent breaks down or when the subordinate social groups are
marginalized to such an extent that their consent is no longer a significant
factor in the maintenance of the dominant position. Such an approach is
useful for understanding the changing social construction of ageing. When
older people are perceived by other, dominant groups to be irrelevant to social
stability, or as a threat, they may be coerced into certain roles and institutions. A policy example might be the widespread use of institutional segrega-
tion in the middle of the twentieth century (Townsend 1962), supported by
the notion of older people as an unproductive burden on economic growth
(Phillipson 1982). However, once older people are of sufficient numbers or
have sufficient means, it may be important to gain their consent (see Chapter
8). Here, the civil rights movements on age inequalities (Vincent 1999) and
the growth of grey consumerism (Sawchuk 1995) have provoked a need for
inclusive public policies. Whatever the policy turn, however, one objective of
public policy would be to maintain the dominant world view and inequalities of power, and justify them in socially acceptable ways. Institutional
incarceration has thus been presented as protecting older adults from a
hostile environment and consumer options, however limited, as the expression of choice in old age. When studying ageing, the question of hegemony
will be intergenerational as well as economic. It will be mediated by other
social inequalities such as race, gender and social class (Estes and Associates
2001). It will also attempt to convince older citizens that their own self-
development is best seen as existing within the dominant hegemony,
discourse or story.

   The work of Michel Foucault is particularly helpful in disentangling the
ways in which consent and coercion influence personal experience. In his
book *Discipline and Punish*, Foucault (1975) examined the ways in which the
creation of a certain category of human behaviour evolves in harness with
professional groups to control that behaviour or social category. Psychiatry did
not, for example, 'discover' forms of mental illness and then cure them.
Instead, forms of madness, criminality and sexual dysfunction were created
from the richness of human diversity, as part of the growth and development
of professional power. The 'professional gaze' refers to the ways in which professional interests create certain methods and intellectual discourses that
define what counts as legitimate knowledge, and in this case legitimate forms

that ageing might take. Indeed, power and knowledge are seen as inseparable, as the ability to establish what is a correct understanding of a problem itself reinforces the professional viewpoint, and power inequalities are thereby perpetuated. The 'professional gaze', then, shapes the observable behaviour of its object, which most specifically is 'inscribed on the bodies' of the person or group of people that is subject to being 'shaped'. It defines what is visible to policy makers, social workers, physicians and nurses and thereby what old age is seen to comprise.

So, according to this view, professions and disciplines do not pre-exist and then apply themselves to a chosen area of study or social problem. The area or problem is actually given shape and form through the process of professional or disciplinary formation. This process creates areas of legitimate knowledge, so that to be seen and heard, or for events to be constructed as a social problem, one has to enter into the discourses that constitute these areas of legitimate knowledge. As such, particular discourses on old age, promoted by and promoting certain professional or disciplinary groups, will 'problematize' the experience of adult ageing in specific ways (Katz 1996; Powell and Biggs 2000).

Foucault (1976) gives two examples of how legitimate forms of knowledge come about, both being related to professional forms of creating information. First, the 'confessional' draws upon the analogy of confessing sin and refers to the collection of case histories. It covers forms of secular scrutiny, including counselling, the psychotherapies and interviewing (Parker 1999). Second, 'normative judgements' are based upon the collection of mass data that allows the categorization of populations into various sub-categories (Katz 1996). Specialized professional methods and techniques can then be used to allocate groups and individuals to ever more specific categories and subject them to forms of observation, monitoring or surveillance.

The interdependence of power and knowledge suggested by this perspective can be traced through a number of professional, disciplinary and policy issues. Estes (1979a) in her book *The Aging Enterprise* shows how growing concerns about an ageing population has led to a multiplication of vested interests who stand to gain from identifying age as a particular sort of problem. This creates a series of powerful voices that drown out the experiences of older people themselves, and restricts the 'problem of ageing' to those that these enterprises can profit from, thus drawing attention away from underlying structural inequalities. The biomedicalization of ageing, for example, has led to age being seen as an individual and corporeal problem to the exclusion of other perspectives based on class, gender and race (Estes and Binney 1989). The ageing body can be seen as a principal site of personal and professional control as issues of age are reduced to those of a malfunctioning body and ever more sophisticated biomedical technologies and assessments to regulate it and deny other experiences arising from adult ageing (Tulle-Winton 2000).

The discovery of elder abuse as a 'new' social problem, in North America in the 1980s and the UK and Australia in the 1990s, can indicate how public policy quickly translates into a new problematization of ageing. Abuse became visible at this time through a wider policy debate on family obligations to care and the erosion of existing welfare services (Biggs 1993). The growth of pressure groups nationally and internationally, the specification of different types of abuse and the increase in the number of interactions that could be labelled abusive quickly followed, plus the deployment of case management as a means of monitoring potentially abusive family situations. Drawing on the work of Foucault, the identification of a new social problem facilitated the policing of all caring situations and the expansion of particular forms of professional power and knowledge. So, while abuse is a real issue, responses to it were shaped by contemporary policy priorities and enterprises (Biggs and Powell 2000). Even the policy of holistic care, benign from a professional point of view, becomes a means of extending the 'professional gaze' so that ever more aspects of private experience become subject to public scrutiny and control (Porter 1997). These processes often appear to give older people what they want, but bring with them discourses that invalidate alternative perspectives, placing power in the hands of others. In each case definitions take shape about successful and unsuccessful ageing and, most importantly, they influence the view ageing adults have of themselves as well as how they are perceived. According to Foucault, these acts of self-surveillance are key to understanding how an acceptable identity is maintained.

In his later thinking Foucault (1988) explored ways in which individuals work on themselves to create a certain sort of personal identity. These he called 'techniques of the self'. Rather than conformity to external control, the emphasis here is on forms of self-development and the ways in which personal subjectivity mediates structural frameworks. These techniques map the degree to which particular ideologies are internalized, recognized and worked on, in and by the self. This perspective recognizes that individuals actively seek out ideas about society and their place within it, and look for ways to fine-tune personal conduct.

Contemporary ageing exhibits a number of techniques that older people might use, including: self-help manuals on appropriate and 'empowering' forms of ageing (Lambley 1995; Sheehey 1996); narrative counselling approaches to mid- and later-life issues in order to 're-story' the self (McAdams 1993; Woolfe and Biggs 1998); the creation of retirement environments that support late-life identities (Kastenbaum 1993; Laws 1995; Phillips *et al.* 2001). They reflect not simply a burgeoning grey consumer market, but also a profound shift in the penetration of ideology into the very sense of how people internalize and eventually experience their own ageing processes. In Gramscian terms, they show us how consent is achieved and maintained on a day-to-day basis.

This section has explored how developments in disciplinary and professional thinking interact with their subjects to form a particular conception of what it is to be old, and how older people are encouraged to 'work on themselves' to conform to these social strictures, which may or may not be in their ultimate interests. Three examples, key to the development of gerontology as a discipline, that underpin many policy initiatives and also provide direction for self-surveillance will now be examined in greater detail.

Active, successful and productive ageing

Attempts to identify the grail of active, successful or productive ageing are well intended. They recognize the growing numbers of older adults plus medical advances that make many of the decrements previously associated with old age modifiable and in some cases reversible (Rowe and Kahn 1987). The debate over successful and productive ageing goes to the heart of ageing studies, and has formed the core of the current disciplinary development of social gerontology. This is because it suggests a means of countering negative stereotyping of older people and increasing their social inclusion. It also raises the question of how far success in terms of ageing should be critical of wider ideological structures and how far to age successfully requires that older people fit into them. When looking at ageing, it is possible to be critical of the stereotypes and to promote approaches that counter those stereotypes, yet still conform to wider values which may not take alternative possibilities for late-life development into account. Posing the question of social ageing in terms of success and productivity draws attention to the ways in which structural and personal components of identity interact, the techniques used to invent the ageing self and the role of public policy in creating an atmosphere that fosters one view of ageing rather than another.

Positive ageing policies are becoming increasingly popular in North America (Estes *et al.* 2001b) and parts of Europe (Walker and Naegele 1999) and are largely replacing assumptions that old age is a time of dependency and decline. This guiding narrative has an effect on both the public legitimacy and the personal identities made available to older people, with a particular emphasis on the value of work and work-like activities (Biggs 2001) and those based on leisure (Katz 2000b). A number of phrases have been used to describe this 'new' approach to ageing, including active, successful and productive forms. Each implies a moral as well as an objective basis on which to grow old as they problematize the question of later life and suggest remedies that can be deployed.

Building on the descriptions of activity and disengagement outlined in Chapter 2, we now examine notions of active, successful and productive ageing, from a critical perspective. In each can be found a vision of what it is to 'age well', as such creating a legitimizing gaze through which theory, policy, professional practice and older people themselves make judgements about what will count toward positive ageing.

Activity

Activity theory, as noted in Chapter 2, made an important and early contribution to social gerontology. It may be more accurate to describe it as an exhortation to a certain form of behaviour, rather than a fully developed theoretical position. It has been described in the following manner:

> The older person who ages optimally is the person who manages to resist the shrinkage of his social world. He maintains the activities of middle age for as long as possible and then find substitutes for those activities he is forced to relinquish.
>
> (Havighurst *et al.* 1963: 419)

Activity theory provided the better fit with a moral 'problem solving' approach adopted by the new discipline. It provided a clear series of objectives and was easy to measure, making it attractive to social workers, nurses and physicians alike. Older people needed to maintain their existing activities for as long as possible and replace those that they had lost with new ones. While much has subsequently been made of the differences between these two explanations of the same Kansas Study (Marshall 1999), both disengagement and activity theories are a response to the problematization of older people as non-productive. One sees the solution to be withdrawal from society, the other as continuing to do things for as long as possible. Indeed, the latter has been satirized by Ekerdt (1986) as 'the busy ethic', as little attention has been paid to the purpose of the techniques involved. Regardless of its limitations, activity theory has gained widespread acceptance in professional circles and among older people as an antidote to the problem of ageing identity (Gubrium and Wallace 1991; Biggs *et al.* 2000). It is, however, unreflective in its attachment to content over explanation (Hendricks and Achenbaum 1999). What it does do is allow the active body to colonize the sense of self, which is then quantifiable and can be turned into measures and regimes. The world is divided into active elders and those described as 'potentially active'.

Successful ageing

The theoretical position described as 'successful ageing' has been explained in the following way:

> [It] takes gains and losses jointly into account, pays attention to the great heterogeneity in ageing and successful ageing, and views the

> successful mastery of goals in the face of losses endemic to advanced age as a result of the interplay of selection, compensation and optimisation.
>
> (Baltes and Carstensen 1996: 397)

The successful ageing approach attempts an understanding of ageing, grounded in the approaches spontaneously arising in elder behaviour (Baltes and Baltes 1990a). It sidesteps the issue of prescribing objectives and contents by engaging with social-psychological processes, thus moving from the 'what' of ageing to the 'how' (Baltes and Carstensen 1996).

Successful ageing is based upon a counter-intuitive observation that older people are by and large satisfied with their lives, often more so than their younger counterparts and in spite of increasing disability or hardship (Rowe and Kahn 1987). Baltes and Baltes (1990b) suggest a 'meta-model' of selective optimization with compensation, or SOC, to explain how older people negotiate the gains and the losses that arise with age with such seeming psychological success. Older people, it is argued, are satisfied because they have found strategies to minimize the losses and maximize the gains. These three processes: selection, compensation, optimization, provide a way to conceptualize the strategies older people use to age well even in the face of loss. The particular recipe for success is, however, elusive. Baltes and Carstensen (1996) point out that one cannot predict any given individual's successful ageing using this model unless 'we know the domains of functioning and goals that the individual considers important, personally meaningful and in which he or she feels competent' (1996: 399).

The theory is illustrated by example. When interviewed by the Baltes, the concert pianist Arthur Rubenstein reported overcoming the challenges of ageing posed in his continuing career. He played a smaller number of pieces (selection), practising them more often (optimization) and slowing down immediately before fast movements to create the impression of speed by contrast (compensation). A senior marathon runner competes against his own age group over easier courses (selection), extends his warm-up periods and varies his footwear (compensation) and increases fitness through a specialist diet (optimization).

The model, according to Carstensen (1993), has the advantage of acknowledging socio-emotional dimensions of ageing and the notion of multiple possibilities for self-development. It is based, then, on the meta-priority of mastering the challenges of ageing, while allowing wide variety in the ways mastery can be achieved.

Successful ageing has been enthusiastically adopted by a number of helping professions, including social care (Usita 2001), nursing, health care and communication with older patients (Hummert and Nussbaum 2001). It is generally perceived as allowing maximum self-control to the patient or client, providing a basis for interaction and grounds for intervention. In other words, it spans the gap between formal ideology and self-surveillance. Everyday existence is converted into successful activities, which are converted into life satisfaction through techniques applied to the self.

It is difficult, however, to identify within the theory the purposes served by all this self-monitoring. Moody (2001) has suggested that the approach successfully divides the population into the 'wellderly' and the 'illderly', and that successful ageing is essentially about survivorship. To be successful is to have life satisfaction for as long as possible. Once satisfaction ends, Moody observes, the next strategy available is euthanasia. At root, successful ageing emerges as a remedial intervention approach, masking a decline model of ageing. It presents a liberal response to age as a natural, manageable problem.

Productive ageing

Successful ageing avoids the issues of content and inequity by focusing on non-judgemental and individualized strategies that older adults are encouraged to monitor in themselves. 'Productive ageing' raises the problem of social conformity head-on, by examining the question of ageing through the lens of economic usefulness. Hinterlong *et al.* (2001) argue that 'society simply cannot afford to continue to overlook the potential of the older population to serve as a resource for social change and economic growth'.

The policy assumption that older people have become a burden is stood on its head as adherents to productive ageing maintain that productivity does not decrease with age. This approach appears radical because it takes as its object the negative stereotyping of older people and is a reaction to intergenerational equity debates in US public policy (Minkler and Robertson 1991). It is pointed out that, rather than sliding steadily into increasing incapacity, most people are healthier for longer then decline very quickly before death – labelled a compression of morbidity (Fries 1980). To this is added the observation that there are many advantages for employers in hiring older workers, including reliability, prior investment in skills and know-how and company loyalty (Schultz 2001). There is a basic connection between continued health and productivity in productive ageing, because 'engagement in productive behaviour requires a certain level of physical, cognitive and emotional functioning' (Butler *et al.* 1990).

Productive ageing originated at the Salzburg conference of 1982 (Butler and Gleason 1985), at which Betty Friedan seen by many as the founder of contemporary US feminism, opined 'We can and must express and facilitate our personal and social productivity as we grow older.' Indeed, much of the discussion around productive ageing has centred around definitions. Caro *et al.* describe productive ageing as 'any activity by an older individual that contributes to producing goods and services or develops the capacity to produce them' (1993: 6). Morgan (1986) suggests 'anything that produces goods and services. It should reduce demand on goods and services produced by others', while Butler and Schechter have proposed, in the *Encyclopedia of Aging*, 'the capacity of an individual or population to serve in the paid workforce, to serve in volunteer activities, to assist in the family, and to maintain himself or herself as independently as possible' (1995: 211).

Bass and Caro (2001) extend their original economic definition to include activities that would otherwise 'need to be done by someone else', but not those done simply for personal gain or self-enhancement. These 'non-productive' activities would include meditation, excursions, carrying on correspondence, worship, or visiting with family and friends. It has been observed that including activities that occur outside the formal market raises problems of measurement and valuation (Morrow-Howell *et al.* 2001).

Thus productive ageing is unashamedly economic in its foundation and uses efficiency as its core argument. The solution to the problem of ageing is, accordingly, to find a way in which older people can be economically useful, either directly or, as some revisionist definitions imply, indirectly. The approach allows the clear measurement of productivity and thus the development of normative judgements, and provides individuals with a clear rationale for monitoring their ageing selves. As such, productive ageing answers successful ageing's liberal avoidance of purpose. The purpose is economic, with the creation of a 'buffer' workforce that can be drawn upon as economic needs demand. Older adults are to find personal value through becoming a pool of surplus labour, although an economic rather than an ideological justification for the claims of formal productivity has been hard to find (Schultz 2001). Indeed, the contradiction between exhorting the old and a continued employer preference for younger workers has led to some interesting twists in Rowe and Kahn's (1998) arguments for linking success with productivity. They note, for example, the importance of productive engagement to health and continued well-being in old age, thus reversing the logic of the earlier statement by Butler *et al.* (1990), that productive behaviour requires a certain level of functioning. However, fundamental to the successful ageing is the emphasis on individual responsibilities. Accordingly: 'The frailty of old age is largely reversible . . . what does it take to turn back the ageing clock? It's surprisingly simple . . . Success is determined by good old-fashioned hard work' (Rowe and Kahn 1998: 102, in Moody 2001).

Productive ageing is a powerful means of reducing ambiguity around the role and place of older people in society. It solves the 'problem' of ageing by capitulation to the dominant values that have contributed to the problem in the first place. Nevertheless, these ideas have become deeply embedded in social policy in both North America (Estes and Associates 2001) and the UK (Biggs 2001), where work and work-like activities have been presented as turning the burden of an ageing population into an asset and an opportunity.

At root the justification of old age lies in not being a drain on social and economic resources, in which productive ageing is the active justification of 'I can still work' and successful ageing the passive justification of 'Look, I'm trying hard not to be a burden on others.' As Katz (2000b) points out, an emphasis on activity as a means to well-being has now become a mechanism for the management of everyday life and a neo-liberal narrative of self.

Issues: ageing for what purpose?

It has been argued above that productive ageing and related themes problem- atize the question of age in a particular way, to the exclusion of alternative meanings and legitimizing limited forms of adjustment. Activity theory advises maintenance with some replacement of old roles with new ones. Suc- cessful ageing examines strategies that achieve a satisfactory accommodation to declining faculties. Productive ageing accepts the ends and means of dom- inant work norms and, by extension, that part of the life course concerned with them. The critical question, however, is not just what to do and how to do it, but for what purpose and in whose interests? To this end, criticisms and alternative perspectives on these approaches will now be examined in more detail.

Cultural specificity

A serious problem with these attempts to define what a viable old age might look like lies in their cultural specificity. The further one steps back from them, the more they can be seen as products of a particular set of historical and social circumstances. Activity looks very much like a midwestern version of the Prot- estant ethic of virtue through 'doing' and the avoidance of sloth. Successful survivorships, and coping with adversity, possibly reflects the experience of European postwar reconstruction. Productive ageing is, perhaps most clearly of the three, a child of the neo-liberal moral economy of the Thatcher–Reagan years.

A number of studies have indicated that, rather than being a universal solution to the personal and structural challenges of ageing, these positions do not travel well. They fail to account for changing and, on occasion, oppos- itional definitions of ageing well that arise through the experience of move- ment from one culture to another, intergenerational expectations arising in non-western cultures and effects on economically subordinate environments.

Torres (2001) has criticized successful ageing from a cultural perspective in so far as it is based on satisfaction and personal control, but fails to examine context. She argues that events such as migration can occasion a significant shift in strategies, depending upon the reference group and motivation of the elder migrant. Strategies may vary depending upon cohort membership and maturational as well as migrational changes.

Phillipson (2001) has also shown that migration can create different associations between social change and satisfaction with ageing. Indeed it is possible to argue that migration problematizes ageing in an entirely different way to the productivity debate and the dominant western characterization of age as loss. Both age and migration can provoke losses and hardships, but in some cases migration has led to adult ageing being associated with new and better circumstances than would have been expected without it.

Fry *et al.* (1997) found that North American associations of successful ageing with self-sufficiency and independent living were met with incomprehension with Hong Kong elders, for whom family willingness to meet their psychological, social and economic requirements was a mark of status. Similarly, the link between longevity and success, which places considerable emphasis on bio-technology, is not universally accepted, with some cultures prioritizing a 'good life and a good death' over length of time spent in old age (Westerhof *et al.* 2001).

It has also been observed that race (Jackson 2001) and gender (Holstein 1992, 1999) may lead to blocked opportunities and different networks to those taken as normative for formal work production, which leads to different conceptions of productivity and success.

Dannefer (2000) has suggested that inequalities and differences between dominant and subordinate cultures, both within and between nations, are interactive. He argues that not only are inequalities played out between cultures but that these affect life opportunities across the life course and even the structure of the life course for different groups. Globally speaking, the lives and life chances of affluent North American elders, Amazonian shamans, street gang members in Los Angeles and child labourers in the third world are linked. By the same coin, certain populations in the supposedly affluent 'North' or 'West' live with inequalities that negate dominant expectations of the life course almost entirely (Newman 1998). Concepts such as productivity retirement and leisure take on different meanings or cease to exist at all.

In each of the above studies cultural difference within and between a variety of communities indicates that productive models of ageing are more diverse and less accepted than the original model would predict. Further, an exclusive preoccupation with autonomy and productivity as the route to a fulfilling old age smacks of a form of cultural imperialism which may have limited validity.

Old age and the work ethic

Whether or not productive ageing is desirable or even desired by older adults, the model significantly underplays structural inequalities that make it an opportunity for some groups and extremely difficult or threatening for others (Estes and Associates 2001; Estes *et al.* 2001b). Holstein (1992), for example, argues that the concept of productivity is gendered, fails to correspond with the life experience of many women, and omits gender-based inequalities in work opportunities and pension rights. Phillipson (2002) argues that pension rights are seriously threatened by global and other economic pressures and that for many groups continued work may not be a choice but an unwelcome necessity.

Each of the above authors would agree that productive ageing contributes to a moral as well as a political economy. The association of success with work is not only unchallenged; it marks a loss of legitimacy for arguments based on social need and eclipses macro problems with an individualized market logic. Ultimately, the privatization of risks, as the responsibility of the older individual that is embedded within the productive model, justifies the retreat of the state services, and thus a further exacerbation of inequity in later life (Phillipson 1998). Productivity provides a solution to the inclusion of older people in the dominant values of society with no need for new services to compensate for the social origins of well-being and barriers to achieving it.

Moody (2001) has noted that the use of work values to evaluate later life marks a move away from valuing the 'past contributions' made by older citizens and bases their status upon current productivity or lack of resource use. A moral dimension comes into sharp focus when this coin is flipped over and what one did earlier in life is seen to deliver the old age one deserves. Research that indicates that health, self-care, economic advancement and probity determines your success and satisfaction in later life (Vaillant and Mukamal 2001) becomes a policy tool to justify the rationing of health care. Further, as Estes *et al.* (2001b) point out, health and illness prevention comes to be interpreted as a biomedical/industrial opportunity, which is marketed to individual consumers. The logic of such a moral economy is that alternatives, such as attention to the fostering of healthy communities, are pushed to the margins of policy agendas. Accordingly, Estes *et al.* (2001b) argue that productive ageing agendas link individualistic solutions to the biomedical industry via market capitalism.

The assumption lying within productive ageing that work is intrinsically good fails to allow space for questions such as 'work for whom' and to 'what end', which are key to understanding the power relationships outlined above. In other words, it is marked by an uncritical acceptance of the master–subordinate social relationships that are integral to work relations and how this is nuanced by issues of age and intergenerational power. Biggs (2001) has observed that, while positive ageing policies in the UK appear to offer greater choice and flexibility to identity following retirement, they are driven by economic needs based on the changing demography of the British workforce and an unwillingness to meet pension needs. The call for greater social inclusion promises inclusion under very restricted criteria, driven by the priorities of other social groups. In fact, productive ageing provides a powerful counterblast to the postmodern view of ageing as a time of consumption and associated identity building. It constitutes not so much an extension of leisure and self-maintenance beyond midlife as an extension of midlife values about work to the whole of the adult life course, which is now seen in terms of workplace values (Sicker 1994: 165). Indeed, Moody (1993) has argued that equity based on productivity builds unequal competition between generations into common-sense thinking about the social value of older people. Impossible goals and standards may be set for older people as intergenerational competition would be premised on the values and baseline capacities of a younger workforce. According to the views expressed above, power relations are being generated, tacitly combining age and work-based inequalities, in ways that reinforce the subordinate status of older people.

Anti-productive ageing

The criticisms voiced in the preceding section claim that productive ageing fails to examine how identity and inequality are socially mediated. The current section extends that argument by considering how definitions of success and productivity are socially contested. As we have seen, activity, success and, most notably, productivity have contributed to a complex construction of age-based and economic hegemony. This promotes a positive image of old age only in so far as one has suspended criticism of an existence that privileges active and 'productive' behaviour. Such an approach is unable to accommodate the diversity of adult ageing. A core issue here is the degree to which such a dominant view eclipses alternative visions and possibilities in later life.

Social connection and solidarity

Because productive and successful ageing are largely concerned with individual conduct, little is said about linking to others and sustaining one's story through others. This has, however, been a continuing theme in the literature on the maintenance of self in later life (Ruth and Coleman 1996). Pillemer *et al.* (2001) have highlighted the value of social integration in the continued well-being and citizenship of older adults. Based on the view that contemporary society holds a series of threats to social integration, including: geographical dispersion and loss of significant others; the increase in the numbers of people living alone; the threat of declining health; social isolation through the loss of work roles; and reliance on care-based relationships, these researchers suggest that future policy should seek to enhance integration through connectedness to others and social embeddedness. Andrews (1991) and Vincent (1999) have both emphasized the importance of political beliefs and continued activism as a source of social connectedness for many older people. While political activity around issues of ageing has often been difficult to organize and reflects social divisions existing already in society, Vincent points to the fact that there has always been an alternative history of ageing, based on resistance to exploitation and oppression. Key to such activity, as has been argued by the Gray Panther movement (Kuhn 1977), has been the creation of intergenerational solidarity around issues that concern younger and older people alike. The Panther perspective on work is complex, in so far as forced exclusion from work is seen as a major source of inequality in the North American context. European pensioners' movements have tended to focus on opposition to work and the need for state-funded economic support following retirement. Overall, these viewpoints do not simply indicate an alternative to productivity as a basis for success in old age; they are actively hostile to the continuance of work-based forms of oppression.

Everyday acts of resistance

Katz (2000b) has noted that there are behaviours which are common to older people, but which simply defy categorization by the normative judgements of productive ageing. One such is 'napping' – the act, presumably rewarding, of taking short periods of sleep and reverie during the 'working' day. Unfortunately, this cannot even be classed as 'potential activity', unless one expands one's criteria to consider dreaming, which is, of course, difficult to give an economic value to. He also cites a number of interviews in which retirement community residents scorn and pour irony on the culture of activity and 'joining in'. In a similar vein, Frank (1998b) discusses how chronic illness can be reclaimed from medical appropriation through the encouragement of personal storytelling.

Several writers have proposed that later life provokes a radical shift rather than a continuity of values with age. Adult ageing raises an alternative series of questions and purposes to those of the first half of life that is dominated by work. Cole (1992) emphasizes existential questions provoked by the second half of life and, eventually, closeness to death, which are often ignored by contemporary western culture. Biggs (1999a) goes further to suggest that the priorities of the first half of life lead to the suppression of human potential which distorts personal and social development. In later life, as work ceases to dominate people's lives, these suppressed or projected parts of the self can be re-owned, resulting in a fuller and more self-conscious sense of identity. This increase in individual development contributes to the diversity of the ageing population and resists simplifying, stereotyping and classification. Tornstam (1996) has argued that adult ageing provokes a process of gerotranscendence. Here, higher degrees of social activity and life satisfaction occur simultaneously with a sense that social activity is actually less important for personal development. As such, gerotranscendence attempts to combine elements of activity and disengagement as part of success in ageing. Gerotranscendent coping patterns include an ability to deal with complexity, a loosening of fixed roles and relationships, a detached interest in others, the discovery of hidden aspects of the self, spirituality and 'big' philosophical questions such as the meaning of life and death. Each of these examples allow us to imagine ways of being old which in Tulle-Winton's words 'defy dominant narratives of old age and look for spaces of resistance where they are least expected' (2000: 82).

Unproductive ageing

A focus on activity, success and productivity gives no answer to the question of what to do with the 'unproductive'. Yet those who will not or cannot conform to the 'busy ethic' pose the greatest threat to the maintenance of a predictable and managed old age. Even in the most advanced stages of mental or physical incapacity, older people have been seen to resist the management of their problems. Thus Katz (1999) has proposed that we see the loss of bodily control as a form of resistance and Terry (1997) shows how even the most damaged stroke victim can, in the course of psycho-dynamic counselling, confront oppressive practices.

Phillipson (1998) has argued that health and social care have formed the base on which to construct an ageing identity for most of the twentieth century and that contemporary threats to the welfare state continue to be an assault on social ageing. A policy emphasis on the active citizen, continually volunteering to organize others less fortunate than themselves or going out to a low-skilled and poorly paid job, divides the world into participative and non-participative old ages (Phillipson 2002). This has led, in UK policy, to a debate on the 'capacity' of older people to make their own decisions and thus the point at which formal services can legitimately make decisions for or protect the person in question (Brammer and Biggs 1998). While participating elders can be trusted to develop self-surveillance, through various 'techniques of the self', non-participators, including victims of abuse or chronic illness, stroke or dementia, may be subject to more direct forms of external monitoring and control. It is possible, following this logic, that older adults will need to nego-tiate the coexistence of different narratives of ageing within social policy. The fault-lines between different forms of policy, based on different models of ageing, have been proposed as a major source of risk to identity in later life (Biggs and Powell 2003).

Concluding comments

A critical analysis of productive ageing indicates that it is a very effective means of ensuring the continued hegemony of work and work-related activ-ities as the key to a socially legitimized form of ageing. When achieved by consent, older people can exist within the dominant generational and eco-nomic narrative, aimed at social inclusion without threatening the dominant discourse on personal and social value. As such, productive ageing exhibits the qualities of a public policy which convinces otherwise resistant minorities to maintain their subordinate status.

Active, productive and successful ageing provide professional rationales and personal techniques whereby older people can be monitored and engage in self-monitoring. At one level there is little that is wrong with this – everyone wants to be healthy and happy and be in control. However, one can also discern the restriction of ageing to a limited and socially conforming set of possibilities. These limited options are presented as the pinnacle of choice and social value, reinforced by and themselves reinforcing a particular profes-sionalized version of legitimacy, which older adults are encouraged to police within themselves. In fact, self-surveillance is key to each of the approaches outlined above. This can be seen in an emphasis on individualized strategies, often lacking a critical understanding of their social context and in the unreflective repetition of market values and personal responsibility. The injunction to stay active and productive, however well-meaning, is neverthe-less a form of social control.

A critical gerontology goes beyond appearances to ask questions about the motivating forces underpinning the functions of what it is to age well. Theoretical statements and policy positions require embedding in their socio-economic and historical contexts so that they can be fully understood. When viewed in this way each of the positions identified in this chapter have implications for the construction of policy and for the more personal task of constructing the self.

6 Biomedicalization, ethics and ageing

Key points:

- Anti-ageism, political economy and experiential challenges to biomedicine.
- Biomedicine as a hegemonic force.
- Commercial drivers of biomedical advance.
- Bioethics regulating professional relationships with older people.

Biomedicine: common-sense beginnings

To the casual onlooker, the critical debate that continues to rage around biomedical innovation may appear difficult to understand. Why is something that appears so obviously a good thing, the abolition or amelioration of physical and mental suffering in old age, the subject of so much dispute? The answer to this question lies in the claims that are made for biomedical approaches to ageing, the breadth of their explanatory value, their availability, and the implications for aspects of age, relationship and causality that are implied or ignored. As noted previously in this book, biomedicine has exercised a major influence in the field of gerontology. This chapter examines the role of biomedical perspectives in more detail, assessing the range of factors which have created this situation.

Biomedicine refers to medical techniques that privilege a biological understanding of the human condition and rely upon pharmacological and technical innovation for their impetus. However, it is contended here that the issue is not simply a matter of individual diagnosis and cure, but rather that biomedicine subsists upon and perpetuates a whole series of structural, interpersonal and symbolic imbalances.

Medicine, objectivity and progress

The narrative of the biomedical sciences holds much in common with other positivist approaches to the human condition. This view, that collecting knowledge about age is a progressive activity that has lost its past errors and incorporated new discoveries, is highly persuasive. Indeed, the reach of the biomedical is so vast, and includes so many different aspects of human existence within its biological, psychological, cultural, interpersonal, social, structural and ethical dimensions, that it is at times difficult to see beyond it. However, such an approach can also contain severe problems.

Hoffmaster, for example, critiques the method of rational abstraction in bioethics that tends to isolate issues from their concrete reality. Reliance on deductive modelling and formal notions of rationality in applied ethics, he cautions, leads from rationality to morality as: 'The rationality involved in the construction of a consistent, coherent system of valid moral norms is taken to engender normativity' (Hoffmaster 1991: 216). There is an unsettling affinity with decision-making processes assumed by economists, as rational agents are expected to act to maximize their expected utility. Critics argue that the assumptions of such forms of rationality are class- and gender-biased (Gilligan 1986; Larabee 1993).

The claims to objectivity which are so much a part of the ideological power of biomedicine offer a certain impartiality but also detach the social actor from human concerns. It is essentially a question of method that offers little in terms of impartiality of access to services, with which it is so often confused. Its claims to demythologize unscientific beliefs about ageing and healing contain the assumption that biomedicine can also tell us what ageing is 'really about', to the exclusion of alternative perspectives and explanations. In other words, such is the contemporary power of forms of explanation that depend upon the body and medicine's ability to counteract illness and disability, that they come to stand for everything that ageing might be about. This is both the power and the great fear associated with any explanatory systems that approach hegemony, that once it is perceived to be necessary, it is taken to be sufficient. Biomedicine is not then seen as a technique, a useful way of fixing the body so that other things can be done in other situations, but becomes a universal panacea. The tension and seductiveness of biomedicine is that, even if it cannot adequately explain the social and psychological experience of adult ageing, it can still do us a lot of good. We need it, but not necessarily in the ways in which it is being presented and provided.

A particular aspect of the biomedical, which arises from its close association with the European enlightenment and a belief in scientific progress, is that the past is not perceived to be particularly important. This is because scientific progress is presented as always riding the crest of a wave, and the present as the accumulation of best practice plus the weeding out of past errors (Williams 2002). Under such circumstances, and the urgency of an ever more efficient pursuit of well-being and alleviation of suffering, why, the argument goes, waste time on history and experience? An answer lies in three directions.

First, in order to understand the blind spots of current thinking it is important to know how we have arrived where we are now. We may be there, not because of the spread of reason, but because of other drivers, such as the desire for profit. There may be a number of influences on contemporary belief and practice that are eclipsed by hegemonic positions. In the case of bio-medicine this would include the structural, economic and political influences of how problems are made visible and given value. Much of the energy of a political-economy critique has been aimed at uncovering the range of inequal-ities that can result (Phillipson 1998; Estes *et al.* 2001a).

Second, a concentration on objectivity alone does a certain violence to the relational nature of human interaction. It separates off the holder of 'real' knowledge from the rest. Validity, in other words, becomes colonized by exclusively professional understandings of adult ageing. Within the hegem-ony of biomedicine and the supposed objectivity of this position, power rela-tions are eclipsed by claims to universal truth. As Foucault (1980) reminds us, power and knowledge reinforce each other so that the collection of infor-mation of a certain sort buttresses the powerful positions of those who do the collecting. However, intergenerational communication is intimately relational; it is created between people and becomes contested if one party attempts to ride roughshod over the perspectives of another. Recognizing the relational nature of interaction between professional helpers and patients who are often also younger and older adults, opens the door to the daily experience of health and illness (Frank 1998a) and power imbalances that can influence the effectiveness of helping interventions (Powell and Biggs 2000).

Third, a denigration of the past and a preoccupation with the here and now exerts a symbolic as well as a practical force. It compromises personal continuity and the use of personal and collective experience. Particularly in relation to older age, it privileges a meta-communication that it is only the present and the young that have real value, while age and experience do not (Moody 1992; Biggs 1998). Distinctions between young and old are at the same time subject to elision, through the promotion of the idea that all are addressed dispassionately and simply in terms of whether a technique will work or not. Indeed, the discontents of old age may eventually be erased com-pletely. As such, biomedicine changes the way in which old age is perceived. Primarily, age becomes associated with illness, and if illness can be abolished, perhaps also can age.

Each of these factors – the structural, the interpersonal and the symbolic – interact. Each is a site upon which hegemonic and dominating discourses are deployed, but also a site upon which they can be resisted and alternative visions of later life can be provoked.

This chapter critically assesses the power that 'medicalization' holds over contemporary ageing. Medical solutions to the problems of ageing are needed to ensure continued agency in later life, and yet they exact a price. The price can be thought of in terms of the dominance of medical definitions of the problems faced in old age and what constitutes success, particularly when it appears that other explanations or remedies are eclipsed (Estes and Binney 1989). It is in this sense that the biomedicalization of ageing seals itself off from other explorations. A consequence of this is that thinking of age in a biomedical way creates a self-contained world in which to grow old. It, for example, forms a basis for definitions of well-being, satisfaction, security, comfort and moral integrity. It provides a basis for the legitimizing discourses held by professional helpers and a ground on which professional–patient interactions take place (Estes *et al.* 1984; Estes and Binney 1989). In addition to undoubted innovation in technique and the alleviation of suffering, it contributes to an atomizing discourse on what it is to grow old. Often ageing is reduced to an individual complaint, the problems of bodily and mental dysfunction, resulting in a fragmentation of lived experience. The focus is more narrowly on medical care, ignoring the vast majority of care and resources most needed by the ageing including public health measures of housing and nutrition, preventive care, chronic and long-term care. Not surprisingly, the substantial profits that can be made through biomedical innovation contribute to an ever increasing definition of what counts as a medical condition, fuelled by both the legitimizing processes of insurance coverage and the aggressive marketing of biomedical solutions. There is little room, here, for the critical analysis of disabling social environments, the effects of disadvantage, history and experience, the power imbalance contained within interpersonal relationships, or structures of care provision and social policy.

The hegemonic solutions suggested by biomedicine are, however, subtly different from those associated with notions of productive ageing (see Chapter 5), although, as Moody (2001) points out, the two are also interdependent. Biomedicine does not imply agelessness, as it appears in policy moves toward productive ageing. Rather, emphasis is placed on the avoidance of or remedy to ageing. As such, biomedicine sidesteps the criticism aimed at the productivity argument that the negative consequences of ageing are being denied. For biomedicine, awareness of the ageing process as a negative experience is a necessary part of the picture, otherwise why bother to try and remedy it? While productive ageing addresses a fear of ageing through denial, biomedicine engages with the promise of avoidance, and bodily repair as necessary. Issues of access and availability to the benefits of biomedicine have therefore become a key component of this debate.

Anti-ageism, medicine and access

Butler's description of gerontology as an optimistic amalgam of science and advocacy (in Moody 1993) reflects a view that the real problem that emerges when medical advances meet ageing adults concerns access. In other words, older adults are discriminated against, relative to other age groups in the provision and availability of the latest drugs, techniques and technologies of effective health care (Age Concern England 2000). Beauchamp and Childress (2001) point out that much of the debate within biomedical ethics has concerned the degree to which older adults have a right to services and can be protected from certain risks. Such interpretations have been influential in the formulation of public policy on both sides of the Atlantic.

In the UK, for example, the 2001 *National Service Framework for Older People* began with the statement that

> Older people don't expect special treatment. They just expect the same level of service and care as everyone else. But that's not always been the case in the past. There are many areas of excellent care for older people. But there are also examples of poor, unresponsive and insensitive treatment, and sometimes simply because of age.
>
> (Department of Health: 2001: 1)

Key areas for service development include a restatement of the long-standing NHS position that all patients should receive treatment on the basis of clinical need, the dropping of age as a criterion for eligibility and the provision of more specialist staff. This position is attractive to gerontologists, activists and many older people because, as with the policy shift toward productive ageing, it appears to address many of the issues that have been raised by these groups in the past. It also reinforces a commonly held ethical belief in the justice of equity in health care and provision. This, it is argued, has been eroded by ageist attitudes and should be rebuilt.

However, by concentrating on civil rights with an emphasis on equity rather than diversity, anti-ageist approaches to the medicalization of old age encounter certain limitations. 'Clinical need', for example, is not an access issue pure and simple. If it is interpreted as a question of access to the same service as everybody else, differences in need between age groups may be underplayed, and the dominance of one age group in defining what might reasonably be expected, overplayed. There is also a focus on the distribution of existing resources within systems. This has the dual disadvantage of tacitly accepting the parameters of what is already available, and tending to overlook the micro interactions of power and hierarchy that perpetuate the daily realities generated by the systems themselves.

Bioethics in the USA has delved substantially into the debate surrounding the moral justifications for age-based rationing in health care (Callahan 1987). The bioethical framing of this debate has embraced the concepts of generational equity, moral rights and responsibilities regarding societal resources, the framing of which has been an effective linguistic weapon in the larger struggles over the state, the citizen and social provision, such as the entitlement to retirement security (Estes *et al.* 1996a).

An example of the difficulties that can follow an uncritical pursuit of what is fair and equal can be seen in the debate on Quality Adjusted Life Years or QALYs. QALYs arose as an attempt to find a value-free means of managing limited health care resources. In essence, the QALY relies on a crudely utilitarian attempt to measure expected quality of life. 'If an extra year of healthy (i.e. good quality) life expectancy is worth one, then an extra year of unhealthy (i.e. poor quality) life expectancy must be worth less than one' (Williams 1988: 285). It has been promoted by Williams in the UK, and Daniels in the USA, both publishing in 1988, as a means of making decisions about the value of specific clinical interventions. Priority was given to treatments that would increase the quality of the largest number of years of life. However, as younger adults usually have a potentially greater number of years to live than older adults, the QALY assessment was tacitly biased against older patients. In essence, the fewer years you can reasonably be expected to live, the less you qualify under this measure.

The QALY approach has been questioned by the President's Commission for the Study of Ethical Problems in Medicine and Biomedical and Behavioral Research as early as 1982 in the USA and by the UK *National Service Framework for Older People* in 2001 (Department of Health 2001).

QALYs arose within an historical period in which non-clinical considerations, including economic recession and a fiscal squeeze on health and welfare spending, had a disproportionate influence on models for the care and support of older adults. It was also a period where the US political Right was raising the issue of generational inequity which, as they saw it, consisted of excessive spending on older people at the expense of younger age groups (Minkler and Robertson 1991). In this context, Daniels argued that care should be provided for a 'normal lifespan', while Williams suggested the notion of a 'fair innings' in support of measures that effectively institutionalized inequality skewed radically against older adults. Thus, Hendricks *et al.* (1999) have argued that retrenchment in US old age programmes reflects a wider, and largely successful, political agenda to replace the perception of older Americans as worthy due to their lifelong contributions with one in which they are 'over-benefiting' at the expense of younger generations. In ethical terms, this argument constitutes a shift from a 'rights' toward a 'greater good' argument (Gillon 1986) centred upon perceptions of current or potential social productivity. It brings biomedicine closer to decisions based on productive ageing and in so doing introduces an essentially unequal attribution of social worth, based on age.

The debate around QALYs demonstrates the interdependence of socio-political and biomedical judgement in a way that is not immediately apparent within the self-contained discourse on medicine and clinical need. It also underlines the need for anti-ageist approaches to take diversity into account in addition to general principles of equality, when questioning existing practice. The QALY debate has been used here to illustrate a way in which ageism can be institutionalized through a seemingly objective tool to aid clinical judgement and the political agendas that may thereby be insinuated into medical decision taking. It is a continuing theme in policy debates over a much wider issue of rationing and service availability that is picked up in a later section of this chapter. For the present, though, we shall develop a critique within the explanatory framework of political economy.

Political economy, rationing and changing demand

Political economy and the medicalization of age

A political economy approach to age and biomedicine argues that the form medicalization takes and the biases within it are related to social structure and the resourcing of health and welfare systems. The value systems and structural arrangements that determine whether one remedy or group is valued more highly than another are seen, at root, to be economic in origin. Economic inequalities are therefore reflected in health and social care, and an individual or group's deservingness would depend upon their current, or in the case of children, future productivity or their ability to spend.

Estes and Binney (1989) have defined the relationship between biomedicalization and ageing through the social construction of ageing as a medical problem to the exclusion of other factors, combined with the construction of medical expertise and technology as marketable commodities and funding of biomedical research as an economic investment. A key result of these combined processes is a form of biological reductionism whereby the explanation for the positive health effects of social improvements, such as sewerage and sanitary systems, education and housing, are replaced in the public mind by attributions to the forward march of medical techniques applied to individual patients.

The influence of bio-technology as a commercial enterprise can be seen in many areas. Examples arise in the continued search for longevity (Fischetti and Stix 2000); the privileging of pharmacological over social solutions and reactive over-preventive approaches to health issues (Estes *et al.* 2001a); and the unequal allocation of resources in favour of affluent older people in the global North and West at the expense of the South and East (Dannefer 2000).

Each follows a pattern identified by Estes *et al.* (2001a) as the commodification of ageing through medicalization, whereby an understanding of adult ageing is distorted by a desire for new territory to be acquired through a partnership of bio-technical innovation and the discovery of new commercial markets. Key to this process are demographic changes, driven by increased population age and the elimination of many diseases of early life, factors that have led to a concentration of medical and technical attention on old age. Because this concentration of factors has happened within the framework of market capitalism, it is argued that particular processes have also come to dominate decision taking. First, medical expertise has moved away from the remedy of need to the maximization of profit. Second, it has led to the monopoly control of expertise by specialist groups that then profit through the regulation of medical techniques. Estes (1979a) has previously described the growth of an expert culture around ageing as the 'aging enterprise', seeing it as a hegemonizing force for professional interests over folk and older persons' perspectives. In her more recent work (Estes and Associates 2001) she has argued that the free market policies of the late twentieth century have exacerbated the commodification of ageing. By this is meant the intensification of the association of ageing with disease and decrement and the transformation of remedies to those decrements into saleable commodities, a process which she maintains has made the profit motive primary and the relief of suffering secondary. In addition, a drive to intensify profit has led, primarily in the USA and extending through globalizing processes to other nation states, to an increase in the power of multinational commercial enterprises over professional power (Estes and Phillipson 2002). As the search for medically sanctioned profit has expanded, this has resulted in the displacement of risk into the private sphere and the exploitation of unpaid forms of care, mostly in the home and mostly undertaken by women. Thus the dynamic of the market has worked to intensify the extraction of profit through the development of new products, subsuming independent professional judgement under corporate control, and recruiting previously untouched aspects of civil society as fields for exploitation and control. Following Ehrenreich and Ehrenreich's (1971: 166) *The American Health Empire*, it is argued that under such circumstances the 'primary function of the health care system is not the delivery of services but, rather, the pursuit of profits, with secondary functions of research and education'.

Rationing and age

A critical concern with the costs and appropriateness of health care is also reflected in arguments that question the value of provision for older adults. Themes of rationing filled a vigorous moral discourse of bioethics throughout the 1980s coincident with the US political framework of the times, and commencing with President Reagan's policies of cost containment, privatization and entitlement reduction. Thus, the contexts in which moral problems arise and have their 'careers' include 'macro-ideological contexts of political discourse'. Dialogue shifted from issues of autonomy to 'normative claims and obligations specific to age, and moral justification for cost-containment solutions based on claims of age-specific consumption of medical resources' (Estes *et al.* 1996a: 102–3).

Scholars working from a political economy approach would suggest that the contentions that spending on older people should be reduced may be rooted in misplaced notions of productivity and the view that older people are no longer seen as worthy of investment. Thus, market economics would dictate that services should be cut where they become a drain on the competitiveness of national capitalist systems. An alternative position would, however, propose that need should be prioritized above profit and that the most damaged by a system are those most deserving of protection in later life.

The issue of the appropriateness of different forms of care in later life has been taken up, most controversially, by Daniel Callahan (1987, 1990). Callahan argues that, while society should provide good quality care for older adults, this should not include unlimited efforts to extend longevity through the use of public funds. Biomedical innovation (the example he gives is of a 76-year-old woman on Medicare receiving a fully transplanted liver) is seen as having little practical value, given the costs and outcomes involved. Here, Callahan takes the conservative position that increasing expenditure of public money on a rising population of older adults creates an economic burden on younger age groups, which is not sustainable. This position picks up on strands of argument identified in the QALY debate but is much broader in scope. It moves beyond clinical judgement to present an explicit challenge to the social and symbolic place of old age in contemporary society.

In fact, the arguments that Callahan (1987) deploys subtly combine libertarian economics with liberal sentiment. A case is made, for example, for increased long-term care and home care, a cherished liberal position. This would entail giving priority to care for 'chronic' conditions which may be more costly than heroic surgery and acute services using high-tech invasive treatment. This issue, it is argued, particularly affects disadvantaged minorities and women, if not resolved, and parallels Minkler and Estes's (1998) work on the perverse relationship between health and social inequality.

Callahan's case extends beyond costs, however: 'I want to lay the foundation for a more austere thesis: that even with relatively ample resources, there will be better ways in the future to spend our money than on indefinitely extending the life of the elderly' (1987: 110). He contends that this tendency reflects a deeper malaise in society: a 'refusal to accept limits . . . (which has) . . . allowed us to evade some deeper truths about the living of a good life and the place of ageing and death in that life' (1987: 116).

While conclusions differ, these premises resonate with positions taken by humanistic gerontologists such as Cole (1992), Biggs (1993) and Tornstam (1994) concerning the positive value of existential challenges in later life. Callahan (1990) has argued that society needs a forum in which discourse on the value of suffering and decline can take place. He claims contemporary western societies have ignored the 'elderly's particular obligation to the future' and discusses the appropriate life course tasks of different ages. Children prepare for future roles, mature adults raise the next generation and manage present society, while the old become 'moral conservators' serving the young and the future they will not themselves see. One positive consequence of this line of thinking is the contention that older adults have an obligation to serve the young and the young a duty to assist the elderly. However, it is also argued that this must happen within the bounds of the 'natural lifespan': 'One in which the possibilities have on the whole been achieved and after which death may be understood as a sad, but nonetheless relatively acceptable event' (1987: 112).

This is not the vision presented by bio-technology, which aims to extend life for as long as possible. Callahan sets himself against the bio-technical industry in so far as he rejects the research and marketing of life-extending products. To a degree, he would thereby find unexpected bedfellows in eco-logical concerns with duties of stewardship and conservation of resources (Dobson 2000) and global inequities in life chances (Dannefer 2000). Neither is it the view of adult ageing reflected in social constructionism, where the life course is seen as a social rather than a natural progress. And while Callahan (1987) maintains that the life course is 'a biographical not a biological defin-ition', he does appear to believe that it contains natural stages and a natural duration. Death becomes tolerable, it is argued, once life possibilities are accomplished and moral obligations discharged. It is 'an understanding of the process of ageing and death that looks to our obligations to the young and to the future, that recognises the necessity of limits and the acceptance of decline and death, and that values the old for their age, not for their continuing youthful vitality' (1987: 115).

While a complex mixture of often opposing traditions within the US debate on age appear in Callahan's argument, it is rooted in traditional eco-nomic issues of productivity. His final conclusions are consonant with some in the radical US Right and those of Daniels (1988), reflecting concern about the low returns expected from state spending on older citizens. The 'natural life-span' then becomes a reasonable yardstick for judging when collective social obligation should be terminated. Moody (1998a) has pointed out that this argument justifies reductions in state spending, but not individual spending, which is supported under the rubric of personal choice and the class-related access to care based upon the ability of individuals in a capitalist market to pay. Only the poor, it appears, can live too long.

Service systems, lifestyle and demand

The argument for rationing is based on the assumed costs of increased longevity. There is strong evidence, however, that rising costs of medical care are not primarily attributable to increasing population age, and that demand is not solely a consequence of biomedical innovation. US medical cost rises have been shown to be due primarily (in the following rank order) to:

1   rises in the general cost of living;
2   rises in medical care prices;
3   increases in the intensity of services including technological innovation; and
4   population growth that, historically, has comprised less than 10 per cent of rising costs (Newhouse 1994).

From the perspective of critical political economy, the costs associated with an ageing population are more likely a result of the inefficiencies in pluralistic organization and financing systems (rather than universal or single payer systems) in which private profits are extracted from the health care systems themselves. There is no justifiable case that the costs of a society that is ageing are primarily the outcome of demographic trends (Navarro 2000). A study by Evans *et al.* (2001) of British Columbian elders shows, for example, a minimal effect on health care costs of population ageing, but a significant effect of changes in age-specific use patterns. Some of these differences can be explained by changes in the lifestyles of older adults that drive a demand for different, rather than fewer services. However, the most powerful pull on increased expenditure was to be found in changes in treatment style, notably the use of more expensive pharmacology, for which out-of-pocket costs for the US elderly are rising alarmingly fast – as much as 34 per cent between 2001 and 2002 alone (Families USA 2002; Gold and Achman 2002). This increase in drug use was not prompted by changes in the illness profile of the ageing population, the authors claim, but arose partly as a consequence of policies aimed at reducing the length of hospital stays and partly through pressure from powerful medico-industrial lobbying. It is argued by these authors that, while advances in medical technology do not in themselves increase costs, when combined with free-market and anti-welfare policies this tends to be the result. Ebrahim (2002) suggests that the relationship between social explanation, medical treatment and health economics is complex. The fear of health care costs associated with an ageing population, in the UK context, has led to policies that demedicalize old age, such as the move from nursing to social forms of care. This has created a situation in which the health needs of old people are often not recognized and are left untreated. He criticizes the 'natural lifespan' perspective, claiming that it justifies this form of medical neglect.

Patterns of health and social care use have also changed because of changes in the availability of occupational pensions and the effects of this on disposable income in later life (Gilleard 1996; Phillipson 1998). This has led some authors to maintain that ageing is best defined by patterns of consumption, rather than in relation to the economic productivity of older adults (Featherstone and Hepworth 1990; Gilleard and Higgs 2000). Polikva (2001) points out that in this respect bio-technological innovation, consumption, bodily manipulation and lifestyle are closely related. It is claimed that postmodernity has placed 'modern' versions of the life course, dominant in the 1950s and 1960s and influential in the shaping of contemporary health and welfare policy, under increasing strain. As social change and technical advance have gathered pace and have produced therapeutic advances that increase bodily potential, it is argued that there has been erosion of rigid divisions between age groups and experiments with a variety of lifestyles by older people themselves. Demands for health interventions based on lifestyle are thereby in a reciprocal relationship with advances in medical technology. Together they mark a fundamental shift in perceptions of the ageing body, which is now seen both as more of a barrier to lifestyle choice and as more malleable. Medical advances that have contributed to a decoupling of bodily, chronological and social-psychological ageing are said to include: developments in the study of genetics; a cultural fascination with cosmetic surgery, extending to the cloning of body parts; drug use, ranging from hormone replacement therapy to recreational use of steroids; and a growing and sophisticated range of prosthetic options. In their different ways each reflects a changing relationship between the use of medicines and the ageing body.

These developments have contributed, in the popular imagination, to the possibility of reshaping the body and revising the ageing process and are reflected in the growth of best-selling manuals that encourage the reader to maintain a midlife style, or abolish ageing altogether. Chopra (1993) states on the cover of *Ageless Body, Timeless Mind*, for example, that 'Ageing is much more of a choice than people ever dream. One of modern medicine's great breakthroughs is a realisation that the body is not an object, but a process with no pre-ordained limits.'

The body, in other words, need no longer be a barrier to self-enhancement, and therefore something very different is happening to our symbolic understanding of ageing. Ageing, in the minds of many patients, is becoming an option, even though this may simply reflect a heady mixture of public faith in medical science and an unwillingness to adapt consumer lifestyles to new circumstances.

The cultural momentum engendered by this changing relationship to the body is, arguably, familiar to general practitioners who are subject to patients' perplexity and dismay if a convincing remedy cannot be supplied for a particular complaint. There may also be an increase in demand for surgery on bodies that patients 'don't like' on top of ones that 'won't work'. Hodgekin (1996) indicates that such trends evidence a move toward what he has called 'recreational surgery' – in other words, interventions that enhance potential beyond what might be considered normative.

These symbolic changes may help to explain the fact that while there has been a 'compression of morbidity' (Fries 1980) in contemporary western societies, this appears not to have reduced reliance on services. The compression here refers to the fact that people are both surviving longer and remaining healthy for an increasing proportion of their old age. Rather than a gradual decline in capacity, Fries's thesis holds that most old people will experience a 'terminal drop' from a plateau of physical and mental functioning shortly before death (Wilson 1991). An underlying assumption of the compression of decline to a brief period of illness at the very end of the life course was that demand for health care might actually decline as the population ages and, further, the causes of such reductions in demand were seen as lying outside the health care system. This does not appear to be the case. Just as Beveridge (1942) discovered, following the birth of the UK National Health Service, demand has not withered away as existing illnesses are overcome; it has simply changed. It is perhaps ironic that the increase in the well-being of the current cohort of older adults, in part a consequence of comprehensive welfare programmes, has not dampened the perceived threat of apocalyptic demography (Robertson 1999; Gee and Gutman 2000). There is still a common view that the proportion of older people in the population is growing at an alarming rate and that this group has an insatiable appetite for health care while not adding to the productive base of society.

The observations above indicate that demand on service systems is not a simple matter of increasing numbers of older people equalling greater and ultimately unsustainable use of societal resources. Rather, factors such as changes to health systems brought about by market economics, changed expectations and lifestyle choices each appear to influence patterns of use. As Vincent (1999) has pointed out, the medicalization of old age is not an objective scientific process, but rather a series of struggles at local, national and international levels of policy. These struggles to define the nature of ageing and the proper place of medicine within it are between older and potentially old people, helping professionals of different types, entrepreneurs (from family-run care homes through to pharmaceutical companies of global reach) and finally the institutions of the state and the organization and distribution of resources through policy.

The power of capital, as designator of value through relations of production and of consumption, has led us to a contradiction. We appear to have a system which simultaneously celebrates the possibilities of increased longevity and condemns the supposed apocalyptic excesses of too many old people.

According to writers such as Callahan, policy should distinguish between different groups of older people: those who can pay and those who rely on public support. This would generate a distinctly class-biased discriminatory approach, with serious racial, ethnic and gender undertones (Binney and Estes 1990). The point, from a political economy perspective, is the same whether it is medical or social arguments that are at stake.

Under both the Callahan and apocalyptic demography scenarios, the willingness to reserve resources for the care of older adults is dependent on their relationship to a very limited understanding of the productive value of older citizens. Free market systems tend to denigrate older people as contributors to the social good because only economic production is valued. However, the increase in older adults is simultaneously perceived to be a market opportunity, so long as this does not tie investment monies up in state funding. Any argument that older adults are in themselves a burden on society underestimates alternative forms of contribution and intergenerational and gender exchange, as well as the power of market forces to distort the efficiency, effectiveness and equity in the performance of health systems.

Interpersonal relations, medical ethics and dialogical selves

Medical ethics as interpersonal relations

A significant consequence of the structural issues outlined above can be seen in older people's need for appropriate medical care, which they are only able to secure through unequal power relationships.

Many of the issues underlying the discussion so far, for example equality, justice and access, often appear under the rubric of ethics. It is perhaps unsurprising that medical ethics has become an increasingly important aspect of the debate on the proper treatment of older people. Approaching interpersonal relationships through the medium of ethical decision taking is seductive because it appears to offer comprehensive solutions to both structural and personal dilemmas at the point of contact between helping professionals and older patients. It is an approach that resonates with the claim that the medical model should be objective and free from prejudice (Gillion 1986) and also preserves the exclusive context of the patient–physician relationship (Woodhouse and Pengelly 1991). Interaction between older people and their doctors and nurses may thereby be driven by a clear ethical code, a clinical examination of need, and respect for the autonomy of the patient. It becomes a matter of technical gatekeeping within the symbolic space of a special, one-to-one bond. While such an approach directly addresses the inequities that arise from explicit decisions (McKenzie *et al.* 1988), medical ethics has been less able to digest issues of institutionalized ageism (Patel 1990) or imbalances of power between patients and health professionals (Frank 1998a; Biggs and Powell 2001).

Autonomy and structure

The key factors identified in two of the most popular texts on medical ethics (Gillon's (1986) *Philosophical Medical Ethics* and Beauchamp and Childress's (2001) *Principles of Biomedical Ethics*, the latter running to five editions at the time of writing) concern patient choice and autonomy.

Autonomy, the decision-making capacity of the patient, is identified by Gillon (1986) as the primary value in medical ethics. Beauchamp and Childress (2001) elaborate this by stating that physicians' judgements of competence, about technique but also about mental capacity, serve a gatekeeping role in health care. The judgement of health professionals as to whether patients are incompetent to make a decision may lead them to take decisions for them or consult with others, such as informal carers.

This has marked a shift in the argument, from a physician's obligation to disclose information, to the quality of the patient's understanding and consent. Ideally, then, interaction between older patients and health professionals should take place under the principle of autonomous authorization, by the patient, based on adequate information and without coercion.

Within this literature, Gillon (1986) has suggested that claims made on blanket calls for equity alone rarely reflect the diversity of need and clinical decision making that takes place in everyday health care. The autonomy of patients' wishes, wishes that vary across cases even when the presenting clinical problem is the same in medical terms, requires that each case is dealt with on its individual merits. This consideration must, it is argued, always be foremost in the professional judgement of the clinician.

The assumption that 'we are all the same' may apply neither across nor within age groups. Older people do not face the same risks or have the same needs as other age groups, although they should have the same rights. Medical decisions are not simply a matter of access, but access to what and how these interface with specific needs and inequalities. Such access is mediated by the adequacy of communication and the completeness and accuracy of information, all of which are highly problematic in terms of cultural competence for different ethnic, socio-economic, gender and age groups (Commonwealth Fund 2002). Age is not an adequate criterion; once access has been achieved, other issues of appropriateness apply.

However, an underlying emphasis upon the individual relationship implied by such an approach would mark a distinctive difference between Gillon and writers like him, and the political economists. Estes and Binney (1989), for example, point to inequalities which influence the likelihood that different groups within the elderly population will receive unequal treatment as well as between age groups, but they emphasize that these inequalities are structurally determined. There are considerable inequities within the older population itself, based on class, gender, race and other factors, which are exacerbated by free market approaches to health and social care (Estes *et al.* 2001a). Thus there is a clear difference in the theoretical and policy implications of the two positions, which lends a different value to alternative service systems.

Both Gillon (1986) and Beauchamp and Childress (2001) indicate that individual choice and autonomy are best served by free market models of health care, while political economists such as Estes *et al.* (2001a) argue against market systems as they exacerbate inequality of health provision. From the latter perspective, the former simply supply an ideological justification for a very particular set of power relationships and social structures that underpin the debate itself (Estes *et al.* 1996a). The focus on individual autonomy and the responsibilities of health practitioners effectively obscures the underlying dynamics – economic, symbolic and interpersonal – that perpetuate health inequalities.

In so far as ethicists deal in universals, they are likely to ignore the social and historical specificity of their own conclusions. There is therefore little attention to issues outside the ethical bubble and, most particularly, the power environment that shapes ethical discourse itself. Ultimately decisions come down either to the ethical judgement of the clinician in so far as this, paradoxically, allows the patient autonomy, or is left to the universal yet hidden hand of market forces.

It is a key element of Estes's (1979a) critique of the ageing enterprise that political–economic systems directly influence patient–professional interaction. This implies that the way in which alliances and power imbalances are played out varies between service systems. An example of this variation can easily be seen by comparing health care systems in the USA and the UK. In the USA, with its predominantly commercial system, it is not uncommon for patients to be reportedly distrustful of their doctors. This trend has been intensified with the advent of managed care, a system that attempts to reconcile treatment options with insurance liabilities. Physicians are often seen as being in alliance with the insurance companies when making clinical judgements, as the latter determine what can be legitimately prescribed. It is not uncommon for patients to go 'doctor shopping' within the US system in order to gain alternative opinions or interpretations of access criteria to clinical procedures. Under the UK system, however, doctors and most notably general practitioners are most likely to be seen as in alliance with the patient in attempts to secure adequate treatment from a limited state system. However, because patients have to register with one doctor and public services are subject to 'queue' systems, doctor shopping is virtually unknown. Thus, when Beauchamp and Childress (2001) talk about the ethical 'responsibilities to third party interests', speaking from the US context, they are referring to a potential conflict of ethical demands from the patient and from the insurer. In the UK context, this is currently more likely to be interpreted as a debate on the duties to informal carers, mostly relatives, or the implications for wider public health (Powell and Biggs 2000). Further, in state-controlled quasi-markets, increasing politico-economic control of public health services and attacks on professional autonomy are more likely to be engineered through 'quality' processes such as monitoring and audit (Cooper 2001), which are perceived to be a greater threat to professional autonomy than corporate capital.

It is instructive that Beauchamp and Childress (2001) do recognize con-flicts of interest, when the commercial self-interest of the gatekeeper/physician may not correspond to the patient's needs or the interests of third parties. A physician might refer patients to her or his own private practice or clinic, or overuse tests or interventions from which the practitioner or corpor-ate employing interest stands to make financial gain. Alternatively, concerned physicians may overstress the severity of a condition to ensure that it is covered by insurance and the patient receives treatment. Both of these con-flicts are exacerbated by a market or mixed economy of health and care ser-vices and are unlikely to occur within public welfare systems.

Traditional ethical concern about the relationship between professionals and the needs of older people has tended to focus on issues such as: what to divulge to patients about their own health status and in what form; the need for privacy and confidentiality and its limits; and a discussion of conflicts of interest (Beauchamp and Childress 2001). The power/knowledge relationship between professional and user tends to be taken as a given, in such a way that discussion hinges on how and whether the professional should make informa-tion available. Patient autonomy is often presented as the deciding factor, whether an individual patient has the wherewithal and sufficient information to make a judgement. While a laudable objective in itself, it also uncritically reflects decision taking within the traditional one-to-one patient–physician relationship where other factors are theoretically more or less equal. However, it cannot be assumed, within a critical gerontological approach, that the users and providers of biomedicine act as free agents meeting equally in the health and welfare market and then returning to their own private activities. The power of each party is uneven; one is older, the other younger; one a holder of medico-technical expertise, the other a patient; one is usually well and the other ill; one designated an active role, the other more often than not passive. However, this wider circumference of policy and power relations is not addressed as it is assumed that the application of general moral principles rather than the interactive dialogue and legitimizing discourses that shape relationships are sufficient to aid professional judgement.

The medical gaze and patient experience

When seen from the perspective of critical gerontology, the ethicist's solution to interpersonal relations between older people and health professionals appears to ignore group experience of structural inequalities and the power relations that prefigure professional–patient interaction. As such it has become part of the hegemonic arsenal of biomedicine. A further argument, elaborated below, is more Foucauldian in its critique in so far as it examines how the medical gaze modifies the way in which old age and biomedicine are perceived and the self is experienced. Looking at the finer grain of interaction in this way gives further hints as to the means by which the atomization and commodification of the ageing body takes place.

Foucault (1973) has argued persuasively that the birth of the medical profession brought with it a different way of seeing illness and well-being. Most notably, the sick other became an object to be modified. Under the 'medical gaze', people become their bodies, bodies disaggregated into a series of dysfunctional parts. This is useful for the scientific analysis of function and remedy but severely limits any perspective that takes into account interpersonal and wider social factors. Gullette (2003) gives as an example, here, how cracking the genetic code of biological ageing has directed attention away from socially determined life chances in later life. Power relations are eclipsed by narratives of technological application by a skilled professional. Interactions take on a Buberian (1958) I–it quality, whereby the humanity of the other is not seen, excepting as a thing-like material, subject to manipulation and control. As Good (1997) has pointed out, this is often a concern of medical students as they begin their education, but is also often lost as part of their induction into a biomedical culture.

Such a perspective does violence to the relational and dialogical realities of interpersonal exchange. Here, relation and dialogue refer to the ways in which each social situation constitutes a form of negotiation, whereby meaning is constructed mutually between participants and reflects their backgrounds and current circumstances (Hermans and Hermans-Jansen 2001). Exchanges that are mediated by the biomedical are relational only in so far as the relationship between physician, nurse, drug company and the nominated patient serves (or is seen to impede) the efficient execution of the technical procedure. Dialogue only takes place in so far as this generates data for the disclosure of symptoms, the identification of a correct diagnosis, and an understanding of compliance in order that cure can take place. If taken as a very limited series of objectives, to effect a cure and leave the rest of the patient's life alone, perhaps such an approach could be justified. However, it becomes problematic when the part is taken to stand for the whole. This is a particular issue when ageing is considered, where ageing is taken to mean illness and to stand in for that person's total social and personal experience, his or her place in the world. Powell and

Longino (2002) have argued that the disaggregation of the ageing body takes a number of forms. First, the experience of ageing is broken down into a number of separate age categories each with its accompanying medical specialism. Second, the dominance of biomedical perspectives on ageing has led to an acceptance of the association between adult ageing and bodily and mental deterioration. Finally they note that a combination of specialism and a separation of mind from the body has compromised the gendered experience of bodily ageing. If the remedy is seen to be the expansion of the medical gaze to ever wider aspects of a nominated patient's life, then not only is the privacy of the individual compromised, but legitimacy is extended only to what can be seen within the gaze itself. The development of 'holistic care', for example, has been criticized because it legitimizes the expansion of biomedical explanation while driving out alternatives before it (Porter 1997). If ageing becomes associated with illness, and the avoidance of ageing with cure, then an expansion of medical discourse to include ever more aspects of the older person's life world leaves two alternatives: subsumption of the self under the rubric of a sick body or a continual flight from the 'symptoms' of ageing. Both depend upon biomedical hegemony. It follows from the above analysis that a biomedical approach to ageing encourages the evacuation of certain forms of experience, through the reclassification of experience into symptoms which can then be addressed separately from interpersonal and wider social impacts.

Despite this powerful dynamic, a number of writers have attempted to explore the experiential and relational construction of meaning in health-related settings. Moody (1993) argues that bioethical versions of decision making, as an ability to make choices based on sufficient information and without duress, provide too weak a view of what it means to be an ageing adult. Common-sense assumptions of health service contexts and the history of institutions and social structure are not questioned, nor are the very problematic cultural differences in understanding, experiences and ability to secure access, financially or otherwise, to care and services. In reality, these service systems reflect the different attention and options offered to different ages and social groups (Adelman *et al.* 1991), the use of strategies, routines and masquerades deployed by professionals and older patients in health settings (Biggs 1993), and the complex relationship between the experience of illness, of ageing and the emotional labour of being a patient in care (Berman 1994).

As if a witness to the tacit yet coercive power of professionalized interaction, Berman (1994) notes an account made by Florida Scott-Maxwell that

> I must do my work of being a patient . . . patients must like and dislike
> as little as possible . . . Then the rage I knew so well rose in me and
> threatened all. I heard the animal growl in me when they did all the
> things it is my precious privacy and independence to do myself. I
> hated them while I breathed 'thank you nurse'.

(1994: 153)

Frank (1998b) argues that the ability to tell one's own story of illness is by no means straightforward. If, as Foucault (1976) claims, the maintenance of existing power relations depends not on the use of force, but on the ability to persuade active subjects to reproduce those relations for themselves, then the telling of narratives will always be suspect.

According to this perspective, the scope of ideas such as patient autonomy will always be limited and problematic because the frameworks that are used to explain and understand our own illness experience to ourselves are themselves compromised. Frank (1998b) poses the almost unanswerable question: when does self-care turn into a technology for producing a certain sort of self? Personal narratives, particularly for older people in health settings, remain both a means of taking care of oneself and conformity to a restricted legitimizing discourse.

Holstein and Cole (1996) and Hermans and Hermans-Jansen (2001) suggest that the development of an ageing self, even in situations of chronic illness, can only be understood dialogically. That is to say, meaning is created between people and through dialogue between internal and external 'voices'. This is particularly true when older people suffer from chronic illness, first because they have to

> preserve a sense of self when they have lost the ability to act within their former frameworks and when their bodies become a paramount concern . . . The older person must find a way to integrate into reconfigured narrative the voices of their families, their care providers and other significant 'actors' in their current life.
>
> (Holstein and Cole 1996: 18)

These significant others become the interdependent means of translating the self from 'possibility into reality'. In other words, it is part of the nature of health and illness that a biomedical hegemony makes its force felt at times when individual patients are at their weakest and most vulnerable. The problem lies in the simultaneous tendency to individualize, objectivize and symptomatize lived experience, such that enduring factors in the construction of self, of collective identities, life chances and power imbalances are effectively sidelined.

Market relations and medical ethics

One of the themes that has emerged from this chapter is the close fit between traditional ethical guidance and the biomedical domain, which Estes *et al.* (1996a) label the 'bioethicalization' of problems. This process brings issues about adult ageing within the realm of a particular professional expertise and moral authority. Thus, while the ethical explanation of relationships tends to individualize the subject and universalize the remedy, the medical gaze objectifies and turns each problem into a technical fix. Both fit well within the hegemonic rubric of biomedicine, with its emphasis on exclusive scientific truths and decontextualized asocial discourse.

It will be recalled that the ethicist solution to problems arising from exclusively professional expertise, relies on ensuring autonomy in decision making and access to information. When seen through the lens of a critical gerontology grounded on political economy, issues such as access and autonomy can be seen to be close cousins to the conduct expected by a market model of interpersonal relationships. Given the intimate relationship between biomedicine, commodification of the body and corporate interests, this relationship is at first glance difficult to recognize. Under a market model it is supposed that otherwise free and equal individuals meet to undertake some bargain or exchange. Here those individuals constitute the older patient and the generally younger health professional. Autonomy needs to be maintained in order to perpetuate an illusion of disinterested choice, while access is defined in terms of the availability of market information. Neither examine structural as opposed to individual constraints on the choices being made, the construction of meaning that the market itself implies, or the underlying imbalances of power and resources which are nevertheless played out within the market itself and in interactions between the holders of specialist knowledge and those who need it. The professional's role as a sort of gatekeeping adviser itself contains profound interpersonal inequalities, and real or potential conflicts of interest, in terms of who controls and allows access to scarce medical and social resources, which simultaneously interact with the economic, social and cultural capital of the practitioner and the patient both within and beyond the clinic.

The biomedical approach tends to present choices between free market, meritocratic and needs-based approaches to the medicalization of old age as if they are outcome-neutral moral options. For older people this is unlikely to be the case, as market approaches have historically led to an erosion of the welfare state on which many older people depend and has exacerbated existing inequalities (Phillipson and Biggs 1998). Merit- and market-based approaches, particularly if they unquestioningly reflect the values of dominant social groups, may either focus on current contribution – as has been examined in our discussion of productive ageing – or on past contributions, which also tend to reflect cumulative disadvantage and advantages (Schultz 2001). Provision based on need may do more to validate the support of disadvantaged or vulnerable groups of which older people form a part. However, even this is not a simple outcome, as the identification of need is mediated by mechanisms that may hold tacit bias, as the debate on QALYs and rationing exemplifies.

The close relationship between services and profit, a tendency to talk in terms of material and not social cost, and of over-expenditiure but not of profit making, drives out competing definitions and experiences of old age inequalities. Without examining how particular options predetermine the nature of the arguments that can be had, discussions of health status can easily degenerate into a moral economy of individual worthiness. A moral imperative to stay healthy privileges the individual character of earlier lifestyle choices as opposed to risks and deprivations one has been exposed to, and organizes them into a moral capital of the life well lived. Stay healthy and have money, we are told; failing that, have family. Like the market, biomedicalization emerges as a self-contained symbolic space that attempts to push all else before it and in so doing reshapes its quarry in its own image.

Conclusions

It has been suggested that biomedicine and medical ethics have a dominant position within contemporary thinking about ageing. The scope includes structural, interpersonal and symbolic effects on the position of old age in society and perceptions about the nature of ageing.

Structurally, the close association between biomedicine and corporate power makes a virtue of profit over need. It thereby contributes to a division of the ageing population into the virtuous who can afford to pay for themselves, and those who cannot. This results in significant paradoxes within public policy such as a rush toward longevity research while simultaneously admonishing the success of a welfare state that has produced what alarmists label an apocalyptic demography. While 'productive ageing' trades on the denial of old age, the biomedical approach subsists of a fear of age, reduced to illness, and its avoidance. In this respect it has been able to include both the expansion of market opportunities into hitherto unexploited areas of the life course and the consumption of its products to fit emerging late-lifestyles. These processes have taken place in harness with the increased exploitation of the private sphere, with a disproportionate and deleterious effect on women and minorities. The structural distortions that have influenced the development of biomedicine have resulted in it offering us things we need in ways that may be against our wider interests.

Interpersonally, the close association of biomedicine, traditional ethics and the logic of the market have had a damaging effect on relationships between older persons and society, and older patients and helping professionals. A focus on bodily dysfunction and individualized relations has contributed to a reliance on medical hierarchy and power relations as givens, with a tendency to place professional helpers in active and older people in passive roles. While a part of the healing process, it also reinforces a wider perception of elders as a social group that are acted upon at the bottom of the pecking order. Seeing the dysfunctional body as separate from the self lends itself to seeing older patients as objects and in terms of physical dysfunction or disease. While this has a certain technical appeal, it separates mind and body in such a way as to split decision-making processes away from the 'body' under scrutiny. This process is exacerbated in the case of older people through the influence of wider structural inequalities and social prejudices.

Symbolically, biomedicine has become so powerful that it may effectively exclude other perspectives, such that illness comes to stand ever more force-fully for old age in the popular imagination, and that solutions to the prob-lems of adult ageing are seen as being solved exclusively through biomedical intervention. This is in spite of clear evidence of the much larger contribution of 'social' factors (including race, class, gender and other environmental and behavioural influences) in explaining the relationship between health, illness and ageing. The individualizing dynamic of technical fixes contributes to the trends, noted in Chapter 3, characterizing old age identity as a battle between individuals and their ageing bodies. Symbolically, biomedicine transforms its object and the experience of ageing and therefore modifies what old age is perceived to be.

7 Ageing and globalization

Key points:

- Global challenges to the nation state and implications for policy on ageing.
- The role of intergovernmental organizations in the new order of later life.
- Transnational ageing, migration and ageing in developing countries.
- Caring across borders, global care chains and institutional responses to old age.

Introduction

So far in this book, we have been exploring a range of theories and issues directly connected with debates and studies about the nature of growing old. This chapter widens the discussion with an exploration of how global social changes are transforming the experience of ageing. Globalization, defined here as the process whereby nation states are influenced (and sometimes undermined) by transnational actors (Beck 2000a), has become a major force in shaping responses to population ageing. Growing old has itself become relocated within a transnational context, with international organizations and cross-border migrations creating new conditions and environments for older people. Globalization, it will be argued, has produced a distinctive stage in the social history of ageing, with a growing tension between nation state-based solutions (and anxieties) about growing old and those formulated by global actors and institutions. Ageing can no longer be viewed as a 'national' problem or issue. Local or national interpretations of ageing made sense in a world where states were in control of their own destiny; where social policies were being designed with the aim or aspiration of levelling inequalities; and where citizenship was still largely a national affair (and where there was some degree of confidence over what constituted 'national borders'). The crisis affecting each of these areas, largely set in motion by different aspects of globalization, is now posing acute challenges for ageing in the twenty-first century.

The new context for ageing marks a radical departure from the era of reform associated with the rise of the welfare state. Services and support from the state are being reconstructed as posing economic problems for future generations, with the market and privatization proposed as the main alternatives (World Bank 1994; Peterson 1999). This development is being played out within an environment dominated by organizations such as the World Bank (WB), OECD (Organisation of Economic Cooperation and Development), IMF (International Monetary Fund) and World Trade Organisation (WTO), each of which has challenged various aspects of public provision for old age (Estes and Phillipson 2002). To review these developments this chapter examines five main areas:

- first, the institutional changes associated with the postwar reconstruction of ageing, with a particular focus on the role of the welfare state, retirement and the intergenerational contract;
- second, the nature of globalization and the role of global capital, and the relevance of both for the study of ageing;
- third, the influence of global actors on areas of public policy;
- fourth, the impact of globalization on less developed countries; and
- fifth, the role of gender and migration.

Institutionalizing old age

The first task is to examine the way in which growing old was transformed in the two decades following the ending of the Second World War. In virtually all industrialized societies, with varying degrees of emphasis, responses to ageing were formed around the institutions and relationships associated with welfare, retirement and what became known as the 'intergenerational contract' (Bengston and Achenbaum 1993; Walker 1996). The associated discourses were fundamental in determining social identity in old age. At the beginning of this period, social provision for older people was still built upon relatively fragile foundations. A variety of studies in Europe and the USA demonstrated the extent to which retirement, to take one example, met with hostility within working-class culture (Townsend 1957; Phillipson 1993). Moreover, as critics such as Gouldner (1971) and Estes (1979a) were to point out, the welfare state (in its weak and stronger versions) itself produced dependency in various forms, these reflecting class, gender and ethnic dimensions.

But what Titmuss (1993) and later Esping-Andersen (1994) were to characterize as the 'moral purpose of the welfare state' must also be emphasized.

Relieving social deprivation was undoubtedly the first concern of government programmes. However, an underlying theme was that of moving society to a higher ethical ground. Lowe (1993) suggests that the welfare state (and social security more generally) was seen as being able to 'elevate society by institutionalising a deeper sense of community and mutual care'. Older people were central to this idea of welfare as embodying a sense of 'moral progress'. Growing old was associated from the 1950s onwards with new ideas about 'social rights' and 'social citizenship' (Phillipson 1998). The idea of sharing the risks attached to growing old was further associated with the theme of intergenerational solidarity. Society was more accepting of the idea of ensuring proper standards of health and well-being across the life course (a theme reflected in the 1948 United Nations *Universal Declaration of Human Rights*).

If welfare and social security provision created – or set out to create – a new identity for old age, it is precisely the transformation of these institutions that has posed a major challenge to the position of older people. Old age has been progressively displaced from the framework created by retirement and the welfare state, and the idea of the 'generational contract'. Instead have come multiple work endings, the creation of welfare as an individual risk rather than a collective right, and the ideology of intergenerational conflict (World Bank 1994; Central Intelligence Agency 2001). Such changes are reinforced by a questioning of the competence of the state in meeting the needs of citizens for a variety of health and social care, and income maintenance programmes. The role of the state has itself been transformed to that of promoting and funding market solutions and placing greater responsibility upon the individual (Estes and Associates 2001). The *globalization* of capital has further extended and heightened the stakes in these hotly contested arenas. To examine some of the causes of this, we shall first consider the nature of globalization as a political and economic process.

Global transformations

The developments discussed thus far can be viewed as part of a new political economy shaping the lives of present and future generations of older people. The change has been variously analysed as a move from 'organized' to 'disorganized capitalism', to a shift from 'simple' to 'reflexive modernity', and to the transformation from 'fordist' to 'post-fordist' economies (Lash and Urry 1987). Essentially, this concerns the change from the mass institutions which defined growing old in the period from 1945 through to the late 1970s, to the more individualized structures – privatized pensions, privatized health and social care – which increasingly inform and reflect the transformation of policies in the period from the 1980s onwards.

This new period of ageing is further defined by its location within a global-ized world where transnational actors and communities are major players in a reconfigured political economy. In their book *Global Transformations*, David Held and his colleagues (1999: 49) set the scene as follows:

> Today, virtually all nation-states have gradually become enmeshed in and functionally part of a larger pattern of global transformations and global flows . . . Transnational networks and relations have developed across virtually all areas of human activity. Goods, capital, people, knowledge, communications and weapons, as well as crime, pollu-tants, fashions and beliefs, rapidly move across territorial boundaries . . . Far from this being a world of 'discrete civilisations' or simply an international order of states, it has become a fundamentally inter-connected global order, marked by intense patterns of exchange as well as by clear patterns of power, hierarchy and unevenness.

This transformed political economy is underscored by the emergence of a more aggressive form of capitalism, one contrasted with the more controlled and regulated capitalism of the 1950s and 1960s. Hutton and Giddens (2000: 9–10) describe the essential features of what has been termed 'turbo-capitalism' as follows:

> Its overriding objective is to serve the interests of property owners and shareholders, and it has a firm belief, effectively an ideological one, that all obstacles to its capacity to do that – regulation, controls, trade unions, taxation, public ownership, etc – are unjustified and should be removed. Its ideology is that shareholder value must be maxi-mised, that labour markets should be 'flexible' and that capital should be free to invest and disinvest in countries at will . . . It's a very febrile capitalism, but for all that and its short-termism it has been a very effective transmission agent for the new technologies and for creating the new global industries and markets. It's a tool both of job gener-ation and of great inequality.

Social policy has been affected by globalization in a variety of ways. Yeates (2001: 2), for example, argues that the relationship between social policy and globalization is best conceived as a 'dialectical' or 'reciprocal' and that: '. . . far from states, welfare states and populations passively "receiving" [and] adapt-ing to globalization . . . they are active participants in its development'. In understanding the relationship between social policy and ageing in this era of globalization, the role of *postindustrial capital* is pivotal. Indeed, a key issue involves the relation of old age policy to the economics and politics of markets and the power of corporate capital around the world. In this respect, globaliza-tion functions both as an ideology and a process. At the ideological level, globalization has been particularly important in promoting the idea of the inevitability of competitive global forces and the purportedly inexorable 'choices' that corporations are 'forced' to make (Stiglitz 2002). De Martino (2000: 2) argues that the dominant ideology is one of global neoliberalism where the: '. . . activities of disconnected economic actors [investors, firms, consumers] . . . are rapidly displacing explicit government direction in determining the flow of goods, services, and finance within and across national borders'.

As such, the *ideology* of globalization serves to obfuscate and render as apolitical (and rational) what actually is the intensely political content of (and conflict in) corporate policy, backed by an increasingly deregulated state (Estes and Associates 2001). As a *process*, globalization raises profound questions concerning:

- first, the role of the nation state and the politics therein, including whether the nation state is 'finished' or whether the state is more essential than ever to regulate relations and maintain conditions of capital accumulation in the context of global competition (Du Boff and Herman 1997);
- second, the concept of citizens and the rights of citizenship and the consequences for both (e.g. social rights of citizenship for elders or any other social group), within the orbit of nation states and in the global community at large (Held and McGrew 2002);
- third, whether globalization is, in itself, 'an' issue or 'the' issue and, alternatively, whether the power of capital is 'the' issue (Tabb 1999);
- fourth, the (decreasing) possibilities of any truly non- or anti-capitalist options, or even the possibilities of significant change in the present world order.

Globalization simultaneously brings home – and exports – the processes of privatization, competition, rationalization and deregulation as well as the transformation of all sectors of society through technology and the flexibilization and deregulation of work (Castells 1989). As a process, debate centres on the 'uses' of globalization as the rationale and means by which corporate capital may transnationally pursue new low wage strategies and weaken the power of labour, women and minority populations. As Klein (2000) and others demonstrate, globalization greatly extends the corporate capacity of capital to 'exit' a nation (and thereby to escape corporate responsibility and/or taxation) in periods of economic crisis and conflicts with labour. As successive crises in Latin America and East Asia have demonstrated, this is likely to have major destablizing effects on older people in key areas such as pensions, social security and health care (Stiglitz 2002).

Anthony Giddens (1999) describes two views on globalization: first, that of 'sceptics', which sees globalization as a myth, and not altogether different from earlier transformational changes in society; and second, that of 'radicals', which understands globalization as real, and with consequences that are indifferent to national borders. Giddens takes the view of the 'radicals', noting that globalization is revolutionary on multiple economic, political, cultural and social levels. He argues that globalization is characterized by a complex set of forces, embodied by contradictory, oppositional processes that pull away power and influence from the local and nation state level while also creating new pressures for local autonomy and cultural identity.

Such tensions are highlighted in Appadurai's (1996) exploration of the 'disjunctures' between economy, culture and politics. These disjunctures occur around five dimensions of global cultural flows: ethnoscapes (the shifting landscape of people moving around the globe); technoscapes (the global configuration of technology); financescapes (the movement of global capital); mediascapes (media images of the world); and ideoscapes (ideologies and counter-ideologies relating to state power). The suffix – scape – is used to refer to the

> . . . fluid, irregular shapes of these landscapes, shapes that characterize international capital as deeply as they do international clothing styles. These terms . . . also indicate that these are not objectively given relations that look the same from every angle of vision but, rather, that they are deeply perspectival constructs, inflected by the historical, linguistic, and political situatedness of different sorts of actors: nation-states, multi-nationals, diasporic communities, as well as sub national groupings and movements . . . and even intimate face-to-face groups . . . The individual actor is the last locus of this perspectival set of landscapes [that are] navigated by agents who both experience and constitute larger formations . . .
>
> (Appadurai 1996: 33)

These landscapes are the building blocks for what Appadurai describes (following Benedict Anderson) as 'imagined worlds':

> . . . that is, the multiple worlds that are constituted by the historically situated imaginations of persons and groups spread around the globe. An important fact of the world we live in today is that many persons on the globe live in such imagined worlds (and not just in imagined communities) and thus are able to contest and sometimes even subvert the imagined worlds of the official mind and of the entrepreneurial mentality that surround them.
>
> (Appadurai 1996: 33)

Globalization and the state

An important element in Appadurai's 'global cultural economy' concerns what William Tabb (1999) depicts as the perils of monetary globalization, defined as 'cross-border movements' of loans, equities, direct and indirect investments and currencies. He describes a key process of globalization as the 'imperialism of finance' in which uncontrolled and rapid movements of capital may quickly destabilize national economies. Following this, Susan Strange (1986) has characterized the international financial sector as a 'casino' in which assets are traded increasingly by non-bank, private financial institutions, entirely for speculative profit.

Severe difficulties are inherent in the capacities of individual nation states to 'fix' or 'correct' problems that may result from the pressures of financial markets with few controls and little social regulation. When things go wrong, costly bail-outs by the state can be expected for financial speculators. Tabb (1999: 6) observes that the 'logic of [this] financial hegemony' is to 'decrease government expenditures and state intervention through privatization and contracting out and do away with capital contributions'. This situation produces a 'tension between international economic integration and possibilities for progressive politics', the social costs of which may be 'severe and potentially catastrophic' (Tabb 1999: 3).

At the level of the state, it is clear that globalization may have a variety of influences on economic and social policies. Kagarlitsky (1999) notes, on the one hand, a weakening role for nation states within the context of the growing importance of global markets and international governmental organizations (IGOs). Yet, on the other hand: '. . . it is equally indisputable that despite this weakening, the state remains a critically important factor of political and economic development. It is no accident that transnational corporations constantly make use of the nation state as an instrument of their policies' (Kagarlitsky 1999: 294). And Yeates makes the point that the growth of global financial capital does not in itself deny states the power to regulate it or any other fraction of capital. She concludes from this that

> Far from capitulating to globalization, states are pursuing a variety of strategies to steer globalization and advance their national interests. These strategies range from the now unfashionable dirigiste control of national economies, exemplified in the developmental states of East Asia, to active participation in the development of regional and international blocs to establish a common set of rules governing exchange, accumulation, distribution and development.
>
> (Yeates 2001: 166)

On the other hand, it is equally clear that states vary greatly in the extent to which they may control and influence the process of globalization. Moreover, it is undoubtedly the case that global institutions are increasingly influential in setting agendas around key social policy issues (especially when acting in partnership with dominant players such as the USA). Joseph Stiglitz (2002: 21–2), former Chief Economist at the World Bank, observes that

> . . . we have a system of *global governance without global government* [author's emphasis], one in which a few institutions – the World Bank, the IMF, the WTO – and a few players – the finance, commerce, and trade ministries, closely linked to certain financial and commercial interests – dominate the scene, but in which many of those affected by their decisions are left almost voiceless.

(See also Steans 2002.) Some illustrations of this, in relation to policies for older people, will now be considered.

International governmental organizations and older people

Thus far, discussion of the impact of globalization has been restricted to questions concerning the extent to which there is a 'race to the bottom' among nation states to see how much and how fast social expenditures may be reduced in order to transfer more national wealth to the corporate sector (Alber and Standing 2001). This is certainly an issue of immense importance in respect of the quality of life of older people. Bob Deacon (2000), for example, argues that certain global conditions are undermining the prospects for equitable social provision. He cites four key tendencies:

- the World Bank's belief that governments should provide only minimum levels of social protection;
- the concern of the OECD's Development Assistance Committee (DAC) to focus funding on only basic education and health care;
- the self-interest of international non-governmental organizations (NGOs) in substituting for government provision of services;
- moves being made within the World Trade Organisation (WTO) to open the global market in private health care, education and social insurance.

Yet, as Deacon himself observes, to focus solely on the economic drivers of globalization would be a mistake. Moreover, the empirical evidence to date raises questions about whether globalization inexorably leads to minimal levels of social protection (Navarro 2000; Alber and Standing 2001). Instead, we should look to a broad and highly stratified range of effects on the lives of older people. In the developed world, the magnitude and absolute size of expenditure on the elderly invariably mean that their programmes are among the first to be targeted with financial cuts (just as they were among the first beneficiaries of the welfare state). In less developed countries, elderly people (women especially) have been among those most affected by the privatization of health care, and the burden of debt repayments to agencies such as the World Bank and the IMF. Additionally, globalization, as a process that stimulates population movement and migration, may also produce changes that disrupt the lives of older people (Phillipson 2001).

But older people have also been affected by the way in which IGOs have fed into what Estes (1991a) has identified as the 'crisis construction and crisis management' of state policies for the elderly. Bob Deacon (2000) argues that globalization generates a global discourse within and among global actors on the future of national and supra-national policy. He illustrates this theme with the observation that 'The future of social policy at the national and supra-national levels is being shaped by a struggle between supranational organisations for the *right to participate* in shaping policy, and within and between supranational organisations for the *content* of social policy' (Deacon 2000: 2). The most obvious example here has been in the field of pension policy where Yeates (2001: 122) observes that 'Both the World Bank and IMF have been at the forefront of attempts to foster a political climate conducive to the residualization of state welfare and the promotion of private and voluntary initiatives.'

The report of the World Bank (1994), *Averting the Old Age Crisis*, has been highly influential in promoting the virtues of multi-pillar pension systems, and in particular the case for a second pillar built around private, non-redistributive, defined contribution pension plans. In a further elaboration Holtzman (1997), in a *World Bank Perspective on Pension Reform*, has argued the case for reducing state pay-as-you-go (PAYG) schemes to a minimal role of basic pension provision. This position has influenced both national governments and key transnational players such as the International Labour Organization (ILO), with the latter now having made concessions to the World Bank's position with their advocacy of a mean-tested first pension, the promotion of an extended role for individualized and capitalized private pensions, and the call for OECD countries to raise the age of retirement.

In Deacon's terms this debate amounts to a significant global discourse about pension provision and retirement ages, but one which has largely excluded perspectives which might suggest an enlarged role for the state, and which might question the stability and cost-effectiveness of private schemes. Significantly, as well, this discourse has excluded the groups most affected (e.g. older people, women and those on low incomes). The ILO has itself made the point that 'Investing in financial markets is an uncertain and volatile business:

under present pension plans people may save up to 30 per cent more than they need – which would reduce their spending during their working life; or they may save 30 per cent too little – which would severely cut their spending in retirement' (ILO 2000). But this observation hardly squares with the advocacy of market-based schemes, which are often saddled with crippling administration charges, and reliance on optimistic assessments of long-term and risk-laden performance of stock markets (Blackburn 2002).

While the impact of IGOs on the pension debate is reasonably well known, their influence upon questions relating to the delivery of health and social services is much less understood. Increasingly, however, the social infrastructure of welfare states is being targeted as a major area of opportunity for global investors. Consistent with the ideology of neo-liberalism, the World Bank has propounded the belief that the public sector is less efficient in managing new infrastructure activities and that the time 'has come for private actors to provide what were once assumed to be public services' (Whitfield 2001). This view has been strongly endorsed by a variety of multinational companies, especially in their work with the WTO.

This is, however, an area of some controversy since, as indicated at the beginning of this chapter, such services have, from a historical perspective, been linked in many developed countries with issues of citizenship and associated rights to health and social care, as well as minimum levels of social protection. With the exception of the USA, virtually all industrialized countries have established universal systems of health care based upon general taxation or social insurance principles. The public sector also tends to be dominant in the provision of health services, but with some (tightly regulated) for-profit providers. Such arrangements have, however, come under intense scrutiny from the World Trade Organisation (with enthusiastic support from the USA).

The WTO enforces more than twenty separate international agreements, using international trade tribunals that adjudicate disputes. Such agreements include the General Agreement on Trade in Services (GATS), the first multilateral legally enforceable agreement covering banking, insurance, financial services and related areas. Barlow and Clarke (2001: 84) note that the current round of GATS negotiations has put 'every single social service on the table and is only the first of many rounds whose ultimate goal is the full commercialization of all services'.

Indeed, the WTO has itself called upon member governments to 'reconsider the breadth and depth of their commitments on health and social services' (Yeates 2001: 74). According to Pollock and Price (2000: 38), 'The WTO intends a tighter regulatory framework that will make it more difficult for member states to keep rules that protect public services from foreign investors and markets. The ultimate aim is to increase pressure on member states to open their public-sector services to foreign investment and deregulation.'

Price *et al.* (1999) observe that the WTO have three main objectives: first, to extend coverage of GATS; second, to toughen procedures for dispute settlements so that members can more easily be brought into line; third, to change government procurement rules to create market access. They highlight the call from the US-based Coalition of Service Industries (CSI) for foreign ownership to be allowed for all health facilities:

> We believe we can make much progress in the negotiations [at the WTO meeting in Seattle] to allow the opportunity for USA businesses to expand into foreign health care markets . . . historically health care services in many countries have largely been the responsibility of the public sector. The public ownership of health care has made it difficult for USA private-sector health care providers to market in foreign countries.
>
> (Cited in Price *et al.* 1999: 1990)

Older people are a major target for private investors, not only in the pension field, but also in the area of health and social services. Elder care has already been identified by the CSI as a service area to be included in a comprehensive GATS agreement. Some European governments (notably successive Conservative and Labour administrations in Britain) have begun to take the lead in encouraging private sector involvement in the development of the welfare infrastructure. Since 1997 the Labour government in Britain has encouraged privatization of a wide range of health and social care services. An important mechanism for achieving this has come through the Private Finance Initiative (PFI). PFI is a particular method of encouraging private investment in the designing, building, financing and operating of public facilities. As one illustration of this, Whitfield (2001: 36) notes that Labour has extended PFI to the 'social infrastructure of the welfare state' (hospitals, social services etc.), and that the capital value of public sector PFI projects has increased from £7 billion [US$10.25 billion] (in 1997) to £25 billion [US$36.5 billion] (in 2000) (including 67 major hospital projects). Areas such as residential home care for older people, home care support and nursing homes are now dominated by different kinds of private (for-profit) providers. In global terms the significance of these developments is to extend private provision ahead of a new GATS agreement. According to Whitfield (2001: 33),

> Outsourcing, strategic partnerships and private finance projects have a significant role in the corporate welfare complex. The private delivery of public services is growing apace, fuelled by Labour's third way policies and underpinned by the modernisation and making-markets ideology. Britain is the leading European . . . country in marketing private services *in advance* (original emphasis) of the [WTO's GATS]

negotiations. The markets, and hence the stakes, are enormous. For example, the annual education market in Britain and the USA is estimated to be worth $706 billion or $2000 billion globally. The global health market is even larger at $3000 billion.

The USA represents the most significant case of privatization as an element in the globalization agenda, and offers a glimpse of what may come to pass for the broader community of nations (Estes 1991b). Pressures for more and more privatization mount on the US state, as exemplified by the growth of the highly profitable $1.2 trillion largely private medical industrial complex, which more than tripled in size during Ronald Reagan's two presidential terms during the 1980s alone. Indeed, the medical industrial complex, and the ageing enterprise within it, comprise nearly 15 per cent of the US economy – even though an alarming 16 per cent (44 million) of US citizens are uninsured for health care. The federal government finances around 40 per cent of US health care, while the state limits its own activities to supporting and complementing the market (Estes *et al.* 2001a).

State policy in the USA expands opportunities for private capital through civil law and regulation by protecting the market, encouraging proprietary health entities, and subsidizing various parts of the medical industrial complex (including more than $30 billion in tax subsidies to employers for the purchase of private health insurance) (Estes and Associates 2001). Current policy debate rages around the privatization of the two bedrock state programmes of the US state for the elderly – Social Security and Medicare. Multinational health enterprises are an increasingly important component of the US medical industrial complex. As early as 1990, 97 US companies reported ownership of 100 hospitals with 11,974 beds in foreign countries. Pharmaceutical firms are also major global corporate players, with the total value of exported and imported pharmaceuticals estimated in excess of $110 billion in 1998 (Tarabusi and Vickery 1998). Crucially, as Estes and Associates (2001: 183) observe,

> After three decades devoted to market rhetoric, cost containment, and stunning organizational rationalization (e.g. for-profit managed care), the net result is the complete failure of any of these efforts to stem the swelling tide of problems of access and cost . . . Moreover, there are alarming increases in the uninsured population among African Americans, Latinos, and the middle class.

In 2001, health care costs in the USA were rapidly rising once again, producing growing strains on government, business and individuals, who face 10–20 per cent rises in the cost of private health insurance (if they are able to obtain coverage at all). Cost-shifting to consumers limits access to needed services, particularly for those with limited incomes. Meanwhile, long-term care in the USA remains virtually a private family (women's) responsibility, with public provision (primarily to pay for much-dreaded nursing home care) through Medicaid only for those who are poor, blind or disabled.

It bears emphasis that – despite being in the vanguard of privatization and despite allocating proportionately more national resources to health care than any other developed nation – the health care system of the USA ranks near the bottom of all industrialized nations in terms of the health status of its citizens; for example, the USA is sixteenth in female life expectancy, seventeenth in male life expectancy and twenty-first in infant mortality (Andrews 1995).

Pollock (2001: 10) concludes that no country in the world has delivered universal public services on the backs of for-profit providers:

> The costs are too high, the risks too great, and markets cannot be orientated towards social equity goals. Europe sought to protect public services from the market for these reasons. Before they rush to engage in [PFIs] and dismantle their public services, removing rights their populations have enjoyed for 50 years, the rest of Europe might pause to reflect the UK's growing inequalities and the widening gap between rich and poor in health and wealth.

Ageing in developing countries

But while the new global discourse is reshaping welfare states in the developed world, its impact on developing countries has proved to be even more dramatic (Polivka 2001). Already the majority of the world's population of older people (61 per cent or 355 million) live in poorer countries. This proportion will increase to nearly 70 per cent by 2025. For many countries, however, population ageing has been accompanied by reductions in per capita income and declining living standards. Epstein (2001) notes that between 1950 and the late 1970s, life expectancy increased by least 10 per cent in every developing country in the world, or on average by about 15 years. However, at the beginning of the twenty-first century, life expectancy remains below 50 in more than ten developing countries, and since 1970 has fallen or barely risen in a number of African countries (WHO 2000). The AIDS epidemic is certainly a major factor, but development loans requiring the privatization of health care have also had a devastating impact. Epstein (2001) reports, for example, that by the mid-1990s the African continent was transferring four times more in debt repayment than it spent on health or education. More generally, HelpAge International (2000: 5) argue that

> . . . older people's poverty is still not a core concern in the social, economic and ethical debates of our time. Their right to development

is routinely denied, with ageing seen as a minority interest or case for special pleading. Poverty and social exclusion remain the main stumbling blocks to the realisation of the human rights of older people worldwide.

Elderly people are also affected in different ways by inequalities in the global distribution of income. Income inequalities within and between countries and regions may create a number of pressures upon older people, increasing the risk of poverty but also disrupting social networks as younger people abandon rural areas for cities, or attempt long distance migrations to wealthier regions or countries. Wade (2001) summarizes data indicating that incomes became markedly more unequal in the period from the late 1980s to the early 1990s. He reports one study which found the share of world income going to the poorest 10 per cent of the world's population falling by over a quarter, whereas the share of the richest 10 per cent rose by 8 per cent. Wade comments here that

> It is remarkable how unconcerned the World Bank, the IMF and global organisations are about these trends. The Bank's *World Development Report* for 2000 even said that rising income inequality 'should not be seen as negative' . . . Such lack of attention shows that to call these world organisations is misleading. They may be world bodies in the sense that almost all states are members, but they think in state-centric rather than global ways.
>
> (Wade 2001: 97)

This argument raises important issues about the limitations of global institutions in their attempts to respond to population ageing. Two points might be made here: first, about the nature of what Amartya Sen (2000) refers to as the 'global architecture' represented by economic institutions such as the IMF, World Bank and OECD; second, the democratic deficit of globalization and possible responses to this. On the first point, we need to question whether arrangements derived from the Bretton's Wood Conference, following the Second World War, really provide an adequate response to the social changes (notably in relation to demography) which have unfolded in the intervening period. Sen (2000: 9) makes the point that

> The world was in fact very different in the forties, when the bulk of Asia and Africa was still under colonial rule of one kind or another, when the tolerance of insecurity and of poverty was much greater . . . and when there was little understanding of the huge global prospects of democracy, economic development and human rights in the world.

And we might also add when concerns about the social and economic impact of population ageing had yet to appear on a world stage.

Institutions apart, it is also clear that the neo-liberal consensus operating within globalization has undermined effective responses to many of the social and economic problems facing older people (Scholte 2000). Indeed, neo-liberalism, as practised by dominant organizations such as the IMF and WB, have often intensified the difficulties facing elderly people: for example, with pressures to privatize core public services and reduce pensions as key elements in packages of economic restructuring (Estes and Phillipson 2002; Stiglitz 2002).

Gender, transnational communities and globalization

The pressures associated with globalization have had a particular impact on women in developed and less developed countries. Jill Steans (2002) makes the point that questions about whether globalization is 'good' or 'bad' for women are not always easily answered. She suggests:

> First, there is no one single category or group called 'women' who have identical interests, although there are, it seems, unifying problems and experiences among very different groups of women in different local and national locations. Second, women are not ever the 'victims' of global capitalism. Critical feminism emphasizes that women are agents who to some extent shape globalization. As Jacqui True has noted, there has been little analysis of gender as a site of globalization, that *shapes* and is *shaped* by global market forces.
>
> (Steans 2002: 94; original emphasis)

Women in fact experience globalization in profoundly contradictory ways. On the one hand, neo-liberal rhetoric stresses globalization as offering new opportunities in areas such as employment and family life. On the other hand, it actively promotes (and intensifies) the dual role of women as agents of productive and reproductive labour. Again, to quote Steans (2002: 94–5):

> While the ideology of neoliberalism espouses certain egalitarian values, the changes associated with globalization and restructuring have sometimes worked to 'privatize' women's labour and, consequently, resulted in a loss of power and autonomy. The neoliberal emphasis on consumer choice, the rational distribution of resources and the efficacy of the market pays no regard to the socially embedded nature of 'economic' activity. Neoliberalism ignores the significance of unremunerated labour, usually performed by women, to the

local, national and global economy. By concentrating on markets and the appropriate role and function of the state, it is possible to over-look how women's activities, though profoundly important to the social welfare of families and communities, have been demoted to the 'private' sphere . . .

Given that ageing has a crucial impact upon women in particular (Ginn *et al.* 2001), and that each nation's sex and gender system is an important determinant of state provision, it should be noted that the globalization of ageing and the efforts of transnational organizations to reduce or privatize state activities will be especially detrimental to older women. Moreover, with women performing long-term care work 'free', but at great financial, physical and psychological hardship, the continuing and deepening themes and patterns of privatization globally are likely to jeopardize women's lives further as population ageing is extended and more and more older people require assistance.

Robert Connell (1987) speaks to gender through globalization, observing that, in the west, the gender order focuses upon a single structural fact: 'the global dominance of men over women'. Mittelman and Tambe (2000: 88) demonstrate how globalization, marginalization and gender form an inter-connected matrix that 'shape[s] patterns of poverty [and] other distributional outcomes' that is particularly disadvantageous to women. They go on to argue:

> Central to the chain of relationships are the varied ways in which economic globalization marginalizes large numbers of people by reducing public spending on social services and delinks economic reform from social policy. This type of marginalization manifests a gendered dimension inasmuch as women constitute those principally affected by it.
>
> (Mittelman and Tambe 2000: 75)

This last aspect is illustrated by the emergence of what may be described as 'global families' – these arising from the communities that emerge from inter-national migration. Arlie Hochschild (2000) makes the point that most writing about globalization focuses on money, markets and labour flows, with scant attention to women, children and the care of one for the other. But older people may be added to this list, representing a significant part of the global flow: they grow old as migrants, and may go backwards and forwards from one home to another (Levitt 2001; Gardner 2002). In consequence, globalization is producing a new kind of ageing in which the dynamics of family and social life may be stretched across different continents and across different types of societies.

This development is also producing great diversity in respect of the social networks within which growing old is shaped and managed. Typically, older people's networks have been examined within national borders, and their experiences of care and support assessed within this context (Phillipson 1998). But migrants bring important variations with responsibilities that may cover considerable physical as well as cultural distances. This is likely to be a particular issue for women and men migrating in search of work or for women who leave home for a new country.

Such developments may create forms of 'structured dependency' which play differently in a global as opposed to a national context. Structured dependency theory in critical gerontology has been criticized from a number of perspectives: for playing down human agency on the one hand, and for an undue emphasis on social inequality on the other (arguments developed most recently in a British context by Gilleard and Higgs 2000). Yet in a global context structured dependency arguments are of considerable value in addressing the widening inequalities between nation states (as demonstrated by Robert Wade (2001) among others) and the crisis this generates in the communities supporting older people.

The structured dependency argument is especially significant when related to gender and the problems facing women within what have been termed 'transnational communities'. Thomas Faist (2000) argues that transnational communities may be said to arise from a context in which those '. . . who leave a country and those who stay may remain connected through social and symbolic ties, these maintained over time and across space in complex patterns of exchange and support'. From an anthropological perspective, Pnina Werbner (2002: 6) defines transnationals as '. . . persons who sustain their home culture away from home. They build around them surrogate cultural worlds which serve to shield them from the local culture into which migration or forced exile has inserted them.'

For societies in the twenty-first century, communities of families and relations sustained across wide geographical distances are likely to play an increasingly influential role in daily life. The demographer Douglas Massey (2000) argues that, barring some calamity or a radical shift in family planning trends, '. . . migration will play a greater role than reproduction in determining the strength and tenor of our societies' (an observation especially applicable to Europe). For many western societies immigration has become the main driver of population growth, with legal immigration accounting for in excess of two million people annually in the USA and Europe combined (with illegal immigration accounting for another million) (*The Economist*, 2 November 2002).

The growth of transnational communities has had a major impact on the women who stay behind in the villages and cities of less developed countries, and those uprooted through the process of migration. Papastergiadis (2000) suggests that the feminization of migration is a growing trend still overlooked in many studies. He suggests that stereotypical images of the 'male urban peasant' may have little resonance in the context of globalization with its 'turbulent and more dispersed streams of movement'. He concludes that

> The specific position of women and the dynamics of spatial trajector-
> ies have been overlooked in the majority of studies on migration.
> Women were not seen as active agents in the great migration stories;
> they were either left behind, or taken along as part of the man's
> family.
>
> (Papastergiadis 2000: 131)

Arlie Hochschild (2000) has identified the development of 'global care chains', which she defines as '. . . a series of personal links between people across the globe based on the paid or unpaid work of caring'. Gulati's (1994) study *In the Absence of their Men: The Impact of Male Migration on Women* is one of the few investigations to examine the lives of those who remain at home (see also Miltiades 2002). Gulati studied male migration from the Indian state of Kerala to West Asia, noting the challenges facing women coping with managing alone with a new family, but with a long period of separation from a husband to whom they may have been married for just a few weeks. Conversely, the arrival of women through family migration has been an important aspect of migration trends in Europe over the past two decades, one which has posed significant issues both for the women and the communities in which they settle (Phillipson *et al.* 2003).

The increased importance of migration and mobility is raising more general issues for gerontological work in a global context. Three points might be highlighted in the context of the discussion in this chapter. First, the processes associated with globalization and migration raise the possibility of additional forms of ageism affecting older people in the twenty-first century. Elderly male and female migrants in particular may become the inhabitants of what Zygmunt Bauman (1998) refers to as 'the second world'. Bauman (1998: 89) argues that

> [for the] inhabitants of the first world – the increasingly cosmo
> politan, extraterritorial world of global businessmen, global culture
> managers or global academics, state borders are levelled down, as they
> are dismantled for the world's commodities, capital and finances. For
> the inhabitants of the second world [on the other hand], the walls of
> immigration controls, of residence laws and of 'zero tolerance pol
> icies', grow taller; the moats separating them from the sites of their
> desire and of dreamed-of redemption grow deeper, while all bridges,
> at the first attempt to cross them, prove to be drawbridges.

Second, a world of greater mobility should in the long term bring benefits of cultural diversity. But in the short term the increase in racism and associated forms of oppression are undeniable and may produce conflicts among older people. Certainly, from research looking at the lives of elderly people in deprived urban areas and from cross-national studies, recognizing the import-ance of forming age-based coalitions which cross ethnic lines will be an important task in the short and medium term (Phillipson *et al.* 2001; Jackson and Antonucci 2002).

Third, transnational communities raise major issues for social policy, with the development of groups holding together care tasks or financial responsi-bilities that may be stretched across continents. Moreover, the experience of migration – with people in middle and older age settling into new cultures or bearing the strain of moving from one culture to another – raises questions about the adequacy of support in areas such as housing, income and social services. On the one hand, migrant groups bring new forms of social capital to hard-pressed urban areas (indeed, they may be said to revitalize such com-munities in significant respects). On the other hand, they may represent a significant challenge for traditional models of delivering health and social care.

Conclusion

An important theme of this chapter has concerned the tension between the global architecture of intergovernmental forums, IGOs and multinational cor-porations, and the global transition towards demographic ageing. Major chal-lenges and threats are posed for the public provision of services, rights to health and social care, public pension provision, and the meaning of citizen-ship across the life course, and most especially in old age.

It is highly salient that, in the developed nations, older people are more dependent upon the contemporary welfare state for social provision for eco-nomic and health security than are most other population groups (Estes and Associates 2001). And among those older persons who are most dependent upon state provision are women, minorities and those on low incomes. Thus, any changes and challenges to the social contract between generations and other social groups, and particularly those forged within the most developed capitalist economies, will be highly consequential for older people around the globe.

A key issue arising from the globalization of ageing concerns the extent to which older women, older minorities and the poor elderly will be a major (or even minor) voice in the new global economy. This is part of a larger question of globalization – the influence of politics in constructing the present and the future. The process of globalization represents both an historical transition and an opportunity for the development and testing of political power and political strategy involving a balance between consent and coercion. As

Sassoon (2001) suggests, one needs to ask about the opportunities or 'spaces' that open up for the politics of ageing in the complex, contradictory and highly contingent processes that are under way. Thus far, older people have been absent from influential debates such as those initiated by the World Bank (over pay-as-you-go pensions) or the WTO (over the commercialization of care services). The major players in these debates have either been governments (from rich countries) wishing to deregulate state provision, or corporations wanting to expand into lucrative areas of work. But it is also the case that older people (and their organizations) have been marginalized in the various forums that are now raising concerns about globalization, despite what Walker and Maltby (1997) view as an upsurge of political activity among pensioners in a number of countries. A starting point, therefore, must be the linkage of organizations representing older people with the larger organizations and forums that are attempting to formulate a global agenda on social issues. Formulating policies that can have an impact on key transnational bodies is set to be a major task over the next few years. We shall return to this theme in the last chapter of this book, where we set out an agenda for social theory and social change in relation to the future of ageing.

8   The politics of ageing

Key points:

- Possibilities and limitations of old age activism.
- The role of the state and bureaucratic responses to the politics of ageing.
- Social movements and diversity in old age.
- Rights in old age and the notion of citizenship.

Introduction

The previous chapter identified the challenges for ageing populations generated by the social and economic changes associated with globalization. From the perspective of critical gerontology such developments have also been important with respect to debates around the politics of old age, which have been driven by the crisis affecting welfare states and the problems attached to certain aspects of demographic change. For a politics of ageing this raises complex issues about the relationship between interest groups and the state, the extent to which people vote and behave collectively as older persons, and the links between and within birth cohorts. Such themes have been examined in varying degrees of detail by the extensive literature in this area. Typically, research has examined questions concerning voting patterns among older people compared with younger age groups (Pinner *et al.* 1959; Binstock 2000; Vincent *et al.* 2001); the impact of interest groups in shaping policies affecting older people (Pratt 1976; Binstock 1972; Torres-Gil 1993; Street 1999; Vincent 1999); and variations across countries and in different welfare state regimes (Pratt 1993; Walker and Naegele 1999). Much of this work has been brought together in systematic overviews of the literature, notably from Estes (1979a, 1979b, 1986) and Walker (1986) and later by Coombs and Holladay (1995) and Binstock and Quadagno (2001).

This chapter aims to build upon this work by arguing that the politics of ageing is entering a new phase of development in the context of globalization on the one hand and welfare state restructuring on the other (Estes and Phillipson 2002). In this chapter we take a 'politics of old age' to mean, first, activities undertaken by older people themselves in asserting claims to resources of different kinds. Second, we refer to activities by organizations acting as representatives and advocates for older people, and third, the activities and politics of other agents and entities (e.g. Generation X or Y and other) undertaken under the rubric of and/or in reaction to age and ageing. A fourth aspect is the behaviour of the state and agents of corporate capitalism in shaping the social construction and distribution of resources for older people (Estes and Associates 2001; Blackburn 2002), and a further dimension concerns the extent to which there is a collective consciousness about old age and ageing (Estes 1979b) that motivates a politics of ageing. Such consciousness may develop either among the elderly alone or among a broader intergenerational cross-segment of society such as caregivers, or both.

All the above elements are undergoing radical alteration at the present time, driven by changes in the political and economic environment surrounding the lives of older people. To explore these developments the chapter covers four main areas. First, some of the key concepts relevant to the politics of old age are defined and analysed. Second, current debates in the 'politics of old age' literature are summarized. Third, an alternative framework for understanding the development of political organization and influence in old age is presented. Fourth, the chapter examines some future trends in the politics of ageing. In each section of the chapter comparisons and contrasts are drawn where possible between the USA and Britain, with additional links to other western countries where relevant.

The political sociology of ageing: conceptual and theoretical issues

Critical perspectives in the political sociology of ageing emerged in the early 1980s, notably with contributions from Myles (1984), Walker (1986) and Estes (1979a, 1986). This work developed at a point of ideological crisis in respect of care and support for older people. In the context of the Reagan and Thatcher administrations, emphasis was placed upon the commodification and privatization of a range of services along with attacks on the welfare state, public provision and anything non-market (e.g. non-profit providers). These policy developments were themselves underpinned by the construction of population ageing as representing a crisis for economic and social institutions. Increasingly, the political sociology of ageing was built around a number of dominant themes: for example, that old people were consuming a disproportionate amount of resources and denying groups such as children an equitable share (Preston 1984); that an ageing population was itself a factor in the economic crisis affecting global capitalism (Longman 1987), and that the increase in numbers of elderly people was producing a growing chronic illness burden, leading to unrealistic expectations about support into advanced old age (Callahan 1987). Johnson *et al.* (1989: 9), in the introduction to *Workers versus Pensioners: Intergenerational Justice in an Ageing World*, focused on the problem of population ageing and the inevitability of intergenerational conflict:

> It seems inevitable that the interaction of current demographic trends and current welfare policies will impose a large ... and possibly unsustainable fiscal burden on the productive populations in developed nations. Since there can be no immediate change in the population age structure, and a rise in fertility would only raise still further the number of 'dependents' ... it may seem that an obvious way to cope with the rising financial burden of an ageing population is to alter in some fundamental way the welfare contract that operates to transfer resources from the young to the old.

And the authors concluded with the alarming view that

> If no action is taken, the competition for resources between workers and pensioners will break the fiscal basis of modern welfare systems, and quite possibly this will undermine the democratic consensus upon which the western economies are based.
>
> (Johnson *et al.* 1989: 15)

This new political landscape was to raise a number of critical issues about the role of the state, the nature of power and the experience of ageing within the context of late capitalist societies. Estes (1999: 20) argues that the study of the state is central to the understanding of old age since it has the power, first, to allocate and distribute scarce resources to ensure the survival and growth of the economy; second, to mediate between the different segments and classes of society; and third, to ameliorate social conditions that could threaten the existing order. However, as Estes points out, the state also plays a crucial role in the formation and transformation of a wide spread of social relationships. In particular, categories such as 'age' and 'older person' are themselves constituted and contested within the framework of state relations.

This perspective is especially significant for understanding the change in the relationship between the state and its support for groups such as older people. Over the period from the 1950s to the 1970s, most western governments were characterized by a significant degree of agreement about the need to develop and expand services directed at meeting the needs of elderly people. Alan Walker (1986: 33) suggests that

> This broad political consensus on policy toward the elderly was accompanied by the consolidation of a conventional wisdom about politicians' sensitivity to the potential power of the pensioner vote. No government, it was argued, would dare to challenge the position of elderly people as the most deserving of all minority groups.

By the 1980s, however, neo-liberal policies were advancing the cause of a 'minimalist state', one which, as Carroll Estes (1991b: 61) argued, '. . . [was] hostile to anything that might impede the order of the market (and its natural superiority)'. This development created a dual crisis for older people when contrasted with the earlier period. On the one hand, the legitimacy of the state came under attack with respect to its ability to tackle problems affecting groups such as elderly people. Services and pensions provided by the market, to take two examples, were proposed as a more efficient option than direct state support (Estes and Associates 2001). Equally, considerable emphasis was laid upon the role of the family, neighbours and volunteers in supporting older people; part of what neo-liberal social policy in Britain (and elsewhere) referred to as 'care by' rather than 'care in' the community (Phillipson 1996). On the other hand, from the late 1970s onward, the legitimation crisis of the state also resulted in the undermining of what had historically been viewed as the 'deserving status' of older people. Resource allocation to the elderly became 'contested' rather than 'consensual', with complex struggles at national, local and, increasingly, global levels (Estes and Phillipson 2002).

This new environment itself changed the social construction of power relationships running through the lives of older people. Vincent (1999: 14) cites Max Weber's influential definition of power as the 'ability to enforce one's own will on others' behaviour'. Intrinsic to this notion is the idea of relationships – at both macro and micro levels – as characterized by a balance of power with associated mechanisms of domination and subordination. Vincent (1999: 19) argues that a number of questions follow from this approach:

> The questions to ask about old age and politics must be about social process not about categories. Understanding old age and politics requires an understanding of political processes – how differentiation and domination affect the lives of older people. These processes are interconnected – who is dominated depends upon who dominates. These processes cannot be considered in some abstract ahistorical manner but as specifically situated in particular times and places. So the questions we need to ask about the politics of any given situation include: who are the different kinds of people involved? What is the

broader historical and social context? Who dominates and how is this achieved? What is the process whereby some people become dominant and others dominated? What part does age play in this?

Such questions were played out in a variety of ways in the contrasting historical contexts taking the period up to the 1970s as compared with that since the 1980s. In the case of the former, power relationships were forged within the context of different welfare state regimes (liberal, corporatist and social democratic in Esping-Andersen's (2000) typology). These provided a variety of approaches to questions such as universalism versus targeting, market versus state provision, and the pursuit of egalitarianism. While power relationships varied within each regime, the idea of transforming or utilizing the resources of the state to improve the lives of old people and other groups was a common theme. At the same time, with respect to the exercise of power, this was a period when older people were locked into a distinctive pattern of inequality: first, through the way in which the welfare state emphasized forms of 'structured dependency' (Townsend 1981, and see further below); second, through the experience of marginalization created by compulsory retirement; third, through the influence of more generalized patterns of discrimination – subsequently termed 'ageism' – experienced by older people (Butler 1975).

Power relations were further transformed in the drive towards the privatization and marketization of care relations, from the 1980s onwards. At an ideological level this was often presented as an attempt to free people from the perceived limitations of state-run services. This approach was reinforced through the promotion of ideas about 'productive ageing' (see Chapter 5) along with what has been viewed as the individualization of social relations characteristic of late modern societies (Bauman 1998). In some respects this approach may be regarded as consistent with the scapegoating of older people as a selfish welfare generation (Binstock, see further below), with demands for greater individual responsibility over the process of ageing. From a critical perspective, inequalities of power are no less apparent than they were in the earlier phase; the causal mechanisms are, however, clearly very different. These range from widening inequalities in the context of pension and welfare state restructuring and the fracturing of class relationships in a context of deindustrialization and globalization, to the new ambiguities affecting transitions through the middle and later phases of the life course (Dannefer 2002).

Finally in this section, an additional factor affecting the politics of age concerned the advent of globalization, as reviewed in the previous chapter. Globalization is an important influence in reshaping state relations, but with the addition of new actors over which older people (in common with other age groups) have very limited control. Ramesh Mishra (1999: 130) summarizes these trends as follows:

The main problem [appears to be] that those conditions and social forces which made *national* welfare states possible, e.g. the existence of a state with legitimate authority for rule-making and rule-enforcement, electoral competition and representative government, strong industrial action and protest movements threatening the economic and social stability of nations, nationalism and nation-building imperatives, are unavailable at the international level. Moreover, globalisation is disempowering citizens within the nation-state as far as social rights are concerned without providing them with any leverage globally. At the same time transnational corporations and the global marketplace have been empowered hugely through financial deregulation and capital mobility.

These developments have, as we note in Chapter 7, raised major issues for the politics of ageing. Increasingly, older people are required to assert their presence at international and global forums, both through their own groups and through international non-governmental organizations. But this itself raises important issues about the power imbalance between older people's groups and the substantial bureaucracies in charge of bodies such as the World Trade Organisation, the International Monetary Fund and the World Bank (Estes and Phillipson 2002). This is leading to a dramatic extension of the unequal power relations between older people on the one hand, and providers and professionals on the other (Estes 1979a, 1993). The extent to which this is creating a new politics of age is an issue to which we shall return in the final section of this chapter. In the next section, having established some of the theoretical context behind the politics of ageing, we assess how this has played through in the history of pensioner organization over the past 50 years.

Old age activism: optimism or pessimism?

At the beginning of a new century, the research literature on the politics of ageing can be read in at least two ways. First, that (and in line with the preceding discussion on globalization) changes at both macro and micro levels will almost certainly lead to greater political activism on the part of older people. Walker (1999), for example, identifies the way in which the 'crisis construction' of ageing will intensify the involvement of older people in all spheres of politics, with a spread of pensioner action groups in local and municipal politics but with action within national and supra-national groupings as well. Taking examples from the European Union, Alan Walker (1999: 11) argues:

> ... in a short space of time, the EU has seen a mushrooming of pensioners' action groups at local and national levels and, with them, the

emergence of what appears to be a newly radicalized politics of old age. Of course the new social movements among older people involve only relatively few pensioners – activism is a minority pursuit in all generations – but many more are involved than previously and more actively so. Furthermore, the nature of political participation and representation is changing: there are more and more examples of direct action by senior citizens, and the new action groups are grass roots organizations composed of older people who want to represent themselves.

Other research suggests, however, that the political power of older people peaked in the 1980s/early 1990s and that its influence on national politics may be declining (McKenzie 1993; Binstock and Quadagno 2001). Some relevant factors include: first, the diversity of older people in relation to income and access to health and social care; second, the power of social movements built around issues unrelated to age; and third, the limited salience of age as a basis for political identity – especially for the 'baby boom generation' (Torres-Gil 1993; Vincent 1995; Rix 1999). Vincent *et al.* (2001: 155), in their analysis of older people and the political process, suggest that

> It is difficult to find at the close of the twentieth century any evidence of a growth in the political strength of the older age groups. Evidence for an apparent lack of influence of older people . . . is twofold, first, in the character and activities of older people's organisations and, second, in the low priority given by party political elites to older voters.

Summarizing the British data, Vincent *et al.* (2001: 155) conclude that

> . . . there is little evidence of increased responsiveness by governments or political parties to organised groups of older people. It is difficult to find examples of political parties having been particularly enthusiastic or efficient in the identification of issues that are important to older voters, or having been sensitive to presenting issues in a manner that appeals to older voters.

But the evidence about political influence can be read in at least two ways. At one level, older people may indeed be alienated from formal mechanisms within political organizations. Walker (1998: 24), for example, reviewing the European scene, notes the way in which '. . . the political representation systems of some countries effectively exclude older people from key institutions'. And he goes on to argue that '. . . few of the established political parties in Europe provide an organisational context for pensioners or make special efforts to include them in their machinery' (Walker 1998: 24). The same may also be said, though with notable exceptions such as Italy and the UK, about the relationship of trade unions and their retired members. After leaving employment, older workers may find themselves cut from involvement in a significant and influential forum within society. Union membership after retirement may be especially low for certain groups such as women and those from minority ethnic groups.

In other respects, however, older people remain an important force within national politics. At the level of voting in national elections in Europe and the USA, older people invariably record the highest turnout of all age groups. Indeed, in many countries voting among those 75 and over exceeds that for the 18–30 age group. Turner *et al.* (2001), viewing US data, point out that older adults have been voting at higher rates than other groups over the past three decades and that while the voting rate for younger cohorts has been in decline, that of older cohorts has increased slightly. Binstock (2000) provides a note of caution about the implications of this, pointing out that older voters tend not to vote in a monolithic bloc, their votes being cast in roughly the same pattern as the electorate as a whole. Yet Binstock's qualifying argument is also instructive – namely, that interest groups of older people retain an important source of power, '. . . based on their symbolic representation of a larger constituency, and the concomitant possibility that they *might*, someday, be able to "swing" the votes of a sizeable number of older voters' (p. 29). He concludes that

> Although the political legitimacy of [interest] groups [of older people] has been on the wane during the past decade, politicians still do focus on the potential cohesiveness of older voters and attempt to position themselves accordingly when undertaking governmental actions and election campaigns – responses that are politically significant.
>
> (Binstock, 2000: 29)

This is consistent with Estes's (1979b) argument, also advanced by scholars who use reputational methods such as Floyd Hunter (1963), that the reputation for power in itself confers, if not reflects, a degree of power. Such arguments build on W. I. Thomas's (1970) insight that if people believe that something is so (e.g. that the elderly have political power), it becomes so through a form of self-fulfilling prophecy.

In any event, it remains the case that future cohorts (notably those from the two baby boom generations) are likely to contribute to a new politics of ageing, with alliances between generations and coalitions of interest groups being an important feature of political life (an argument developed further below).

An additional set of issues, however, concerns the way in which policies and resources affecting older people have been socially constructed in different ways over the second half of the twentieth century (Estes and Associates 2001).

In the next section, and building on the frameworks outlined by Torres-Gil (1993) and Walker (1991), we identify three phases in the politics of old age, taking the period from the late 1940s to the early years of the twenty-first century. These we describe as: first, the rise of the bureaucratic lobby; second, activism and the new politics of age; third, social movements and social diversity. These phases are analysed in terms of what they tell as about the impact of older people both on the political process and in respect of their wider social identity.

Growing older: the bureaucratic lobby

The period from the 1950s to the mid-1970s was one of considerable significance in redefining the politics of old age. The state itself began to play a more prominent role in respect of legislation and in adopting age as one of several criteria for defining eligibility and for identifying those in need of care and assistance (Torres-Gil 1993). Binstock and Quadagno (2001: 338) highlight what they see as the 'tremendous expansion' in the number of old age organizations in this period, both in relation to membership and their overall profile:

> In contrast to the earlier groups and movements in the United States, these have been stable and enduring organizations, and some of them have substantial bureaucracies . . . In the United States alone there are over 100 national organizations focused on ageing policies and concerns . . . these include mass membership groups representing older people in general or subgroups of the elderly, single issue advocacy groups, and organizations of professional and service providers . . . [a] diverse array of . . . age-based political organizations have also emerged in Australia, Canada, Japan and throughout Europe . . .

In essence, the growth of such groups reflected the substantial expansion in services and programmes for older people (part of what Estes (1979a) was to term as the 'ageing enterprise'). In broad outline the period up to the late 1960s was characterized by, following Binstock (1983), 'compassionate concerns about the status of older people'. In addition to the actions of government, these concerns were reflected in the growth of charitable organizations such as Age Concern and Help the Aged in Britain and the emergence of old age interest groups (notably the American Association of Retired Persons) in the USA.

For the first two decades in the period after the Second World War, however, it was the experience of poverty that exerted the strongest influence over the lives of older people and representative organizations. In 1960, in the USA, one-third of older men and 40 per cent of older women still had incomes below the poverty line (cited in Quadagno 1991: 39; see also Harrington 1963).

Research by Cole and Utting (1962) and Townsend and Wedderburn (1965) reported similar findings on the extent of poverty affecting older people in Britain. Even into the 1970s, the Royal Commission on the Distribution of Income and Wealth (1978) was reporting that one in every three elderly families had incomes on or below the poverty line and that nearly three in every four lived in or on the margins of poverty.

The political response to old age poverty, however, followed different paths in the two countries. In Britain, an expanding welfare state (at least up until the economic recession of the early 1970s) had the effect of delivering welfare provision while limiting political mobilization among older people. Peter Townsend (1981: 22) viewed the organization of welfare as creating a form of 'structured dependency' whereby 'the elderly are usually viewed as the grateful and passive recipients of services administered by an enlightened public authority'. Pratt (1993) highlighted the division in the British case between lobbying organizations such as Age Concern and pensioner organizations devoted to campaigns around the state pension – a distinction that has persisted to the present day. The lobbying groups contributed to what has been described as the 'welfarization' of old age, focusing on a narrow set of concerns relating to service provision and support (Fennell *et al.* 1988). Pensioner groups (such as the National Federation of Retirement Pensions Association) provided a challenge to this approach, but in reality had a somewhat limited impact as a national force (Bornat 1998).

Three factors operated in Britain in the 1950s and 1960s that tended to limit the political influence of interest groups of older people. First, although issues about ageing had a high degree of legitimacy in this period (reflecting what was seen to be the sacrifices of older people through the depression of the 1930s and in wartime), older people often came a poor second behind other economic and social priorities. Despite the emergence of a pensions lobby in the 1950s (led by seminal figures such as Richard Titmuss and Peter Townsend), state policies maintained their role in structuring poverty and deprivation in old age. The 'rediscovery' of poverty in the 1960s tended to give greater emphasis to issues relating to child poverty, educational disadvantage and inner city deprivation (Phillipson 1982). Blaikie and Macnicol (1989: 79) make the point that 'Significantly, no pensioners' lobby was formed equivalent in political influence to the Child Poverty Action Group. In the 1960s, the elderly were not a cause upon which political reputations were made'.

A second factor influencing the nature of pensioner organizations was their relative isolation from the Labour movement. This provided a significant contrast to the prewar period, when bodies such as the Trades Union Congress (TUC) and individual trade unions were heavily involved around campaigns for better pensions (Macnicol 1998). And it contrasts as well with the period from the 1970s, when trade unions became involved once again in providing organizational assistance to more militant groups of pensioners such as the

British Pensioners Trade Union Action Association (BPTUAA) (Phillipson 1982).

Finally, to repeat an earlier point, the politics of ageing also reflected the impact of the welfare state, not just with respect to resources but also in terms of older people's social identity (Phillipson 1998). Elderly people drew heavily upon the moral framework associated with welfare provision in defining their relationship with society more generally. Yet the price was high: an element of security on the one hand, but with the stultifying sense of dependency analysed by Townsend, Walker and others. Moreover, these aspects were reinforced by the retention of earlier forms of welfare provision. In this context, although the 1950s and 1960s may be properly viewed as part of what Torres-Gil (1993) refers to as the 'modern aging period', in the case of Britain the treatment of older people retained many of the characteristics of a 'pre-modern era'. This was reflected in the continued use (notably for residential and hospital care) of institutions built under the Poor Law (Townsend 1962), and also in the payment of state pensions at below subsistence level.

In political terms, the USA offers an interesting contrast with Britain in the period up to the mid-1970s. In the first place, organized labour was to play an important role in improving social security benefits. Quadagno (1991: 39) cites Derthick's observation that

> In building the social security program, organized labor was by far the most important ally of the Social Security Administration. It supported the SSA inside the advisory councils and lobbied and testified for the agency's legislative proposals. It largely conducted and financed the public campaigns for Medicare . . . Perhaps most important of all, labor was an unofficial outlet for proposals that SSA officials were not free to promote themselves because they lacked approval from political superiors.

A substantial amount of the work to develop the legislation for Medicare in the USA also reflected union activity and support. In his classic work on *The Politics of Medicare* (2000: 18), Ted Marmor observes that 'Organized labor was the most powerful single source of pressure . . . Organisations of the aged were the result more than cause of . . . demands [for Medicare]. The National Council of Senior Citizens, formed in 1961 with AFL/CIO financial support, claimed by 1962 a membership of 600,000 (Rose 1967: 422).'

Yet ultimately (and again in contrast with Britain) union influence was to take a back seat compared with the growth in interest groups claiming to represent older people. Throughout the 1970s older people continued to be viewed as a legitimate and deserving target for economic and social support, reflected in the Older Americans Act of 1965 (Estes 1979a), the 20 per cent increase in social security benefits passed in 1972, and in the same year the indexing of benefits to inflation (the Cost of Living Adjustment or COLA). Quadagno (1991: 41) argues that

> The 1972 amendments represented a turning point for social security, a watershed for USA welfare-state development. Between 1967 and 1984, the average income of elderly family units rose by 55 percent, despite a large drop in the average amount of earned income, while poverty rates dropped from over 25 percent to less than 15 percent. Further, social security benefits gained in importance as the total share of elderly income derived from social security [rose] from 28 percent in 1967 to 36 percent in 1984. For the first time in USA history, the middle class was fully incorporated into a national welfare program whose benefits determined the well-being of a large proportion of the nation's elderly.

These developments created services and entitlements which older people were keen to defend. And while unions contributed to the expansion of social security, interest groups representing elderly people became a more prominent force in seeking to protect what had been achieved. This was to form the basis for the growth in the bureaucratic lobby represented by organizations such as the American Association of Retired Persons (AARP) (founded in 1958 but with a substantial growth in membership in the 1970s and 1980s), and smaller groups such as the National Council of Senior Citizens (NCSC) (founded by the American Federation of Labor/Committee for Industrial Organization (AFL/CIO) in 1962 and later renamed Alliance for Senior Citizens). Finally, this activity was itself framed within an ideology of retirement which (for middle-class retirees at least) had begun to offer an alternative to the idea of ageing as a form of dependency and disengagement. Retirement, for a minority of older people in this period, was seen to embody both 'a way of life and a way of thinking about the experience of being old' (Graebner 1980: 241). Politically, this was to give greater emphasis to the importance of protecting social security in its role both of alleviating poverty and in supporting (for some) leisure-based lifestyles.

Activism and the new politics of old age

In the context of a developing welfare state, the politics of ageing up until the early 1970s were built around a consensus regarding the need to expand resources directed at elderly people. As Walker (1999: 9) puts it:

> ... pressure groups representing older people were bargaining for public policy advances within a context of shared understanding about the possibilities of politics, the assumption of both progressive

welfare development and the deservingness of the case they espoused.

These elements were to be called into question over the next two decades with an economic crisis driving an ideological debate concerning equity between generations. By the middle of the 1980s, older people had moved from being a 'deserving' to a 'selfish welfare generation' (Thomson 1989) or 'greedy geezers' in the more direct language of North Americans (*New Republic*, 28 March 1988).

The theme of crisis, first identified by Estes in 1979 (1979a), now became a central motif in shaping public policy towards older people (Estes 1991b). With the rise of neo-liberal governments in the USA and Britain, economic crisis was used to justify the imposition of cost-containment policies that transferred responsibility from the state to individuals. Commenting on the Reagan legacy and the situation facing elderly people in the 1980s, Estes (1991b: 77) argued that

> Aging people in the United States and the policies designed to deal with them are in a war zone. This is so because the real and constructed crises of both capital and the state have been transported into the field of health and social policy. At the ideological level, the elderly are accused of ... ripping off the country's youngsters. The material consequences of this assault are reflected in a complex struggle between forces seeking drastic cutbacks in state financing for the aged, a major retrenchment of the welfare state, with publicly-financed resources redirected ... through the restitution of market forces ... One result, and one source of contradiction, is the simultaneous commodification of health care for the elderly (increased privatization) where profits are to be made and decommodification (increased family care/responsibility) where costs are high and women's work is involved.

This background generated what Walker (1998: 17) came to define as a 'new politics of old age'. At a macro level this was reflected in concerns (highlighted from the mid-1980s onwards) about the costs of population ageing, expressed both at the level of the nation state and subsequently by global actors such as the World Bank, OECD and IMF (Estes and Phillipson 2002). At the micro level of pensioner organization and lobbying the responses were, however, complex and with some variation across western countries. Walker's (1999: 18) analysis of political action by older people in the European Union points to a 'rapid increase in direct political involvement on the part of older people', listing the rise of groups such as the German Grey Panthers, the Danish C Team and the British National Pensioners' Convention. In the USA existing lobby groups such as AARP and NCSC were joined by groups such as the

National Committee to Preserve Social Security and Medicare, the Gray Panthers and the Older Women's League.

A key role for these groups has been seeking to protect existing legislation and developing new policy initiatives. Street (1999: 113) makes the point that age-based interest groups can exercise political power in at least three ways: first, by vetoing policy decisions they dislike; second, by framing the parameters of age-based policy debates; third, by setting the policy-making agenda. Judged on these terms, the record of old age organizations has been a mixture of successes and setbacks. In the American case, the proliferation of interest groups in the 1970s through to the early 1990s undoubtedly sharpened awareness about the potential impact of demographic ageing on the political process. The largest senior organizations became heavily involved during this time in seeking to protect social security, most notably in the period around Presidential elections (Street and Quadagno 1993). Moreover, together with smaller organizations such as the Gray Panthers, they started to exert an influence in raising broader issues relating to age discrimination in fields such as employment and service provision.

More generally, interest groups of older people encouraged important moves forward at the level of ideology, notably in challenges to the extremes of the intergenerational equity debate. Pressure groups such as Americans for Generational Equity (AGE) peaked in influence by the early 1990s. The intergenerational war paradigm – the notion that there is a war between the generations (Binney and Estes 1988) – may still be used to express concerns about the adequacy of economic resources, but its power to mobilize the young against the old (never strong even at its height) appears to be circumscribed. Groups such as AGE have also been unsuccessful in undermining public support (maintained across all age groups) for social security. This has been especially important in the context of moves towards privatization. Again, older people's organizations, along with other groups, have been of considerable significance in influencing the debate in this area – especially in getting politicians to declare their position in relation to social security. Fearing the political power of the elderly, conservative Republican strategists in the 2002 US midterm elections disavowed the term 'privatization', calling instead for use of the term 'choice', as the rationale for private investment accounts under social security. This symbolic camouflage, supported by a well-funded political media campaign, sufficiently confounded the voting public that the Republicans regained their Senate majority.

Marmor has identified three key features of US pressure group alignment around the passage of Medicare that are enduring:

> First, the adversaries who are 'liberal' and 'conservative' [on the Medicare issue] are similarly aligned on other controversial social policies ... Second, the extreme ideological polarization promoted by these

groups has remained markedly stable despite significant changes in the actual object in dispute . . . Illustrat[ing] the . . . structure of conflict over 'redistributive' issues in America, . . . [that] resemble 'class war' (Lowi 1964: 707). Finally, public dispute continued to be dominated by the AFL-CIO and the AMA . . . characterized as a 'slugging match' . . . The AMA has rallied groups against Medicare behind the slogans of freedom of choice, individualism, distaste for bureaucracy, hatred of the welfare state, collectivism and higher taxes. Under such banners have trooped organizations distantly related to health insurance legislation: professional organizations, business and fraternal groups, farm organizations, and various right wing protest groups.

(Marmor 2000: 18–19)

These same features of pressure group alignment are reflected in the contemporary politics of ageing surrounding the privatization of social security and Medicare. The politics are highly conflictual, with struggles that are intensely polarized along with major policy issues to be resolved. There has, however, been an evolution of capitalism – from industrial to finance capital and from nation state to global politics, with enormous consequences for nation states and their citizens. Privatization proponents comprise the dominant players in global finance including Wall Street, the banking and insurance industries and (in the case of health care) the multi-trillion dollar for-profit medical–industrial complex (Estes *et al.* 2001a). In this context, the idea that these are just 'interest groups' is no longer defensible. The very concept of 'interest group' requires critical reformulation, as such 'interests' extend well beyond simple organizations and mere collections of individuals or organizations that share a concern – instead these interests are major structural forces comprised of complex interwoven industries and sectors that possess formidable technological and communication tools as well as political and financial resources in a globally networked society. Privatization pressures are focused and orchestrated through a conservative right-wing agenda that pervades the US Congress and the White House, and reflects conservative think tanks and corporate interests, all of which are increasingly echoing the pronouncements of the giant financial interests (the IMF and the World Bank) that western democracies can no longer afford the welfare state because of population ageing. On the other hand, privatization opponents draw from a chastened and weakened union movement, the Democratic Party left wing, and disparate organizations for the ageing, whose interests (more or less) resonate with social movement advocates for civil rights and social and economic justice for women, children, racial and ethnic groups, the working poor and other vulnerable groups. The match-up of these adversarial forces appears unequal at present.

In Britain, the formation of the National Pensioners' Convention in 1979 led to determined lobbying characterized by mass demonstrations, an annual Pensioner Parliament with upwards of 2000 delegates, and regular campaigns focusing upon the declining value of the state pension (Goodman 2002). This activity had the benefit of producing more focused campaigns on pensioner issues, the development of links with influential trade union leaders, and the involvement of older people in direct political activity. The National Pensioners' Convention now has some 1.5 million affiliated members in local pensioner groups spread through the UK but with strong clusters in particular urban areas. The NPC, along with other pensioner groups, has been especially successful in developing local campaigns around cuts to services utilized by older people, and in working to gain the support of local and national politicians in struggles to increase the basic state pension.

Despite this activity, the dramatic extension of means-tested benefits in the UK (set to cover around half of all pensioners) has been a major setback for a movement which has consistently argued for an end to this kind of approach (Ginn 2001). Moreover, the goal of restoring the indexation of the basic state pension to wage as well as price movements seems further away than ever, with the Labour administration continuing to resist calls from the pensioner movement for restoration of the value of the pension (currently set to become a declining share of pre-retirement income).

Additionally, the strengthened link with trade unions, while having undoubted organizational (and some political) benefits, has raised issues about the extent to which the needs of groups such as women and minority ethnic groups are fully acknowledged. Jay Ginn (cited in Bornat 1998: 189) argues that the neglect of gender and race is a direct result of the strength of the movement's ties with the trade union movement: 'As women, ethnic minorities and disabled people know to their cost, trade unions have often been slow to recognise and respond to these needs.' This situation is gradually changing – not least because women are themselves exerting a more influential role both within trade unions and in pensioner organizations. But certain groups may continue to feel excluded, especially those without an organizational or ideological connection to the trade union movement.

Social movements and social diversity: towards a new politics of ageing

The period of the 1980s and 1990s produced undoubted benefits to the pensioners' movement. Building on the earlier, bureaucratic phase, this was a time when consciousness about age was enhanced, and when the organizations representing older people exerted a higher national and international profile. But this was also a time of considerable struggle and crisis for older people, one experienced in a variety of ways depending on social class, gender and ethnic affiliations. By the end of the 1990s, political organization among older people reflected a number of divisions, these enhanced by the rising inequalities that accompanied neo-liberal policies. This aspect forms the backdrop to the current phase of pensioner politics, one in which there will almost certainly be greater diversity among organizations representing older people. Torres-Gil (1993: 254) summarizes this in an American context in the following way:

> Although elders and their interest groups will continue to have a collective voice on specific issues, such as preserving social security benefits, differences among subpopulations of the elderly, and interest group politics, will create competition among the elderly on many other issues, such as means-testing and higher eligibility ages, especially in the face of budget deficits. Increased age consciousness, coupled with inter- and intra-cohort relationships, will increase the potential for divisiveness and conflict, since the neediest, regardless of age, will be at a disadvantage; well-organised, relatively well-off elderly carry more weight, are more age conscious, and can play the political game.

Vincent *et al.* (2001) link these developments to changes in the labour market, suggesting that this is producing a greater diversity of interests and allegiances in old age. They note that

> The decline of class politics has been widely debated . . . and undermines the power of appeal to the common interest of working people to protect the value of the pension. On the other hand, appeals to common age-based interests have not yet emerged as an alternative basis of solidarity and collective action.
>
> (Vincent *et al.* 2001: 146)

Diversity should also be noted at a cross-national as well as national level. In terms of demography, traditional assumptions about a shared pathway towards population ageing (for example among countries in the developed world) are now being challenged – especially by the contrasting experiences and demographic trends of Europe on the one side and the USA on the other. The former remains set on a path of declining fertility and continued gains in life expectancy, these producing a predicted median age for Europe of 52.7 by 2050 (*The Economist*, 24 August 2002: 23). Here, short of much higher rates of immigration than is presently the case, and a reversal in current fertility trends (presently equivalent to a family size of 1.8 children per woman), ageing will still be a dominant issue of concern within the public domain.

Equally, the position of older people as a social and cultural force may indeed remain high, especially given the likely decline in public provision and protection of retirement income support and welfare services. New data project that the American demographic case is likely to be very different, given the rise in fertility rates (to just below 2.1 children per woman) and the maintenance of high levels of immigration (producing a predicted median US age of 36.2 by 2050). These contrasting demographic realities, with a relatively youthful US population and an older European population, could well have an important bearing on the future politics of ageing in the two countries with, for example, arguments about generational equity still influencing debates in Europe while losing their force to some extent in the USA. It is interesting that under the new population projections, the themes of crisis and the unsustainable burden of ageing continue to dominate US political discourse even though the USA is likely to have the lowest population ageing among all western industrialized nations. Thus, it would appear that 'demography is not destiny' (Friedland and Summer 1999), while the politics and political processing of demography may be.

Variations in responses to population change will also be promoted by the different historical legacies of the old welfare state regimes. Myles and Pierson (2001) reflect this point with their argument that

> The . . . reason for continued diversity in the 'new' welfare states is the same as that which created diversity in 'old' welfare states – workers, employers, women, private insurers and public officials continue to have an important impact on the character of reform, just as they have in the past. Politics, including traditional partisan politics between left and right, remains operative in the reconstruction of the welfare states, albeit in new and sometimes unfamiliar ways.

The developments identified above suggest the likelihood of greater diversity among old age organizations on the one side, but with the potential for some regrouping and coalition building on the other. Traditional themes and forms of organization will certainly persist; but change is also inevitable, as groups representing older people search for more effective mechanisms for articulating their rights in the context of a global political economy. What are likely to be some of the key themes running through a future politics of ageing? First, in terms of financial issues, the struggle to protect core elements of social security (in the USA) and the basic state pension (in Britain) will continue. However, this may preoccupy some groups more than others. In Britain, for example, the campaign to restore the value of the state pension may be a particular issue for older cohorts and for unskilled and semi-skilled workers who are likely to have a limited or non-existent second pension. Women and older people from minority groups will also have a keen interest in challenging further advances in the privatization of financial support in old age. Poverty in old age will remain a crucial concern for women in the medium as well as short term, with moves towards pension privatization being highly discriminatory against women in the context of their role as carers along with gaps in employment and the experience of low-paid work (Ginn 2001).

Second, a new form of politics is emerging among workers anxious to protect their future retirement income. British firms are increasingly moving employees from final salary (defined benefit) into money purchase (defined contribution) schemes (these typically generating a pension around 40 per cent lower at the age of 60 than a final salary (defined benefit) scheme. Surveys among trade unions suggest an increasing propensity to take strike action when faced with employers attempting to change pension schemes or reduce contributions to save money. In Britain, one survey indicated 29 per cent of workers – equal to around 3 million – who would strike if their pension was threatened, and 36 per cent – nearly 4 million – who would join in a protest rally on the issue. Substantial majorities – 66 and 58 per cent respectively – would sign petitions or take their grievance direct to management (*Independent*, 19 November 2002). Such protests have already occurred in the case of France (a country where, as Peter Stearns (1977) has argued, workers have had a long history of fighting for decent pensions and the right to retirement). According to one report of a demonstration in November 2002,

> France's public sector trade unions . . . raised the stakes in their battle to prevent the centre-right government from cutting their pension privileges, by staging a big protest in central Paris. The demonstration representing all parts of the public sector was accompanied by similar protests in other cities along with selective strike action in public transport. Worse affected was French air traffic, with one of the controllers' unions observing a 36-hour stoppage that caused the cancellation of two-thirds of flights at main airports. [The] Paris demonstration, by over 60,000 people . . . was officially to protest against the threat of privatisation. Behind this lay fears that the introduction of private capital would end the special status of public sector employees. Their . . . pension privileges concern job protection and pension contributions that are lower than the private sector but produce a greater pay-out with earlier retirement.
>
> (*Financial Times*, 27 November 2002)

These developments are important in suggesting a new basis for the politics of ageing, one in which issues are followed throughout the life course rather than segregated to one part of it. Crucially it suggests that interest groups of older people will form new alliances with younger workers concerned about the erosion of their prospects for old age. Moreover, in contrast to the generational equity perspective that attempts to pit the younger and older generations against one another, these coalitions are just as likely to be based upon a view of a shared interest across generations in ensuring that rights to state and public pensions are maintained.

Third, building on this last point, older people are just as likely to play a role in broader social movements as they are in activities formed around age alone. John Foster (2002: 45) has made the point that

> The power to upend and reshape society in decisive ways will not come primarily through single-issue movements for reform, but rather through forms of organization and popular alliance that will establish feminists, opponents of racism, advocates of gay rights, defenders of the environment, etc. as the more advanced sectors of a unified, class-based, revolutionary political and economic movement.

Coalition building may be especially characteristic of the 'baby boom generation' for whom wider campaigns and identity movements around problems associated with globalization, issues facing women and minority ethnic groups, environmental questions and related concerns may have as much relevance as those connected with age alone.

Responses to the impact of globalization will almost certainly be crucial. A key issue here concerns the extent to which older people will be a major (or even minor) voice in the new global economy and efforts to reshape the institution of old age and retirement that are occurring across different nation states. The process of globalization represents both an historical transition and an opportunity for the development and testing of new forms of political power – among older people themselves as well as across generations.

Citizenship, democracy and the role of the state

Over the next decade, social struggles will be pivotal concerning the role of the state and social rights as a defining principle of citizenship. As the politics of globalization and ageing unfold, major conflicts are likely to be over the ideology of individualism and the imposition of reward structures (through state policy) that are based upon individual market performance *versus* the ideology of interdependence and the implementation of reward structures that build upon a more communal foundation. Historically, in both the UK and the USA, older people have benefited to the extent that a philosophy of interdependence rather than individualism has prevailed. The tensions are over the distribution of resources and the basis for that distribution; that is, whether state policy reflects the value for

- shared (as opposed to individual) problem solving and responsibility;
- pooling risks through social insurance (as opposed to individual risk); and

- accounting for women's unpaid caregiving by acknowledging the chains of intergenerational relations and exchange across the life course.

Vincente Navarro (2000) cautions against pessimism, instead contending that there is no inevitability about the future of the welfare state. There is a two-edged sword at work. Globalization opens the door to multiple possible outcomes (positive and negative), and there is the threat of the further exploitation of social divisions and differences and the creation of new and widening social inequalities both within and across nation states. However, economic globalization does not automatically preclude progressive welfare states with social democratic policies; nor is globalization, by definition, antithetical to social rights and full employment. Nevertheless, Navarro (2000: 238) notes that not only are such beliefs erroneous, but they have also weakened the commitment of leaders of social democratic parties to expansionist and full employment policies.

> The evidence against the decline of social democracy is so overwhelming that the claim of its demise because of globalization has lost all credibility ... [Instead] ... [the developments in social democracy have] been as a consequence of the adaptation to the process of globalization, with social democratic parties giving up or considerably diluting their traditional expansionist and full-employment policies. The new [and erroneous] version of the globalization theory is that the electoral successes of social democratic parties are based on their abandonment of social democratic policies.

In a related vein, Kagarlitsky (1999: 293–4) contends that the challenge for the Left under current conditions is 'reclaiming the state'. When the Left accepts the idea of the 'impotence of the state' in the face of transnational corporations and 'rejects the idea of the radical transformation of the structures of power', a result may become a self-fulfilling prophecy that 'the established state structures start to appear unshakeable' and the state is symbolically and practically given over as a 'monopoly of the right'. The progressive agenda is to reclaim and democratize the state, for it is only through states that transnational financial institutions can pursue their policies. Otherwise, as Kagarlitsky observes,

> The thesis of the 'impotence of the state' is, then, not so much an observation of fact as a self-fulfilling prophecy. A state that acts strictly according to the rules dictated by neo-liberal ideology and the IMF does in fact become impotent. It is true that this 'impotence' is of

a very peculiar kind. Anyone who tries to issue a challenge to the existing order discovers that the state remains quite strong enough to take up the struggle in defence of that order.

(Kagarlitsky, 1999: 297)

The increasing power of global finance and private transnational bodies raises significant issues about the nature of citizenship, and associated rights to health and social care, in old age. In the period of welfare state reconstruction, rights were defined and negotiated through various manifestations of nation state-based social policy (although the dominance of the USA via the Bretton Woods system is important to emphasize). With globalization, however, issues of citizenship are moved to a transnational stage, and driven by a combination of the power of intergovernmental structures, the influence of multinational corporations, and the pressures of population movement and migration.

Provocative questions concern the nature of citizen rights, and the determinants of 'life chances' available to members of the global society, including older people. Under the pressures of global capitalism and finance, citizen rights have become a hotly contested arena rife with power struggles on multiple levels. In liberal states such as the USA, there are modest universal transfers and means-tested assistance with strict entitlement rules, often associated with stigma. In contrast to the 'largely individualistic and some-times asocial views of the New Right' in which citizen rights are based largely on labour market participation and property, there is the opposing concept of 'social rights' emphasizing notions of interdependence and solidarity.

Two contrasting notions of citizenship are at war here. The concept of social rights of citizenship is 'grounded in the notion of "life course inter-dependence"' (Twine 1994). It is significant that 'quality of life in old age strongly reflects the different costs of "life course interdependencies", of child rearing and employment [and caregiving and long term care in old age], and these vary by social class and gender' (Twine 1994: 34). In opposition to this, the neo-liberal ideology of individualism shapes a different view of citizenship rights, supporting the concept that we are independent, as if independent of society, 'a form of *freedom from society* or more specifically *freedom from the state*' (Twine 1994: 34; original emphasis). The reluctance of neo-liberals to embrace the principle of 'interdependence' stems from the fact that to do so 'would present us with moral obligations to compensate those who bear the costs of our progress'. A critical approach to social policy and ageing is consist-ent with the assumption that, first, 'the material and human reproduction of society involves relations and processes of interdependence' (Twine 1994: 29); and second, it is appropriate for social policy on ageing to reflect (and even more importantly, to compensate for) these life course and society-wide inter-dependencies. The burdens of not doing so are profoundly unequally borne, with women particularly disadvantaged, given that they perform most of the unpaid labour in realizing that interdependence (through their social repro-duction, both biological and in caregiving across generations).

Through struggles over state policy, the reconstruction of the meaning of citizenship is especially complex and problematic within the context of the global community. The complexities mount, as critical work on citizenship demonstrates, given that within single societies/nations, even where policies are designed to assure treatment of individuals 'as equals' under the law, it may be very difficult to achieve any form of substantive 'equality' in the *result* (e.g. in the life experience for older persons) due to the varying attributes, social situations and conditions of different older individuals. As Sassoon (1991: 90) notes, '. . . differences between people according to resources and needs, fam-ily situation and point in life cycle, and life history with regard to the world of work are as significant as equality before the law or equal political rights'.

Conclusion

The aim of this chapter has been to provide a survey of the politics of ageing, with a particular emphasis on developments in the USA and Britain. An important part of the argument developed is that a new set of forces are now shaping political debate and organization among older people. The key issues concern questions about the rights of older people within the context of a globalized world, the power of corporate structures to influence daily life in old age, and the continuing reconstruction of key areas of health and social security provision in old age. The responses from older people are, however, complex. It is certainly the case that a new politics of old age has emerged, built around the increased diversity of older people as a social group. On the other hand, this is almost certainly a politics built around coalitions that cross over generational, gender, class and ethnic boundaries. This fact alone strengthens the case for a more sophisticated political sociology of ageing as a crucial element within critical gerontology. We shall return to this theme again in the concluding chapter of this book.

9 Conclusion: future tasks for a critical gerontology

Introduction

The aim of this book has been to explore, from a critical perspective, problems and perspectives within contemporary social gerontology, with a particular emphasis on social theory and social policy. At this point in the twenty-first century a range of opportunities and challenges present themselves for the study of ageing. On the one side, there is little doubt of the growth in policy interest and funded research across Europe and the USA. This reflects the range of agencies – international, state-funded research councils, charitable and voluntary organizations, private companies – urgently seeking answers to what are perceived to be a range of social, economic and political problems associated with ageing populations. On the other side, social gerontology as a set of approaches to understanding the nature of growing old might be said to be in a state of crisis and disunity. In part this is because the existing conceptual tools and related assumptions and the scholars working with them have either not kept pace with the new set of influences affecting older people, or have uncritically accepted them as unproblematic.

Some of the characteristics of this crisis may be identified in terms of, first, the uneasy relationship between the core social science disciplines and the study of ageing. This often centres on whether it is simply enough to impose sociological, economic or psychological theories and methods onto the study of old age, or whether gerontology requires its own explanation, that can critically inform those disciplines from an age-aware perspective. Second, there is the continued hold of perspectives that fail to acknowledge the profound effects of race, ethnic, gender and class divisions, as well as intergenerational relations, on the experience of ageing. Third, there are profound changes to expectations by and about older people in terms of identity and pressure to 'age well'. New roles are emerging for older people in the developed west around work, family and leisure that legitimate certain normative patterns of ageing and occasion moral sanction on others. Fourth, there are problems associated with welfare state restructuring and the attendant power struggles and implications these carry for the social position, rights and identity of older people.

A more general issue facing gerontology, however, concerns the need to develop a clearer perspective on the pressures facing older people as a result of accelerating global change. A significant weakness of gerontology over the past decade (symptomatic of its marginal status within the social sciences) has been an inadequate grasp of how globalization is transforming the nature of growing old. In this context, the need for a framework to respond to the challenge associated with globalization is a matter of some urgency. The key dimensions here include: the changing and contested form of the nation state, citizenship and nationalism; the enhanced role of supra-national bodies; the increased concentration and power of multinational corporations; and the emergence of new forms of class-based, gender-based and ethnic-based inequalities and divisions. In concluding this book, we develop this theme by highlighting five main issues that a critical gerontology will need to focus on over the next decade:

- developing critical theory;
- theorizing the ageing society;
- globalization, social theory and social rights;
- social divisions and inequalities;
- the critical study of old age identity and intergenerational relations.

Developing critical theory

A cornerstone of the political economy of public policy and ageing is, first, the examination of the social construction of problems and the remedies to deal with them; second, the political and economic influences on their treatment through social policy (Estes 1979a). A central task for theory concerns the need to examine the structural inequalities and power dynamics that perpetuate current understandings of ageing. An analysis that accepts commonly held assumptions about ageing, for example, as a period of inevitable decline, poverty or, for that matter, unending leisure, fails to ask the key questions about why this state of affairs holds true rather than another. Assumptions that contemporary ways and lifestyles are the only or natural ways to grow old ignore cultural and historical variations and possibilities in life patterns. A critical theoretical perspective must move beyond appearances and seek explanations that overturn conformist realities. Importantly, power relations, processes and structures must be examined as they appear in everyday relations, between generations, between professionals and older adults and between different groups based on class, gender and race. Links must be made between macro, meso and micro levels of analysis, so that the pull of social inequalities can be identified, and the experience and daily interpretation of them explored. In other words, each must be made meaningful to the other, an essential ingredient for critical social change.

The above process will have a direct effect on the sort of theoretical development that critical social approaches should encourage. From a critical perspective, some priority areas include studies of discursive constructions of ageing and intergenerational relations; existing and emerging political, economic and cultural structures and institutions; historical and contemporary forms of domination; the politics of representation; and emerging forms of human and political agency – and the effects of each of these on social policy and old age as well as individual and societal ageing. Key to developing a critique of ageing as it is currently constructed would be a creative amalgam of two streams of contemporary social gerontology. On the one hand these would include experiential, humanistic and personal approaches; on the other, those that address macro structural movements and forces. Both require each other for a comprehensive understanding of contemporary ageing to take place. Structural approaches, without the humanistic element, offer limited insight into the humanity of the situations described. Without an understanding of social structure, however, an overly humanistic approach to ageing is isolated from context and history. These two factors, experiential realism and the effects of material circumstances, lie at the centre of a critical understanding of later life.

A strength of this approach to critical gerontology is that it assumes (and interrogates) the interpenetration of the spheres of economics, culture and politics, on both the individual and social structural levels. In connecting social theory to social policy in ageing, an important aim of our project is to understand how the spheres of economics, politics and culture are mutually constituted (Shaw 2002), by whom, and with what consequences for ageing including the race, class, gender and intergenerational relations that comprise these spheres. These consequences must be examined from the personal to the economic and political levels – from human agency, identity and development across the life course, to governance and representation of the generational stake through a transformed and transforming state and economic institutions.

Clearly, such a perspective is predicated on social engagement: that the perspectives taken should have the practical ability to bring radical perspectives to established problems and policies and to the development of alternatives. For critical approaches, research would not necessarily make existing systems run more smoothly, nor iron out problems as they are defined by existing policies. This may often be a consequence of an analysis, but it is not its primary purpose. Rather, priority would be given to discovering contradictions within established structures, establishing the limits of their viability and their purposes in terms of the politics of ageing. At its best, critique also points to alternatives to those systems and work toward social change that increases the self-development and social enhancement of older people and intergenerational solidarity. It is also, then, central to contributing to the conceptual tools people can use to make sense of their daily lives.

A key element of critical social gerontology is praxis or social action. Critical gerontology supplies evidence and perspectives that help groups and individuals assess their situation, make the links between personal experience and structural inequities and engage in collective change.

Theorizing the 'ageing society'

A second set of issues for critical theory concerns the place and nature of the entity known as 'society'. The idea of society as a bounded self-sufficient entity (a theme most associated with the functionalist perspective of Talcott Parsons) has become somewhat taken for granted within gerontological theorizing. In this respect, the focus of mainstream gerontology has been built around questions of how social integration in old age is possible, given some of the changes affecting people in the later stages of the life course – experiences such as retirement, bereavement and chronic illness. Such a formulation assumes that there is a coherent and bounded society into which integration is indeed attainable. This view has been sustained for much of the twentieth century by a relatively small group of western societies, and in particular those associated with the aggressive and often imperialist promotion of nation statehood. The notion of society as a bounded, sovereign entity is, however, profoundly changed with globalization. John Urry (2000: 13) writes:

> . . . there are exceptional levels of global interdependence; unpredictable shock waves spill out 'chaotically' from one part to the system as a whole; there are not just 'societies' but massively powerful 'empires' roaming the globe; and there is a mass mobility of people, objects and dangerous human wastes.

This questioning of the traditional basis to society is a challenging one for gerontology. In a number of senses the old formulation of 'ageing societies' is unhelpful in a globalized world. Global society comprises many demographic realities – ageing Europe certainly, as compared with an increasingly youthful USA, and in stark contrast plummeting life expectancy in Russia and sub-Saharan Africa. But what, in any event, is the 'society' element in this ageing? In a fluid and networked world, growing old is becoming detached from the protective welfare states that were once seen to be at the core of (western) society. But, steering a careful path between Giddens's 'global optimists' and 'global pessimists', it may be argued that a new formulation is required which at the very least maintains the idea of protection associated with welfare provision but also recognizes the diverse and unequal networks in and through which people interact throughout the life course and that produce different types of ageing – national, transnational, sub-cultural and, for some, the wish – and the means – not to age at all (see Chapter 3).

Globalization, social theory and social rights

A major dimension of structural inequality concerns the impact of globalization on the experience of growing old. In general terms, debates around globalization have focused on issues such as the ecological crisis, the power of multinational corporations, problems of debt repayment and related concerns (Klein 2000; Stiglitz 2001). All of these certainly touch the lives of elderly people – many of whom are involved in campaigns around such areas. Yet as a group, as argued in Chapter 7, older people have been presented as marginal to critiques of globalization and related forms of structural change. But the paradox, for older as well as younger generations, is that the macro level has become more rather than less important as a factor influencing daily life. Indeed, one might argue that while social theory in gerontology has retreated from the analysis of social institutions (see Chapter 2), the phenomenon of globalization (as ideology and process, and struggles around both) has transformed the terms of the debate. Even in the case of political economy perspectives, which continue to focus on structural issues (Estes and Associates 2001), globalization has reordered the concepts typically used by researchers. Ideas associated with the idea of society, the state, gender, social class, ethnicity, have retained their importance, but their collective and individual meaning is substantially different in the context of the influence of global actors and institutions (Bauman 1998).

The first argument, therefore, is that accepting the importance of globalization also strengthens the case for reinserting macro level analysis within gerontology. Hagestad and Dannefer (2001) note that the costs of a microfocus have been significant: 'hamper[ing] our ability to address the ageing society in the context of global economic and technological change'. Given the explanatory role of theory, globalization is setting major new challenges in terms of the interaction between individuals, communities and nation states, and the global architecture within which these are nested. Ageing may now be more appropriately analysed in the context of the networks and flows characteristic of global society, these producing a loosening in those attachments which have traditionally anchored people to specific class, nation state and kinship settings (Castells 1996; Urry 2000).

Following the above argument, three distinct phases may be outlined in the development of old age over the past 50 years. In the first phase, the nation state introduced new institutions to manage the growth of an ageing population. The second phase began their fragmentation, with increasing variation in individual and societal responses to growing old. With the third phase of global ageing, these variations are maintained (and indeed enhanced in many respects) but with the influence of transnational communities, corporations and international governmental organizations producing new agendas and challenges for ageing societies. As argued in Chapter 7, globalization is bringing forth new dynamics and new sets of actors and institutions that are shaping the social construction of public policy for old age. The nature of citizenship and associated rights to health and social care in old age are both hotly contested and highly negotiable under the lead of the complex and commanding influences of powerful intergovernmental structures (e.g. the World Bank and IMF), private multinational corporations, and largely western welfare states that are under the major pressures associated with ideological neo-liberalism and population movements and migration. This contrasts sharply with the period of welfare state reconstruction, during which rights were independently defined and negotiated through various manifestations of British, European and American nation building and sovereign state-based social policy.

It may also be argued that rights, in the period of late modernity, have become more fragmented as well as individualized. However, the risks associated with ageing are relatively unchanged – the threat of poverty, the need for long-term care, the likelihood of serious illness. What has changed, as Bauman (2000) argues in a more general context, is that the duty and the necessity to cope with these risks has been transferred to individual families (women carers in particular, as argued in Chapter 4) and to individual older people (notably in respect of financing for old age). The new social construction (and contradiction) of ageing is, on the one hand, the focus upon growing old as a global problem and issue; on the other hand, the social reconstruction of old age as a personal rather than collective responsibility. This development suggests an important role for theory in bringing together macro- and micro-social perspectives with new approaches in order to understand how global processes contribute to the reshaping of the institutions in which the experiences of old age and ageing are embedded.

As previously suggested, ageing must be viewed as a global phenomenon, one transforming developing as much as developed countries. But we need to delineate the ways in which global institutions and global governance might be used to promote the needs and rights of older citizens. The task here must be to construct new theories about the nature of citizenship in light of the more fluid borders surrounding nation states. Important questions concern whether and how older people are advantaged or disadvantaged by the spread of mobile communities along with more varied and contested forms of citizenship – issues which can only be illuminated through the application of research and developments in social theory.

The extent to which such developments will lead to the emergence of a 'global community' and 'global citizenship' in John Urry's sense (2000), is unclear. Nevertheless, old age and ageing will be profoundly influenced by the 'development of a common consciousness of human society on a world scale . . . and an increased awareness of the totality of human social relations as the largest constitutive framework of all relations (Shaw 2002: 11–12). One of the most intriguing and significant questions relates to how the state and globalization shape the politics of the life course in the context of a political economy that is unstable and continually throwing up new challenges for older people.

Social inequality and social policy

A further issue concerns the extent to which gerontological research may challenge the dominant institutions that reproduce and perpetuate social divisions in society. Applications of the policy sciences to ageing take for granted the existing systems of medicine and capitalism as scholars work largely within 'definitions of the situation' that are framed by classical economic paradigms, assumptions, and models of cost-effectiveness and individual level outcomes. The end result is that such investigations consider only a limited array of potentially viable policy options, assuring the serious consideration of only incremental changes that will do little to alter the underlying problems facing older people.

Challenging this context are some of the theories reviewed in this book, namely, political economy perspectives, critical theory, studies of identity and feminist approaches (see Chapters 2, 3 and 4). The substantial intellectual ferment in 'political economy of ageing', 'critical gerontology' and 'humanistic gerontology' has resulted from a combination of, on the one hand, the infusion of theoretical developments in postmodernism, feminism, antiracism and critical theory and, on the other hand, growing concerns over the challenge for the intellectual Left in the wake of the failure of communism, and the lack of what may be perceived as viable socialist alternatives to the capitalist state.

There is a need for projects in the tradition of the Frankfurt School that are multidisciplinary and that examine the structural forces and social processes that profoundly shape social policy on old age and ageing in any single society and in the global community of the first, second and third worlds. Attention needs to be given to rebalancing studies of individual ageing with research on the processing and treatment of the elderly in society, and with emphasis on the 'social', especially on the political, economic and cultural conflicts and struggles that delineate the winners and losers of social policy.

Empirical and theoretical work on social policy and ageing from a critical perspective seeks to illuminate alternative understandings and a vision of 'what is possible' for old age and ageing. It is requisite to lifting the ideological veil of scientific objectivity that obscures and mystifies inequality and social injustice in a society and economy that prioritizes the production of goods and services primarily (if not only) for its economic or exchange value rather than for its social value and capacity to meet human needs.

Critical gerontology and the study of identity

The issues raised in this chapter also pose questions about the relationship between a critical gerontology and the exploration of identity in old age. The key point for a critical theory of identity lies in the recognition that people can take a position, a stance toward the identities available to them, and that these are not simply accepted as givens. However, this possibility is often constrained by a restrictive ideology that defines only a limited number of ways in which to grow old. Definitions of productive ageing and the biomedicalization of ageing are two examples examined in this book, where very limited notions of what it is to age have been promoted by powerful and commercial interests.

By adopting a critical approach, an important distance is opened up between what people are told are the 'choices' available to them and what they might personally and collectively desire. This critical distance itself facilitates an ability to make a stand, to discriminate between what we are led to believe and what we experience, what appears given and what can be taken. It facilitates an ability to resist assaults on an ageing identity and build alternative possibilities for adult ageing. In that way, adopting a critical approach is a determining factor in beginning to take back control of one's own destiny, which is true both for theoretical orientation within gerontology and in the practice of self-development.

A critical analysis of ageing identity would suggest that older adults require elements of continuity and stability of identity as well as options and possibilities for change. Both are essential elements in becoming critically engaged with social identity as well as with wider social and political issues. As stated most forcefully in Chapter 3, ageing identities have been faced by two forms of excess. An excess of structure confines the possibilities of adult ageing to age stages and stereotypes. An excess of fluidity disconnects ageing from the material bases of experience and can lead to insecurity and risk. Both have served to police acceptable forms of contemporary ageing.

Given the above, it is impossible to examine the relationship between ageing and identity without examining the factors that restrict these possibilities for some and not for others. There are certain fundamental criteria that have to be met before a balance can be achieved between enough stablility to ensure confidence and enough flexibility to allow positive change. Mapping inequality, in terms of social, economic, political and psychological capital also maps, then, the existing horizons for identity development which social groups and individual social actors have made available to them. This is not to say that this is the only material available, but that it forms a network of restrictions and expectations that have to be overcome. In terms of old age, the network would include gender, class and cultural expectations that interact with common experiences of inequality and of ageing itself.

A critical appreciation of the often hidden force of inequality has a number of implications for an ageing identity. These may be listed as follows. First, it rebuts the claim that an older adult's particular circumstances are an exclusively personal phenomenon and that they can be explained by individual moral conduct, either in the past or in the here and now. Second, it raises the question of whose voice is being heard in debates on adult ageing, on issues that are charged by intergenerational difference, or by the interests of dominant power groups. Third, it highlights the need to encourage a perception of the ageing self as a conscious agent, in spite of the circumstances social actors find themselves in. Fourth, questions of age and identity are seen to travel beyond a struggle with one's own ageing body to a confrontation with the socially constructed environments that shape the possibilities for ageing well and for social participation. Fifth, it places centre stage the tension between finding constructive conditions within which mature identities can be expressed and those forces that attempt to force it into fixed and inauthentic patterns. Finally, it reintroduces the issue of solidarity, as a challenge to the age-segregation endemic to contemporary western societies, and as a process of discovering common causes rather than disempowering differences between social groups.

Conclusion

This book assesses the state of social gerontology from the perspective of the early part of the twenty-first century. We can certainly identify strengths within the discipline, including advances in empirical studies, greater understanding of variations within the older population, and increased awareness of the impact of different health and social policies. Nevertheless, the weakness of much research is also apparent, notably around issues such as: first, gender and ethnicity; second, the marginal status of social theory; third, the failure to acknowledge or theorize the role of the state; fourth, the limited scope of interdisciplinary work.

From a critical perspective, the lack of what might be termed 'emancipatory gerontology' is a major concern. Critical gerontology has been developing evidence over the past two decades about the injustices and inequalities experienced by older people. The next step, however, must be the development of a clearer vision about ageing relevant to a global community that is characterized by massive economic divisions and complex forms of political oppression. The study of ageing in the twentieth century was largely about the western experience and driven by western assumptions about what a 'good' old age was meant to be. For the twenty-first century, the key issue will be studying ageing as a global phenomenon while at the same time incorporating older people as participants into the processes of research and theorizing. Achieving these goals represents both a major task and an opportunity for critical gerontology in the years ahead.

BIBLIOGRAPHY

Abeles, R.P., Gift, H.C. and Ory, M.G. (1994) *Aging and Quality of Life*. New York, NY: Springer.

Able, E.K. (1986) The hospice movement, *International Journal of Health Services*, 16 (1): 71–85.

Abramovitz, M. (1988) *Regulating the Lives of Women*. Boston, MA: South End Press.

Achenbaum, W.A. (1995) *Crossing Frontiers: Gerontology Emerges as a Science*. Cambridge: Cambridge University Press.

Acker, J. (1988) Class, gender and the relations of distribution, *Signs*, 13 (3): 473–93.

Acker, J. (1992) Gendered institutions – from sex roles to gendered institutions, *Contemporary Sociology*, 21, 565–9.

Acker, J. (2000) Rewriting class, race, and gender: problems in feminist rethinking, in M.M. Ferree, J. Lorber and B.B. Hess (eds) *Revisioning Gender*. Walnut Creek, CA: Rowman and Littlefield.

Adelman, R. (1995) The 'Alzheimerization' of aging, *The Gerontologist*, 35 (4): 526–32.

Adelman, R., Greene, M. and Charon, R. (1991) Issues in physician–elderly interaction, *Ageing and Society*, 11(1): 127–47.

Adler, N.E., Boyce, T., Chesney, M.A., Folkman, S. and Syme, L. (1993) Socio-economic inequalities in health, *Journal of the American Medical Association*, 269 (24): 3140–5.

Age Concern England (2000) *Turning Your Back on Us: Older People and the NHS*. London: ACE.

Alber, J. and Standing, G. (2001) Social dumping, catch-up or convergence, *Journal of European Social Policy*, 10(2): 99–119.

Alford, R.R. (1976) *Health Care Politics*. Chicago, IL: University of Chicago Press.

Allan, G. (1996) *Kinship and Friendship in Modern Britain*. Oxford: Oxford University Press.

Allan, G. and Crow, G. (2001) *Families, Households and Society*. London: Palgrave.

Amann, A. (ed.) (1984) *Social gerontological research in European countries – history and current trends*. West Berlin and Vienna: German Centre of Gerontology and Ludwig-Boltzmann Institute of Social Gerontology and Life Span Research.

Andersson, L. (ed.) (2003) *Cultural Gerontology*. Westport, CT: Auburn House.

Andrews, C. (1995) *Profit Fever: The drive to corporatise health care and how to stop it*. Monroe: Common Courage Press.

Andrews, M. (1991) *Lifetimes of Commitment: Aging, Politics, Psychology*. Cambridge: Cambridge University Press.

Antonucci, T.C. (1990) Social supports and social relationships, in R.H. Binstock and L.K. George (eds) *Handbook of Aging and the Social Sciences*, 3rd edn. San Diego, CA: Academic Press.

Antonucci, T. and Akiyama, H. (1987) Social networks in adult life: a preliminary examination of the convoy model, *Journal of Gerontology*, 4: 519–27.

Appadurai, A. (1996) *Modernity at Large*. Minneapolis, MN: University of Minnesota Press.

Arber, S. and Attias-Donfut, C. (2000) *The Myth of Generational Conflict*. London: Routledge.

Arber, S. and Ginn, J. (1991) *Gender and Later Life*. London: Sage Publications.

Arber, S. and Ginn, J. (eds) (1995) *Connecting Gender and Ageing: A Sociological Approach*. Buckingham: Open University Press.

Atchley, R. (1999) *Continuity and Adaptation in Old Age*. Baltimore, MD: Johns Hopkins University Press.

Atchley, R.C. (1989) A continuity theory of normal aging, *The Gerontologist*, 29: 183–90.

Bailey, J. (1975) *Social Theory for Social Planning*. London: Routledge and Kegan Paul.

Baltes, M.M. and Carstensen, L.L. (1996) The process of successful aging, *Ageing and Society*, 15: 397–422.

Baltes, P.B. and Baltes, M.M. (1990a). *Successful Aging: Perspectives from the Behavioural Sciences*. New York, NY: Cambridge University Press.

Baltes, P.B. and Baltes, M.M. (1990b) Psychological perspectives on successful aging, in P.B. Baltes and M.M. Baltes (eds) *Successful Aging*. New York, NY: Cambridge University Press.

Barlow, M. and Clarke, T. (2001) *Global Showdown*. Ontario: Stoddart.

Bass, S.A. and Caro, F.G. (2001) Productive ageing: a conceptual framework, in N. Morrow-Howell, J. Hinterlong and M. Sherraden (eds) *Productive Aging: Concepts and Challenges*. Baltimore, MD: John Hopkins University Press.

Batley, M., Blane, D. and Charlton, J. (1997) Socioeconomic and demographic trends, in J. Charlton and M. Murphy (eds) *The Health of Adult Britain 1841–1994*, Decennial Supplement No. 12. London: Office for National Statistics.

Bauman, Z. (1995) *Life in Fragments: Essays in Postmodern Morality*. Oxford: Blackwell.

Bauman, Z. (1998) *Globalization*. Cambridge: Polity Press.

Bauman, Z. (2000) *Liquid Modernity*. Cambridge: Polity Press.

Beauchamp, T.L. and Childress, J.F. (2001) *Principles of Biomedical Ethics*. New York, NY: Oxford University Press.

Beck, U. (2000a) *What is Globalisation?* Cambridge: Polity Press.

Beck, U. (2000b) 'Living your own life in a runaway world: individualisation, globalisation and politics', in W. Hutton and A. Giddens (eds) *On the Edge: Living with Global Capitalism*. London: Cape.

Becker, H. (1963) *The Outsiders*. New York, NY: Free Press.

Bengston, V.L. and Achenbaum, W.A. (eds) (1993) *The Changing Contract Across Generations*. New York, NY: Aldine De Gruyter.

Bengtson, V.L. and Schaie, K.W.S. (eds) (1999) *Handbook of Theories of Aging*. New York, NY: Springer Publishing Co.

Bengtson, V.L., Burgess, E.O. and Parrott, T.M. (1997) Theory, explanation, and a third generation of theoretical development, in Social Gerontology. *Journal of Gerontology: Series B, Psychological Sciences and Social Sciences*, 52 (2), S72–S88.

Berger, P. and Luckmann, T. (1966) *The Social Construction of Reality*. New York, NY: Doubleday.

Bergmann, B. (1995) Becker's theory of the family: preposterous conclusions, *Feminist Economics*, 1 (1): 141–50.

Bergthold, L. (1990) *Purchasing Power in Health*. New Brunswick, NJ: Rutgers University Press.

Berman, H. (1994) *Interpreting the Aging Self: Journals of Later Life*. New York, NY: Springer.

Bernard, M. and Meade, K. (1993) *Women Come of Age*. London: Edward Arnold.

Beveridge, W. (1942) *Social Insurance and Allied Services*. London: HMSO.

Biggs, S. (1993) *Understanding Ageing*. Buckingham: Open University Press.

Biggs, S. (1997) Choosing not to be old. Masks, bodies and identity management in later life, *Ageing and Society*, 18 (5): 553–70.

Biggs, S. (1998) Mature imaginations: ageing and the psychodynamic tradition, *Ageing and Society*, 18 (4): 421–39.

Biggs, S. (1999a) *The Mature Imagination*. Buckingham: Open University Press.

Biggs, S. (1999b) The blurring of the life course: narrative, memory and the question of authenticity, *Journal of Aging and Identity*, 4 (4): 209–21.

Biggs, S. (2001) Toward critical narrativity. Stories of aging in contemporary social policy, *Journal of Aging Studies*, 15(4): 303–16.

Biggs, S. and Powell, J. (2000) Surveillance and elder abuse. *Journal of Contemporary Health*, 4(1): 43–9.

Biggs, S. and Powell, J. (2001) A Foucauldian analysis of old age and the power of social welfare, *Journal of Aging and Social Policy*, 12(2): 93–112.

Biggs, S. and Powell, J. (2003) Older people and family in social policy, in V. Bengsten and A. Lowenstein (eds) *Internation Perspectives on Families, Aging and Social Support*. New York, NY: Aldine de Gruyter.

Biggs, S., Bernard, M., Kingston, P. and Nettleton, H. (2000) Lifestyle of belief: narrative and culture in a retirement community, *Ageing and Society*, 20: 649–72.

Biggs, S., Lowenstein, A. and Hendricks, J. (2003) *The Need for Theory: Critical Approaches to Social Gerontology*. Amityville, NY: Baywood Publishing.

Binney, E.A. and Estes, C.L. (1988) The retreat of the state and its transfer of responsibility: the intergenerational war, *International Journal of Health Services*, 18 (1): 83–96.

Binney, E.A. and Estes, C.L. (1990) Setting the wrong limits: class biases and the biographical standard, in P. Homer and M. Holstein (eds) *A Good Age? The Paradox of Setting Limits*. New York, NY: Simon and Schuster.

Binstock, R.H. (1972) Interest group liberalism and the politics of aging, *The Gerontologist*, 12: 265–80.

Binstock, R.H. (1983) The aged as scapegoat, *The Gerontologist*, 23: 136–43.

Binstock, R.H. (2000) Older people and voting participation: past and future, *The Gerontologist*, 40 (1): 18–31.

Binstock, R.H. and Quadagno, J. (2001) Aging and politics, in R.H. Binstock and L. George (eds) *Handbook of Aging and the Social Sciences*, 5th edn. London: Academic Press.

Birren, J.E. and Bengston, V.L. (eds) (1988) *Emergent Theories of Aging*. New York, NY: Springer.

Blackburn, R. (2002) *Banking on Death or Investing in Life*. London: Verso Books.

Blaikie, A. (1999) *Ageing and Popular Culture*. Cambridge: Cambridge University Press.

Blaikie, A. and Macnicol, J. (1989) Ageing and social policy: a twentieth century dilemma, in A. Warnes (ed.) *Human Ageing and Later Life*. London: Edward Arnold.

Bornat, J. (1998) Pensioners organise: hearing the voices of older people, in M. Bernard and J. Phillips (eds) *The Social Policy of Old Age*. London: Centre for Policy on Ageing.

Bortz, W.M. IV and Bortz, W.M. II (1996) How fast do we age?, *Journal of Gerontology: Medical Sciences*, 51A (5): M223–M225.

Bottomore, T.B. (1983) *A Dictionary of Marxist Thought*. Cambridge, MA: Harvard University Press.

Bourdieu, P. (2001) *Masculine Domination*. Stanford, CA: Stanford University Press.

Brammer, A. and Biggs, S. (1998) Defining elder abuse, *Journal of Social Welfare and Family Law*, 20(3): 285–304.

Brown, W. (1995) *States of Injury: Power and Freedom in Late Modernity*. Princeton, NJ: Princeton University Press.

Brush, L.D. (2000) Gender, work, who cares? Production, reproduction, deindustrialization, and business as usual, in M.M. Ferree, J. Lorber and B.B. Hess (eds) *Revisioning Gender*. Walnut Creek, CA: a Division of Rowman and Littlefield.

Buber, M. (1958) *I and Thou*. New York, NY: Scrivner.

Butler, R.N. (1975) *Why Survive? Being Old in America*. San Francisco, CA: Harper and Row.

Butler, R.N. and Gleason, H. (1985) *Productive Ageing: Enhancing Vitality in Later Life*. New York, NY: Springer.

Butler, R.N. and Schechter, M. (1995) Productive aging, in G. Maddox (ed.) *The Encyclopaedia of Aging*. New York, NY: Springer.

Butler, R.N., Overlink, M. and Schecter, M. (1990) *The Promise of Productive Ageing: From Biology to Public Policy*. New York, NY: Springer.

Bytheway, W. (1994) *Ageism*. Buckingham: Open University Press.

Calasanti, T. and Zajicek, A. (1993) A socialist feminist approach to aging: embracing diversity, *Journal of Aging Studies*, 7(2): 117–31.

Calasanti, T.M. (1993) Introduction: a socialist–feminist approach to aging, *Journal of Aging Studies*, 7 (2): 117–31.

Calasanti, T.M. (1996) Incorporating diversity: meaning, levels of research, and implications for theory, *The Gerontologist*, 36: 147–56.

Callahan, D. (1987) Setting limits, in P. Homer and M.A. Holstein (eds) *Good Old Age?* New York, NY: Simon and Schuster.

Callahan, D. (1990) Why we must set limits, in H.R. Moody, *Aging Concepts and Controversies*, 2nd edn. Thousand Oaks, CA: Pine Forge Press.

Caro, F., Bass, S. and Chen, Y. (1993) *Achieving a Productive Aging Society*. Westport, CT: Auburn House.

Carrigan, T., Connell, R.W. and Lee, J. (1987) Towards a new sociology of masculinity, in M. Kaufman (ed.) *Beyond Patriarchy: Essays by Men on Pleasure, Power and Change*. Toronto: Oxford University Press.

Carstensen, L. (1993) Motivation for social contact across the lifespan, in J. Jacobs (ed.) *Nebraska Symposium on Motivation*. Lincoln: Nebraska University Press.

Castells, M. (1989) *The Informational City*. Cambridge, MA: Blackwell.

Castells, M. (1996) *The Rise of the Network Society*. Oxford: Blackwell.

Cavan, R.S., Burgess, E.W., Havighurst, R.J. and Goldhamer, H. (1949) *Personal Adjustment in Old Age*. Chicago, IL: Science Research Associates.

Central Intelligence Agency (2001) *Long-term Global Demographic Trends: Reshaping the Geopolitical Landscape*. Virginia: CIA.

Chopra, D. (1993) *Ageless Body, Timeless Mind*. New York, NY: Rider Books.

Ciscel, D.H. and Heath, J.A. (2001) To market, to market: imperial capitalism's destruction of social capital and the family, *Review of Radical Political Economics*, 33 (4): 401–14.

Clarke, P. and Marshall, V. (2001) Social theory and the meaning of illness in later life. Paper to 17th World Congress of the International Association of Gerontology, Vancouver.

Cochran, M., Larner, M., Riley, D., Gunnarsson, L. Jr. and Henderson, C.R. (1990) *Extending Families*. Cambridge: Cambridge University Press.

Cole, D. and Utting, J. (1962) *The Economic Circumstances of Older People*. Welwyn: Codicote Press.

Cole, T., Van Tassel, D. and Kastenbaum, R. (eds) (1992) *Handbook of the Humanities and Aging*. New York, NY: Springer.

Cole, T., Achenbaum, A., Jakobi, P. and Kastenbaum, R. (eds) (1993) *Voices and Visions of Aging: Toward a Critical Gerontology*. New York, NY: Springer.

Cole, T.R. (1992) *The Journey of Life: A Cultural History of Aging in America*. Cambridge: Cambridge University Press.

Coleman, P. (1996) Identity management in later life, in R. Wood (ed.) *Handbook of the Clinical Psychology of Ageing*. Chichester: Wiley.

Collins, P.H. (1991) *Black Feminist Thought. Knowledge, Consciousness, and the Politics of Empowerment*. New York, NY: Routledge.

Commonwealth Fund (2002) *Cultural Competence in Health Care.* New York, NY: The Commonwealth Fund.

Connell, R.W. (1983) The concept of 'role' and what to do with it, in R.W. Connell, *Which Way is UP?* Sydney: Allen and Unwin, first published in *Australian and New Zealand Journal of Sociology* (1979) 15: 7–17.

Connell, R.W. (1985) Theorising gender, *Sociology*, 19: 262–4.

Connell, R.W. (1987) *Gender and Power: Society, the Person and Sexual Politics.* Sydney: Allen and Unwin.

Connell, R.W. (1995) *Masculinities.* Sydney: Allen and Unwin.

Connell, R.W. (1996) Politics of changing men, *Arena*, 6(56).

Connell, R.W. (2000) *The Men and the Boys.* Sydney: Allen and Unwin.

Coombs, W.T. and Holladay, S. (1995) The emerging political power of the elderly, in J. Nussbaum and J. Coupland (eds) *Handbook of Communication and Aging Research.* New Jersey, NJ: Lawrence Erlbaum Associates.

Cooper, A. (2001) The state of mind we're in, in S. Hall, D. Massey and M. Rustin (eds) *Soundings*, 15: 118–38. London: Lawrence and Wishart.

Costa, P.T. and McCrae, R.R. (1980) Still stable after all these years, in P.B. Bartes and O.G. Brim (eds) *Lifespan Development and Behavior*, Volume 3. New York, NY: Academic Press.

Cowdry, E.V. (1939) *Problems of Ageing.* Baltimore: Williams and Wilkins Co.

Cowgill, D.O. and Holmes, L.D. (eds) (1972) *Aging and Modernization.* New York, NY: Appleton Century-Crofts.

Crawford, M. (1971) Retirement and disengagement, *Human Relations*, 24: 255–78.

Cumming, E. and Henry, W.E. (1961) *Growing Old: The Process of Disengagement.* New York, NY: Basic Books.

Daatland, S. (2002) Time to pay back? Is there something for psychology and sociology in gerontology?, in L. Andersson (ed.) *Cultural Gerontology.* Westport, CT: Auburn House.

Daniels, N. (1988) *Am I My Parents' Keeper?* New York, NY: Oxford University Press.

Dannefer, D. (2000) Whose life course is it anyway?, in R. Stetteron, *An Invitation to the Life Course.* New York, NY: Springer.

Dannefer, D. (2002) Towards a global geography of the life course: challenges of late modernity for life course theory, in J.T. Mortimer and M. Shanahan (eds) *The Future of the Life Course.* New York, NY: Kluwer Publishers.

Dannefer, D. and Uhlenberg, P. (1999) Paths of the life course: a typology, in V.L. Bengtson and K.W. Schaie (eds) *Handbook of Theories of Aging.* New York, NY: Springer.

De Martino, G. (2000) *Global Economy, Global Justice: Theoretical Objections and Policy Alternatives to Neoliberalism.* New York, NY: Routledge.

Deacon, B. (2000) *Globalisation and Social Policy: The Threat to Equitable Welfare*, Occasional Paper no. 5, Globalisation and Social Policy Programme (GASPP). Geneva: United Nations Research Institute for Social Development.

Demetriou, D.Z. (2001) Connell's concept of hegemonic masculinity: a critique, *Theory and Society*, 30: 337–61.

Department of Health (2001) *National Service Framework for Older People*. London: Department of Health.

Diamond, T. (1992) *Making Gray Gold: Narratives of Nursing Home Care*. Chicago, IL: University of Chicago Press.

Dickinson, J. and Russell, B. (1986) *Family, Economy and State: The Social Reproduction Process under Capitalism*. New York, NY: St. Martin's Press.

Dobson, A. (2000) *Green Political Thought*. London: Routledge.

Dowd, J.J. (1975) Aging as exchange: a preface to theory, *Journal of Gerontology*, 30: 584–94.

Dressel, P., Minkler, M. and Yen, I. (1998) Gender, race, class, and aging: advances and opportunities, in M. Minkler and C.L. Estes (eds) *Critical Gerontology*. Amityville, NY: Baywood Publishing.

Dressel, P.L. (1988) Gender, race and class: beyond the feminization of poverty in later life, *The Gerontologist*, 28(2): 177–80.

Du Boff R.B. and Herman, E.S. (1997) Globalization is *an* issue. The power of capital is *the* issue. *Monthly Review*, 49(6).

Ebrahim, S. (2002) The medicalisation of old age, *British Medical Journal*, 324: 861–3.

Edelman, M. (1977) *Political Language: Words That Succeed and Policies That Fail*. New York, NY: Academic Press.

Ehrenreich, B. and Ehrenreich, J. (1971) *The American Health Empire*. New York, NY: Vintage.

Ekerdt, D. (1986) The busy ethic: Moral continuity between work and retirement, *The Gerontologist*, 26(3): 239–44.

Elder, G.H. (1974) *Children of the Great Depression*. Chicago, IL: University of Chicago Press.

England, S.E, Keigher, S.M., Miller, B. and Linsk, N.L. (1987) Community care policies and gender justice, *International Journal of Health Services*, 17 (2): 217–32.

Epstein, H. (2001) Time of indifference, *New York Review of Books*, 12 April: 33–8.

Erikson, E. (1950) *Childhood and Society*. New York, NY: Norton.

Erikson, E., Erikson, J. and Kivnick, H. (1982) *The Lifecycle Completed*. New York, NY: Norton.

Erikson, E., Erikson, J. and Kivnick, H. (1986) *Vital Involvement in Old Age*. New York, NY: Norton.

Esping-Andersen, G. (1990) *The Three Worlds of Welfare Capitalism*. Cambridge: Polity Press.

Esping-Andersen, G. (1994) *After the Golden Age: The Future of the Welfare State in the New Global Order*, occasional paper no. 7. Geneva: United Nations Research Institute for Social Development.

Esping-Andersen, G. (ed.) (1996) *Welfare States in Transition.* Thousand Oaks, CA: Sage Publications.

Esping-Andersen, G. (2000) Three worlds of welfare capitalism, in C. Pierson and F. Castles (eds) *The Welfare State Reader.* Cambridge: Polity Press.

Estes, C.L. (1978) Political gerontology, *Transaction Society,* 15: 43–9.

Estes, C.L. (1979a) *The Aging Enterprise.* San Francisco, CA: Josey-Bass.

Estes, C.L. (1979b) Toward a sociology of political gerontology, *Sociological Symposium,* no. 26, Spring: 1–25.

Estes, C.L. (1981) The social construction of reality: a framework for inquiry, in P.R. Lee, N.B. Ramsay and I. Red (eds) *The Nation's Health.* San Francisco, CA: Boyd and Fraser.

Estes, C.L. (1983) Social security: the social construction of a crisis, *Milbank Memorial Fund Quarterly/Health and Society,* 61(3): 445–61.

Estes, C.L. (1986) The politics of ageing in America, in C. Phillipson, M. Bernard and P. Strang (eds) *Dependency and Interdependency in Later Life: Theoretical Perspectives and Policy Alternatives.* London: Croom Helm.

Estes, C.L. (1991a) The new political economy of aging: introduction and critique in M. Minkler and C.L. Estes (eds) *Critical Perspectives on Aging: The Political and Moral Economy of Growing Old.* Amityville, NY: Baywood Publishing.

Estes, C.L. (1991b) The Reagan legacy: privatization, the welfare state, and aging in the 1990s, in J. Myles and J. Quadagno (eds) *States, Labour Markets and the Future of Old Age Policy.* Philadelphia, PA: Temple University Press.

Estes, C.L. (1993) The aging enterprise revisited, *The Gerontologist,* 33 (3): 292–8.

Estes, C.L. (1998) *Crisis and the Welfare State in Aging.* American Sociological Association. August. San Francisco, CA.

Estes, C.L. (1999) Critical gerontology and the new political economy of aging, in M. Minkler and C.L. Estes (eds) *Critical Gerontology.* Amityville, NY: Baywood Publishing.

Estes, C.L. (2000) The political economy of aging, in G. Maddox (ed.) *The Encyclopedia of Aging.* New York, NY: Springer.

Estes, C.L. (2001a) Crisis, the welfare state, and aging: ideology and agency in the social security privatization debate, in C.L. Estes and Associates *Social Policy and Aging: A Critical Perspective.* Thousand Oaks, CA: Sage Publications.

Estes, C.L. (2001b) Political economy of aging: a theoretical framework, in C.L. Estes and Associates, *Social Policy and Aging: A Critical Perspective.* Thousand Oaks, CA: Sage Publications.

Estes, C.L. (2001c) Sex and gender in the political economy of aging, in C.L. Estes and Associates, *Social Policy and Aging: A Critical Perspective.* Thousand Oaks, CA: Sage Publications.

Estes, C.L. (2001d) Long term care policy and politics. Distinguished Scholar Award Lecture, American Sociological Association Section on Aging and the Life Course, Anaheim, California, 19 August.

Estes, C.L. (2001e) From gender to the political economy of ageing, *European Journal of Social Quality*, 2(1): 28–46

Estes, C.L. and Alford, R. (1990) Systemic crisis and the nonprofit sector, *Theory and Society*, 19(2): 173–98.

Estes, C.L. and Binney, E.A. (1989) The biomedicalization of aging: dangers and dilemmas, *The Gerontologist*, 29 (5): 587–96.

Estes, C.L. and Binney, E.A. (1990) *Older Women and the State* (unpublished manuscript). San Francisco, CA: UCSF Institute of Health and Aging.

Estes, C.L. and Linkins, K.W. (1999) Critical health and aging, in G.L. Albrecht, R. Fitzpatrick, S.C. Scrimshaw (eds) *Handbook of Social Science in Medicine and Health*. Newbury Park, CA: Sage Publications.

Estes, C.L. and Mahakian, J. (2001) The political economy of productive aging, in N. Morrow-Howell, J. Hirtezlong and M. Sheraden (eds) *Productive Aging Concepts and Challenges*. Baltimore, MD: John Hopkins University Press.

Estes, C.L. and Phillipson, C. (2003) The globalization of capital, the welfare state, and old age policy, *International Journal of Health Services*, 32(2): 279–97.

Estes, C.L., Swan, J.H. and Gerard, L. (1982) Dominant and competing paradigms: toward a political economy of aging, *Ageing and Society*, 2 (2): 151–64.

Estes, C.L., Gerard, L., Zones, J.S. and Swan, J. (1984) *Political Economy, Health, and Aging*. Boston, MA: Little, Brown.

Estes, C.L., Binney, E.A. and Culbertson, R.A. (1992a) The gerontological imagination: social influences on the development of gerontology, 1945–present, *International Journal of Aging and Human Development*, 35 (1): 49–65.

Estes, C.L., Swan, J.H., Bergthold, L.A. and Hanes-Spohn, P. (1992b) Running as fast as they can: organizational changes in home health care, *Home Health Care Services Quarterly*, 13(1/2): 35–69.

Estes, C.L., Swan, J.H. and Associates (1993) *The Long Term Care Crisis*. Newbury Park, CA: Sage Publications.

Estes, C.L, Linkins, K.W. and Binney, E.A. (1995) The political economy of aging, in L. George and R. Binstock (eds) *Handbook of Aging and the Social Sciences*, 4th edn. San Diego, CA: Academic Press.

Estes, C.L., Kelly, S.E. and Binney, E.A. (1996a) Bioethics in a disposable society: health care and the intergenerational stake, in J.W. Walters (ed.) *Choosing Who's to Live: Ethics and Aging*. Urbana, IL: University of Illinois Press.

Estes, C.L., Goldberg, S., Shostak, S. *et al.* (2000a) Implications of welfare reform for the elderly: provider, advocate and consumer perspectives in a local community, in *Effects of Devolution on Long Term Care for the Elderly in San Francisco*, Final Report Submitted to the San Francisco Foundation. San Francisco, CA: Institute for Health and Aging, UCSF.

Estes, C.L., Wallace, S. and Linkins, K.W. (2000b) The political economy of health and aging, in C.E. Bird, P. Conrad and A.M. Fremont (eds) *The Handbook of Medical Sociology*, 5th edn. Upper Saddle River, NJ: Prentice Hall.

Estes, C.L., Harrington, C. and Pellow, D.N. (2001a) The medical–industrial complex and the aging enterprise, in C.L. Estes and Associates, *Social Policy and Aging: A Critical Perspective*. Thousand Oaks, CA: Sage Publications.

Estes, C.L., Mahakian, J. and Weitz, T.A. (2001b) A political economy critique of 'productive aging', in C.L. Estes and Associates, *Social Policy and Aging: A Critical Perspective*. Thousand Oaks, CA: Sage Publications.

Estes, C.L. and Associates (2001) *Social Policy and Aging: A Critical Perspective*. Thousand Oaks, CA: Sage Publications.

Evans, R.G., McGrail, K.M., Morgan, S.G., Barer, M.L. and Hertzman, C. (2001) Apocalypse no: population aging and the future of health care systems, *Canadian Journal on Aging*, 20 (suppl. 1): 160–91.

Faber, M. and van der Wiel, A. (2001) Successful aging in the oldest old, *Archives of Internal Medicine*, 161: 2694–700.

Faist, T. (2000) *The Volume and Dynamics of International Migration and Transnational Social Spaces*. Oxford: Clarendon Press.

Falkingham, J. (1998) Financial (in)security in later life, in M. Bernard and J. Phillips (eds) *The Social Policy of Old Age*. London: Centre for Policy on Ageing.

Families USA (2002) *Out of Pocket Medicare Costs*. Washington, DC: Families USA Foundation.

Featherstone, M. (1991) *Consumer Culture and Postmodernism*. London: Sage Publications.

Featherstone, M. and Hepworth, M. (1983) The midlifestyles of George and Lynne. *Theory, Culture and Society* 1 (3): 85–92.

Featherstone, M. and Hepworth, M. (1989) Ageing and old age: reflections on the post-modern life course, in W. Bytheway (ed.) *Becoming and Being Old: Sociological Approaches to Later Life*. London: Sage Publications.

Featherstone, M. and Hepworth, M. (1990) Images of ageing, in J. Bond and P. Coleman (eds) *Ageing in Society*. London: Sage Publications.

Featherstone, M. and Hepworth, M. (1995) Images of positive ageing, in M. Featherstone and A. Wernick, *Images of Ageing*. London: Routledge.

Featherstone, M. and Wernick, A. (1995) *Images of Ageing*. London: Routledge.

Fennell, G., Phillipson, C. and Evers, H. (1988) *The Sociology of Old Age*. Milton Keynes: Open University Press.

Ferree, M.M. and Hall, E.J. (1996) Rethinking stratification from a feminist perspective: gender, race and class, in *Mainstream Textbooks, ASR*, 61 (Dec.): 929–50.

Finch, J. (1995) Responsibilities, obligations and commitments, in I. Allen and E. Perkins (eds) *The Future of Family Care for Older People*. London: HMSO.

Firestone, S. (1979) *The Dialectic of Sex: The Case for Feminist Revolution*, reprint edn. London: The Women's Press.

Fischer, C.S. (1982) *To Dwell Amongst Friends*. Chicago, IL: University of Chicago Press.

Fischetti, M. and Stix, G. (eds) (2000) When life knows no bounds, *Scientific American*, 11(2): 6–7.

Folbre, N. (2001) *The Invisible Heart: Economics and Family Values*. New York, NY: New York Press.

Foster, J. (2002) It is not a postcapitalist world, nor is it a post-Marxist one, Interview in *Evrensel Kultur (Universal Culture)*, September, 129.

Foucault, M. (1973) *The Birth of The Clinic*. London: Tavistock.

Foucault, M. (1975) *Discipline and Punish*. London: Penguin.

Foucault, M. (1976) *The History of Sexuality*, vol. 1. London: Penguin.

Foucault, M. (1980) *Power/Knowledge: Selected Interviews and Other Writings*, edited by C. Gordon. New York, NY: Pantheon Books.

Foucault, M. (1988) *Technologies of the Self*. Amherst, MA: University of Massachusetts Press.

Fox, B. (ed) (1988) *Family Bonds and Gender Divisions: Readings in the Sociology of the Family*. Toronto: Canadian Scholars' Press.

Francis, D. (1984) *Will You Still Need Me, Will You Still Feed Me, When I'm 84?* Bloomington, IN: Indiana University Press.

Frank, A. (1998a) Foucault or not Foucault? Commonwealth and American perspectives on health in the neo-liberal state, *Health*, 2(2): 233–43.

Frank, A. (1998b) Stories of illness as care of the self, *Health*, 2(3): 329–48.

Frankel, V. (1969) *The Doctor and the Soul*. London: Penguin.

Fraser, N. (1997) *Justice Interruptus*. New York, NY: Routledge.

Freud, S. ([1905] 1953) *On Psychotherapy*, Collected Works, Volume 7. London: Hogarth.

Friedland, R.B. and Summer, L. (1999) *Demography is Not Destiny*. Washington, DC: National Academy on an Aging Society, Gerontological Society of America.

Fries, J.E. (1980) Aging, natural death and the compression of morbidity, *New England Journal of Medicine*, 303(3): 130–5.

Frosh, S. (1991) *Identity Crisis: Modernity, Psychoanalysis and the Self*. London: Macmillan.

Fry, C.L., Dickson-Putman, J. and Draper, P. (1997) Culture and the meaning of a good old age, in J. Sokolovsky (ed.) *The Cultural Context of Aging*. Westport, CT: Bergin and Garvey.

Gardner, K. (2002) *Age, Narrative and Migration*. Oxford: Berg.

Gee, E.M. and Gutman, G.M. (2000) *The Overselling of Population Aging: Apocalyptic Demography, Intergenerational Challenges and Social Policy*. Don Mills, Ontario: Oxford.

George, L.K. (1990) Social structure, social processes, and social psychological states, in R.H. Binstock and L.K. George (eds) *Handbook of Aging and the Social Sciences*. San Diego, CA: Academic Press.

George, L.K. (1993) Sociological perspectives on life course transitions, *Annual Review of Sociology*, 19: 353–73.

Gergen, K. (1991) *The Saturated Self*. New York, NY: Basic Books.

Giddens, A. (1984) *The Constitution of Society*. Cambridge: Polity Press.

Giddens, A. (1991) *Modernity and Self-Identity*. Cambridge: Polity Press.

Giddens, A. (1999) *Globalisation*, BBC Reith Lecture 1. BBC On Line Network.

Gilleard, C. (1996) Consumption and identity in later life, *Ageing and Society*, 16: 489–98.

Gilleard, C. and Higgs, P. (2000) *Cultures of Ageing: Self, Citizen and the Body*. London: Prentice-Hall.

Gilligan, C. (1986) In a different voice, in M. Pearsall (ed.) *Women and Values*. Belmont, CA: Wadsworth.

Gillon, R. (1986) *Philosophical Medical Ethics*. Chichester: Wiley.

Ginn, J. (2001) Privatising pensions: new options and new risks for women, in N. Gilbert, *Researching Social Life*. London: Sage Publications.

Ginn, J. and Arber, S. (1995) Only connect: gender relations and aging, in S. Arber and J. Ginn (eds) *Connecting Gender and Aging*. Philadelphia, PA: Open University Press.

Ginn, J., Street, D. and Arber, S. (eds) (2001) *Women, Work, and Pensions: International Issues and Prospects*. Buckingham and Philadelphia, PA: Open University Press.

Gold, D.A., Lo, C.Y.H. and Wright, E.O. (1975) Recent developments in Marxist theories of the capitalist state, *Monthly Review*, 27(5): 29–43.

Gold, M. and Achman, L. (2002) *Average Out of Pocket Health Care Costs for Medicare + Choice Enrollees Increase Substantially in 2002*. New York, NY: The Commonwealth Fund.

Good, B.J. (1997) *Medicine, Rationality and Experience: An Anthropological Perspective*. New York, NY: Cambridge.

Goodman, D. (2002) Campaigning and the pensioners' movement, in B. Bytheway, V. Bacigalupo, J. Bornat, J. Johnson and S. Spurt, *Understanding Care, Welfare and Community*. London: Routledge in association with the Open University.

Gouldner, A. (1970) *The Coming Crisis of Western Sociology*. London: Heinemann.

Graebner, W. (1980) *A History of Retirement: The Meaning and Function of An American Institution, 1885–1978*. New Haven, CT: Yale University Press.

Gramsci, A. (1971) *Selections from Prison Notebooks*. Edited and translated by Q. Hoare, and G. Nowell-Smith. London: Lawrence and Wishart.

Gubrium, J.F. (1986) *Oldtimers and Alzheimers: The Descriptive Organization of Senility*. Greenwith, CT: Jai Press.

Gubrium, J.F. (1993) Voice and context in a new gerontology, in T. Cole, P. Achenbaum, P. Jakobi and R. Kastenbaum (eds) *Voices and Visions of Aging: Toward a Critical Gerontology*. New York, NY: Springer.

Gubrium, J.F. and Holstein, J.A. (1999) Constructionist perspectives on aging, in V.L. Bengtson and K.W. Shaie (eds) *Handbook of Theories of Aging*. New York, NY: Springer.

Gubrium, J.F. and Wallace, J. (1991) Who theorises age? *Ageing and Society*, 10: 131–49.

Guillemard, A.M. (1977) *A Critical Analysis of Governmental Policies on Aging from a Marxist Sociological Perspective*. Paris: Center for Study of Social Movements.

Guillemard, A.M. (1980) *La vielless l'etat*. Paris: Presses Universitaires de France.

Guillemard, A.M. (1983) (ed.) *Old Age and the Welfare State*. New York, NY: Sage Publications.

Gulati, L. (1994) *In the Absence of their Men*. New Delhi: Sage Publications.

Gullette, M.M. (2003) *New Time Machines: Practicing Critical Aging Studies*. Chicago, IL: University of Chicago Press.

Habermas, J. (1975) *Legitimation Crisis*. Boston, MA: Beacon Press.

Hagestad, G. and Dannefer, D. (2001) Concepts and theories of aging: beyond microfication in social science approaches, in R. Binstock and L. George, *Handbook of Aging and the Social Sciences*, 5th edn. San Diego, CA: Academic Press.

Hahn, M. and Kaplan, G.A. (1985) The contribution of socio-economic position to minority health, in M. Heckler (ed.) *Report of the Secretary's Task Force on Black and Minority Health*. Washington, DC: USA Department of Health and Human Services.

Hall, G.S. (1922) *Senescence*. New York, NY: D. Appleton and Sons.

Hall, S., Held, D., Hubert, D. and Thompson, K. (1997) *Modernity*. Malden, MA: Blackwell.

Harding, E., Cummings, S. and Bodenheimer, T. (eds) (1972) *Billions for Band-Aids*. San Francisco, CA: Bay Area Medical Committee for Human Rights.

Harding, S. (1996) Standpoint epistemology (a feminist version): how social disadvantage creates epistemic advantage, in S.P. Turner (ed.) *Social Theory and Sociology: The Classics and Beyond*. Cambridge, MA: Blackwell.

Harrington Meyer, M. (1990) Family status and poverty among older women: the gendered distribution of retirement income in the US, *Social Problems*, 37(4): 551–63.

Harrington Meyer, M. (1996) Making claims as workers or wives: the distribution of social security benefits, *American Sociological Review*, 61 (3): 449–65.

Harrington, Michael (1963) *The Other America*. Baltimore, MD: Penguin.

Harrington, Mona (2000) *Care and Equality: Inventing A New Family Politics*. New York, NY: Routledge.

Havighurst, R.J. and Albrecht, R. (1953) *Older People*. London: Longmans, Green.

Havighurst, R.J., Neugarten, B.L. and Tobin, J.S. (1963) *Disengagement and Patterns of Aging*. Chicago, IL: University of Chicago Press.

Held, D. and McGrew, A. (2002) *Governing Globalization: Power, Authority and Global Governance*. Cambridge: Polity Press.

Held, D., McGrew, A., Goldblatt, D. and Perraton, J. (1999) *Global Transformations*. Cambridge: Polity Press.

HelpAge International (2000) *The Mark of a Noble Society*. London: HelpAge International.

Hendricks, J. (1992) Generations and the generation of theory in social gerontology, *International Journal of Aging and Human Development*, 35 (1): 31–47.

Hendricks, J. and Achenbaum, A. (1999) Historical development of theories of aging, in V.L. Bengtson and K.W.S. Shaie (eds) (1999) *Handbook of Theories of Aging*. New York, NY: Springer Publishing Co.

Hendricks, J. and Leedham, C. (1991) Dependency or empowerment? Toward a moral and political economy of aging, in M. Minkler and C.L. Estes (eds) *Critical Perspectives on Aging: The Political and Moral Economy of Growing Old*. Amityville, NY: Baywood Publishing.

Hendricks, J. *et al.* (1999) Entitlements, social compacts, and the trend toward retrenchment in USA old-age programs, *Hallym International Journal of Aging*, 1(1): 14–32.

Hennessy, P. (1993) *Never Again: Britain 1945–1951*. London: Vintage Books.

Hepworth, M. (1991) Positive ageing and the mask of age, *Journal of Educational Gerontology*, 6(2): 93–101.

Hermans, H. and Hermans-Jansen, E. (2001) Dialogical processes and the development of self, in J. Valsiner and K. Connoly (eds) *Handbook of Developmental Psychology*. London: Sage Publications.

Hernes, H.M. (1987) *Welfare State and Woman Power: Essays in State Feminism*. Oslo/Oxford: Norwegian University Press, distributed by Oxford University Press.

Hewitson, G. (1999) *Feminist Economics: Interrogating the Masculinity of Rational Man*. Edwin Elgar Publications.

Himmelweit, S. (1983) Reproduction, in T. Bottomore (ed.) *Dictionary of Marxist Thought*. Cambridge, MA: Harvard University Press.

Hinterlong, J., Morrow-Howell, N. and Sherraden, M. (2001) Productive aging: principles and perspectives, in N. Morrow-Howell, J. Hinterlong and M. Sherraden (eds) *Productive Aging: Concepts and Challenges*. Baltimore, MD: Johns Hopkins University Press.

Hochschild, A. (2000) Global care chains and emotional surplus value, in W. Hutton and A. Giddens, *On the Edge: Living with Global Capitalism*. London: Cape.

Hodgekin, D. (1996) Medicine, postmodernism and the end of certainty, *British Medical Journal*, 313: 1568–9.

Hoffmaster, B. (1991) The theory and practice of applied ethics, *Dialogue 30:* 213–34.

Holstein, J. and Gubrium, J. (2000) *The Self We Live By*. New York, NY: Oxford University Press.

Holstein, M. (1992) Productive aging: a feminist critique, *Journal of Aging and Social Policy*, 4(3–4): 17–34.

Holstein, M. (1999) Women and productive aging: troubling implications, in M. Minkler and C.L. Estes (eds) *Critical Gerontology: Perspectives from Policial and Moral Economy*. Amityville, NY: Baywood Publishing.

Holstein, M. and Cole, T. (1996) Reflections on age, meaning and chronic illness, *Journal of Aging and Identity*, 1(1): 7–21.

Holtzman, R. (1997) A world perspective on pension reform. Paper prepared for the joint ILO-OECD Workshop on the Development and Reform of Pension Schemes, Paris, December.

Hooyman, N. and Gonyea, J. (1995) *Feminist Perspectives on Family Care: Policies and Gender Justice*. Newbury Park, CA: Sage Publications.

House, J., Kessler, C. and Herzog, A.R. (1990) Age, socioeconomic status, and health, *Milbank Quarterly*, 68: 383–411.

Hummert, M.L. and Nussbaum, J.F. (2001) *Aging, Communication and Health*. New Jersey, NJ: Lawrence Erlbaum.

Hunter, F. (1963) *Community Power Structure*. Chapel Hill, NC: University of North Carolina Press.

Hutton, W. and Giddens, A. (eds) *On the Edge: Living with Global Capitalism*. London: Cape.

International Labor Organization (2000) Press Release, 28 April, Geneva.

Jackson, J. and Antonucci, T. (2002) Attitudes of western countries on immigrants' ageing in place and later life immigration. Paper to Gerontological Association of America, 55th Annual Meeting, Boston.

Jackson, J.S. (2001) Changes over the lifecourse in productive activities: comparison of black and white populations, in N. Morrow-Howell, J. Hinterlong and M. Sherraden (eds) *Productive Aging, Concepts and Challenges*. Baltimore, MD: Johns Hopkins University Press.

Jaggar, A.M. and Rothenberg, P.S. (1984) *Feminist Frameworks*. New York, NY: McGraw-Hill.

Jamieson, L. (1998) *Intimacy: Personal Relationships in Modern Societies*. Oxford: Polity Press.

Johnson, P., Conrad, C. and Thomson, D. (eds) (1989) *Workers versus Pensioners: Intergenerational Justice in an Ageing World*. Manchester: Manchester University Press.

Jones, K. (1990) Citizenship in a woman friendly polity, *Signs*, 15(4): 781–812.

Jung, C. ([1932] 1967) *Collected Works*, vol. 7. London: Routledge.

Kagarlitsky, B. (1999) The challenge for the Left: reclaiming the state, in L. Panitch and C. Leys (eds) *Socialist Register 1999: Global Capitalism versus Democracy*. New York, NY: Monthly Review Press.

Kastenbaum, R. (1993) Encrusted elders, in T. Cole (ed.) *Voices and Visions of Aging*. Charlottesville, VA: University Press of Virginia.

Katz, S. (1996) *Disciplining Old Age*. Charlottesville, VA: University Press of Virginia.

Katz, S. (1999) Fashioning agehood: lifestyle imagery and the commercial spirit of seniors culture, in J. Povlesen (ed.) *Childhood and Old Age*. Odense: Odense University Press.

Katz, S. (2000a) Reflections on *The Gerontological Handbook*, in T.R. Cole and R.E. Ray (eds) *Handbook of the Humanities and Aging*, 2nd edn. New York, NY: Springer.

Katz, S. (2000b) Busy bodies: activity, aging and the management of everyday life, *Journal of Aging Studies*, 14(2): 135–52.

Kaufman, S. (1986) *The Ageless Self*. New York, NY: Meridian.

Kenen, J. (1999) Social Security, Medicare Bankruptcy Delayed, *Los Angeles Times*, 31 March.

Klein, N. (2000) *No Logo: Taking Aim at the Brand Bullies*. London: Flamingo.

Knuttila, M. (1996) *Introducing Sociology: A Critical Perspective*. New York, NY: Oxford University Press.

Kohli, M. (1987) Retirement and the moral economy: an historical interpretation of the German case, *Journal of Aging Studies*, 1: 125–44.

Kohli, M. (1988) Ageing as a challenge for sociological theory, *Ageing and Society*, 8: 367–94.

Kohli, M. (1989) *Lebenslauf, Familie und Generationen*. Berlin: Free University Press.

Krause, E.A. (1996) *Death of the Guilds*. New Haven, CT: Yale University Press.

Krugman, P. (2002) The private interest, *New York Times*, Editorial/Op-Ed. 7/26/02. *www.nytimes.com/2002/07/26/opinion/26KRUG.html?tntemail1*

Kuhn, M. (1977) *Maggie Kuhn on Aging*. Philadelphia, PA: Westminster Press.

Kuumba, M.B. (2001) *Gender and Social Movements*. Walnut Creek, CA: Alta Mira Press.

Lambley, P. (1995) *The Middle Aged Rebel*. Shaftesbury: Element.

Lang, F. and Cartensen, L. (1994) Close emotional relationships in later life: further support for proactive aging in the social domain, *Psychology and Aging*, 9: 315–24.

Larabee, M.J. (ed.) (1993) *An Ethic of Care: Feminist and Interdisciplinary Perspectives*. New York, NY: Routledge.

Lash, S. and Urry, J. (1987) *The End of Organized Capitalism*. Cambridge: Polity Press.

Laws, G. (1995) Understanding ageism: Lessons from feminism and postmodernism, *The Gerontologist*, 35: 112–16.

Lerner, G. (1986) *The Creation of Patriarchy*. New York, NY: Oxford University Press.

Levinson, D. (1986) *The Seasons of a Man's Life*, New York, NY: Knopf.

Levitas, R. (1986) Competition and compliance: the utopias of the New Right, in R. Levitas (ed.) *The Ideology of the New Right*. Cambridge, MA: Polity Press.

Levitt, P. (2001) *The Transnational Villagers*. Berkeley, CA: University of California Press.

Litwak, E. (1960) Occupational mobility and extended family cohesion, *American Sociological Review*, 25: 9–21.

Longman, P. (1987) *Born to Pay: The Politics of Aging in America*. Boston, MA: Houghton Mifflin.

Lorber, J. (1998) *Gender Inequality: Feminist Theories and Politics*. Los Angeles, CA: Roxbury Publishing.

Lowe, R. (1993) *The Welfare State in Britain Since 1945*. London: Macmillan.

Lowenthal, M.F. (1975) Psychological variations across the adult life course: frontiers for research and policy, *The Gerontologist*, 15 (Pt. 1): 6–12.

Lowi, T. (1964) American business, public policy and political theory, *World Politics*, 16: 677–715.

Lynott, R. and Lynott, P.P. (1996) Tracing the course of theoretical development in the sociology of aging, *The Gerontologist*, 36 (6): 749–60.

McAdams, D. (1993) *The Stories We Live By*. New York, NY: Morrow.

McCallister, L. and Fischer, C. (1978) A procedure for surveying personal networks, *Sociological Methods and Research*, 7: 131–47.

McGinnis, J.M. and Foege, W.H. (1993) Actual causes of death in the USA, *Journal of the American Medical Association*, 270 (18): 2207–13.

McKenzie, J.K., Moss, A.H., Feest, T.G., Stocking, C.B. and Siegler, M. (1988) Dialysis decision making in Canada, the United Kingdom, and the United States, *American Journal of Kidney Diseases*, 31: 12–18.

McKenzie, R.B. (1993) Senior status: has the power of the elderly peaked?, *American Enterprise* 4 (3): 74–80.

McKeown, T. (1997) Determinants of health, in P.R. Lee and C.L. Estes (eds) *The Nation's Health*, 5th edn. Sudbury, MA: Jones and Bartlett.

McKinlay, J. and Stoekle, J. (1988) Corporatization and the social transformation of doctoring, *International Journal of Health Services*, 18: 191–205.

McKinlay, J.B., McKinlay, S.M. and Beaglehole, R. (1989) Trends in death and disease and the contribution of medical measures, in H.E. Freeman and S. Levine (eds) *Handbook of Medical Sociology*, 4th edn. Englewood Cliffs, NJ: Prentice-Hall.

McLeod, J. (1997) *Narrative and Psychotherapy*. London: Sage Publications.

McMullin, J.A. (1995) Theorizing age and gender relations, in S. Arber and J. Ginn (eds) *Connecting Gender and Ageing: A Sociological Approach*. Philadelphia, PA: Open University Press.

Macnicol, J. (1998) *The Politics of Retirement in Britain 1878–1948*. Cambridge: Cambridge University Press.

Marcuse, E. (1964) *One Dimensional Man*. London: Penguin.

Markides, K.S. and Black, S.A. (1995) Race, ethnicity and aging, in R. Binstock and L. George (eds) *Handbook of Aging and the Social Sciences*, 4th edn. New York, NY: Academic Press.

Marmor, T.R. (2000) *The Politics of Medicare*, 2nd edn. Hawthorne, NY: Aldine De Gruyter.

Marshall, T.H. (1949) Citizenship and social class, republished in T.H. Marshall *Sociology at the Crossroads*. London: Heinemann.

Marshall, V. (1999) Analysing theories of aging?, in V.L. Bengtson and K.W.S. Shaie (eds) (1999) *Handbook of Theories of Aging*. New York, NY: Springer.

Marshall, V. and Tindale, J.A. (1978) Notes for a radical gerontology, *International Journal of Aging and Human Development*, 9: 163–75.

Marshall, V.W. (1996) The state of aging theory in aging and the social sciences, in R.H. Binstock and L. George (eds), *Handbook of Aging and the Social Sciences*, 4th edn. San Diego, CA: Academic Press.

Marx, K. and Engels, F. ([1888] 1976) *The Communist Manifesto*. London: Penguin.

Massey, D. (2000) To study migration today, look to a parallel era. *The Chronicle of Higher Education*, 18 August, B4–B5.

Matthaei, J. (2001) Healing ourselves, healing our economy: paid work, unpaid work, and the next stage of feminist economic transformation, *Journal of Radical Political Economics*, 33 (1): 461–94.

Matza, D. (1969) *Becoming Deviant*. Englewood Cliffs, NJ: Prentice-Hall.

Mayer, K.U. and Schoepflin, U. (1989) The state and the life course, *Annual Review of Sociology*, 15: 187–209.

Meador, K. (1998) The embodied and contingent self in later life, *Aging and Identity*, 3(3): 119–31.

Miltiades, H. (2002) The social and psychological effect of an adult child's emigration on non-immigrant Asian Indian parents, *Journal of Cross-Cultural Gerontology*, 17: 33–55.

Minkler, M. and Cole, T. (1991) Political and moral economy: not such strange bedfellows, in M. Minkler and C.L. Estes (eds) *Critical Perspectives on Ageing: The Political and Moral Economy of Growing Old*. Amityville, NY: Baywood Publishing.

Minkler, M. and Cole, T. (1999) Political and moral economy: getting to know one another, in M. Minkler and C.L. Estes (eds) *Critical Gerontology: Perspectives from Political and Moral Economy*. Amityville, NY: Baywood Publishing.

Minkler, M. and Estes, C.L. (1991) *Critical Perspectives on Aging: The Political and Moral Economy of Growing Old*. Amityville, NY: Baywood Publishing.

Minkler, M. and Estes, C.L. (1998) *Critical Gerontology*. Amityville, NY: Baywood Publishing.

Minkler, M. and Estes, C.L. (eds) (1999) *Critical Gerontology: Perspectives from Political and Moral Economy*. Amityville, NY: Baywood Publishing.

Minkler, M. and Robertson, A. (1991) The ideology of age–race wars, *Ageing and Society*, 11(1): 1–22.

Mishra, R. (1999) *Globalization and the Welfare State*. Cheltenham: Edward Elgar.

Mitchell, J. (1966) *Women: The Longest Revolution*. Boston, MA: New England Free Press.

Mittelman, J.H. and Tambe, A. (2000) Global poverty and gender, in J.H. Mittelman, *The Globalization Syndrome: Transformation and Resistance*. Princeton, NJ: Princeton University Press.

Moghadam, V.M. (2000) Gender and the global economy, in M.M. Ferree, J. Lorber and B.B. Hess (eds) *Revisioning Gender*. Walnut Creek, CA: a Division of Rowman and Littlefield.

Mohanty, C.T. (1991) Introduction: cartographies of struggle, third world women and the politics of feminism, in C.T. Mohanty, A. Russo and L. Torres (eds) *Third World Women and the Politics of Feminism*. Bloomington and Indianapolis, IN: Indiana University Press.

Moody, H.R. (1988a) *Abundance of Life: Human Development Policies for an Aging Society*. New York, NY: Columbia University Press.

Moody, H.R. (1988b) Toward a critical gerontology: the contributions of the humanities of theories of aging, in J.E. Birren, V.L. Bengston and D.E. Deutchman (eds) *Emergent Theories of Aging*. New York, NY: Springer.

Moody, H.R. (1992) *Ethics in an Aging Society*. Baltimore, MD: Johns Hopkins University Press.

Moody, H.R. (1993) Overview: what is critical gerontology and why is it important?, in T.R. Cole (ed.) *Voices and Visions of Aging: Toward a Critical Gerontology*. New York, NY: Springer.

Moody, H.R. (1997) *The Five Stages of the Soul*. New York, NY: Doubleday.

Moody, H.R. (1998a) Should we ration health care for older people?, in *Aging: Concepts and Controversies*. Thousand Oaks, CA: Pine Forge Press.

Moody, H.R. (1998b) *Aging*, 2nd edn. Thousand Oaks, CA: Pine Forge Press.

Moody, H.R. (2001) Productive aging and the ideology of old age, in N. Morrow-Howell, J. Hinterlong and M. Sherraden (eds) *Productive Aging Concepts and Challenges*. Baltimore, MD: Johns Hopkins University Press.

Moody, H.R. (2002) The changing meaning of aging, in R. Weiss and S. Bass, *Challenges of the Third Age*. Oxford: Oxford University Press.

Morgan, J. (1986) Unpaid productive activity over the life course, in Committee on an Aging Society, *Productive Roles in Older Society*. Washington, DC: National Academy Press.

Morrow-Howell, N., Hinterlong, J. and Sherraden, M. (2001) *Productive Aging: Concepts and Challenges*. Baltimore, MD: Johns Hopkins University Press.

Mutari, E. (2001) . . . As broad as our life experience: visions of feminist political economy, 1972–1991, *Review of Radical Political Economics*, 33 (1): 379–99.

Myles, J. (1984) *Old Age and the Welfare State*. Lawrence, KS: University of Kansas Press.

Myles, J. (1996) Social security and support of the elderly: the western experience, in J. Quadagno and D. Street (eds) *Ageing for the Twenty-First Century*. New York, NY: St. Martin's Press.

Myles, J. and Pierson, P. (2001) The comparative political economy of pension reform, in P. Pierson (ed.) *The Politics of the Welfare State*. Oxford: Oxford University Press.

Naurigh, J. (1996) 'I am with you as never before': women in protest movements, Alexandra Townships, South Africa, 1912–1945, in K. Sheldon (ed.) *Courtyards, Markets, City Streets: Urban Women in Africa*. Boulder, CO: Westview Press.

Navarro, V. (1978) *Class Struggle, the State, and Medicine*. Oxford: Martin Robertson.

Navarro, V. (1984) Political economy of government cuts for the elderly, in M. Minkler and C.L. Estes (eds) *Readings in the Political Economy of Aging*. Amytiville, NY: Baywood Publishing.

Navarro, V. (1990) Race or class versus race and class: mortality differentials in the USA, *Lancet*, 336: 1238–40.

Navarro, V. (2000) Are pro-welfare state and full employment policies possible in the era of globalisation? *International Journal of Health Services*, 30 (2): 231–51.

Neugarten, B.L. (1964) *Personality in Middle and Late Life: Empirical Studies*. New York, NY: Atherton.

Neugarten, B.L. (1968) *Middle Age and Aging.* Chicago, IL: Chicago University Press.

Neugarten, B.L. and Hagestad, G.O. (1976) Age and the life course, in R.H. Binstock and E. Shanas (eds) *Handbook of Aging and the Social Sciences.* New York, NY: Van Nostrand Reinhold.

Neugarten, B.L., Havinghurst, R.J. and Tobin, S.S. (1968) Personality and patterns of aging, in B.L. Neugarten (ed.) *Middle Age and Aging: A Reader in Social Psychology.* Chicago, IL: University of Chicago Press.

Newhouse, J.P. (1994) An iconoclastic view of health cost containment, (Supplement), *Health Affairs,* 155.

Newman, K. (1998) Place and race, in R.A. Schweder (ed.) *Welcome to Middle-age.* Chicago, IL: University of Chicago Press.

Öberg, P. (1996) The absent body – a social gerontological paradox, *Ageing and Society,* 16: 701–19.

O'Connor, J. (1973) *The Fiscal Crisis of the State.* New York, NY: St. Martins.

O'Connor, J. (1993) Gender, class, citizenship in the comparative analysis of welfare state regimes: theoretical and methodological Issues, *British Journal of Sociology,* 44: 501–18.

O'Connor, J. (1998) *Natural Causes.* New York, NY: Guilford.

O'Connor, J.S., Orloff, A. S. and Shaver, S. (1999) *States, Markets, Families: Gender, Liberalism and Social Policy in Australia, Canada, Great Britain and the United States.* Cambridge: Cambridge University Press.

O'Kane, J. (2002) Capital, culture, and socio-economic justice, *Rethinking Marxism,* 14 (2): 1–23.

Olson, L. (1982) *The Political Economy of Aging.* New York, NY: Columbia University Press.

Omi, M. and Winant, H. (1994) *Racial Formation in the United States.* New York, NY: Routledge.

O'Rand, A. and National Academy on Aging (1994) *The Vulnerable Majority: Older Women in Transition.* Syracuse, NY: Syracuse University National Academy of Aging.

Orloff, A.S. (1993) Gender and the social rights of citizenship: the comparative analysis of gender relations and welfare states, *American Sociological Review,* 58(3): 303–29.

Ortner, S.B. (1996) *Making Gender: The Politics and Erotics of Culture.* Boston, MA: Beacon Press.

Pahl, R. and Spencer, L. (1997) Friends and neighbours, *New Statesman,* 26 September: 36–7.

Pampel, F. C. (1994) Population aging: class context and age inequality in public spending, *American Journal of Sociology,* 100 (1): 153–9.

Papastergiadis, N. (2000) *The Turbulence of Migration.* Cambridge: Polity Press.

Pappas, G. (1994) Elucidating the relationship between race, socioeconomic status, and health, *American Journal of Public Health,* 84: 892–3.

Pardes, H., Manton, K.G., Lander, E.S. *et al.* (1999) Effects of medical research on health care and the economy, *Science*, 283: 36–7.

Parker, I. (1999) *Deconstructing Psychotherapy*. London: Sage Publications.

Parsons, T. (1942) Age and sex in the social structure of the United States, *American Sociological Review*, 7: 604–16.

Pascall, G. (1986) *Social Policy: A Feminist Analysis*. London and New York, NY: Tavistock Publications.

Passuth, P. and Bengston, V. (1996) Sociological theories of aging: current perspectives and future directions in J. Quadagno and D. Street (eds) *Ageing for the Twenty-First Century*. New York, NY: St. Martin's Press.

Patel, N. (1990) *A Race Against Time*. London: Runnymede.

Pateman, C. (1989) *The Disorder of Women: Democracy, Feminism, and Political Theory*. Stanford, CA: Stanford University Press.

Pescosolido, B.A. and Kronenfeld, J.J. (1995) Health, illness and healing in an uncertain era, *Journal of Health and Social Behavior*, Extra Issue: 5–33.

Peterson, P. (1999) How will America pay for the retirements of the baby boom generation?, in J.B. Williamson, D.M. Watts-Roy and E. Kingston (eds) *The Generational Equity Debate*. New York, NY: Columbia University Press.

Phillips, J., Bernard, M., Biggs, S. and Kingston, P. (2001) Retirement communities in Britain, in S. Peace and C. Holland, *Inclusive Housing in an Ageing Society*. Bristol: The Policy Press.

Phillips, J., Bernard, M. and Chittenden, M. (2002) The experience of working carers of older adults, *Joseph Rowntree Foundation Findings*, July.

Phillipson, C. (1982) *Capitalism and the Construction of Old Age*. London: Macmillan Books.

Phillipson, C. (1993) The sociology of retirement, in J. Bond, P. Coleman and S. Peace (eds) *Ageing and Society: An Introduction to Social Gerontology*. London: Sage Publications.

Phillipson, C. (1996) Interpretations of ageing, *Ageing and Society*, 16: 359–69.

Phillipson, C. (1997) Social relationships in later life: a review of research literature, *International Journal of Geriatric Psychiatry*, 12(5): 505–12.

Phillipson, C. (1998) *Reconstructing Old Age: New Agenda in Social Theory and Practice*. London: Sage Publications.

Phillipson, C. (2001) Globalization, critical gerontology and the political economy of ageing. Paper to the Gerontological Society of America, 54th Annual Meeting, Chicago, October.

Phillipson, C. (2002) *Transitions from Work to Retirement: Developing a New Social Contract*. Bristol: The Policy Press.

Phillipson, C. and Biggs, S. (1998) Modernity and identity: themes and perspectives in the study of older adults, *Journal of Aging and Identity*, 3: 11–23.

Phillipson, C. and Walker, A. (eds) (1986) *Ageing and Social Policy: A Critical Assessment*. Aldershot: Gower.

Phillipson, C., Bernard, M., Phillips, J. and Ogg, J. (2001) *The Family and Community Life of Older People: Social Support and Social Networks in Three Urban Areas*. London: Routledge.

Phillipson, C., Ahmed, N. and Latimer, J. (2003) *Women in Transition: A Study of the Experiences of Bangladeshi Women Living in Tower Hamlets*. Bristol: The Policy Press.

Pillemer, K., Moen, P., Wethington, E. and Glasgow, N. (2001) *Social Integration in the Second Half of Life*. Baltimore, MD: Johns Hopkins University Press.

Pinner, F.A., Jacobs, P. and Selznick, P. (1959) *Old Age and Political Behaviour*. Berkeley, CA: University of California Press.

Piven, F.F. and Cloward, R.A. (1997) *The Breaking of the American Social Compact*. New York: New Press distributed by Norton.

Polivka, L. (2001) Postmodern aging and the loss of meaning, *Journal of Aging and Identity*, 5(2): 225–36.

Pollack, A. (2001) Private sector cured by £30 billion public goldrush. *Observer*, 8 July.

Pollock, A. and Price, D. (2000) Rewriting the regulations: how the World Trade Organisation could accelerate privatization in health care systems, *Lancet*, 356: 1995–2000.

Porter, S. (1997) The patient and power: the politics of holistic care, *Health and Social Care in the Community*, 5(1): 17–20.

Powell, J. and Biggs, S. (2000) Managing old age: the disciplinary web of power, surveillance and normalization, *Journal of Aging and Identity*, 5 (1): 3–14.

Powell, J. and Longino, C. (2002) Embodiment and the study of aging, in V. Berdayes, *Interdisciplinary Perspectives on Embodiment*. New York, NY: Routledge.

Pratt, H.J. (1976) *The Grey Lobby*. Chicago, IL: Chicago University Press.

Pratt, H.J. (1993) *Gray Agendas: Interest Groups and Public Pensions in Canada, Britain and the United States*. Ann Arbor, MI: University of Michigan Press.

Preston, S. (1984) Children and the elderly: divergent paths for America's dependents, *Demography*, XXI: 435–57.

Price, D., Pollock, A.M. and Shaoul, J. (1999) How the World Trade Organisation is shaping domestic policy, *Lancet*, 354: 1889–92.

Quadagno, J. (1988) *Transformation of Old Age Security*. Chicago, IL: University of Chicago Press.

Quadagno, J. (1990) Race, class, and gender in the USA welfare state, *American Sociological Review*, 55(1): 11–29.

Quadagno, J. (1991) Interest-group politics and the future of USA social security, in J. Myles and J. Quadagno (eds) *States, Labour Markets and the Future of Old Age Policy*. Philadelphia, PA: Temple University Press.

Quadagno, J. (1994) *The Color of Welfare*. New York, NY: Oxford University Press.

Quadagno, J. and Reid, J. (1999) The political economy perspective of aging, in V.L. Bengtson and K.W. Schaie (eds) *Handbook of Theories of Aging*. New York, NY: Springer.

Randall, W. and Kenyon, G. (1999) *Ordinary Wisdom*. Westport, CT: Praeger.

Redclift, N. and Mingione, E. (eds) (1985) *Beyond Employment: Household, Gender, and Subsistence*. Oxford and New York, NY: Blackwell.

Relman, A. (1980) The new medical industrial complex, *New England Journal of Medicine*, 303: 963–70.

Renaud, M. (1975) On the structural constraints of state intervention in health, *International Journal of Health Services*, 5 (4): 559–71.

Rice, D.P. (1996) Medicare beneficiary profile, *Health Care Financing Review*, 18 (18): 23–46.

Riley, J.W. (1971) *Aging and Society. Vol. 3: A Sociology of Age Stratification*. New York, NY: Russell Sage Foundation.

Riley, M.W. (1998) Successful aging, *The Gerontologist*, 38 (2): 151.

Riley, M.W. and Riley, J.W. (1994a) Structural lag, in M.W. Riley, R.L. Kahn and A. Foner (eds) *Age and Structural Lag*. New York, NY: Wiley.

Riley, M.W. and Riley, J.W. (1994b) Age integration and the lives of older people, *The Gerontologist*, 34 (1): 110–15.

Riley, M.W. and Riley, J.W. (1994c) Structural lag: past and future, in M.W. Riley, R.L. Kahn and A. Foner (eds) *Age and Structural Lag: Society's Failure to Provide Meaningful Opportunities in Work, Family, and Leisure*. New York, NY: Wiley.

Riley, M.W., Johnson, M. and Foner, A. (1972) A sociology of age stratification, in M.W. Riley, A. Foner, M.E. Moore, B. Hess and B.K. Roth (eds) *Aging and Society*, Vol. 3. New York, NY: Russell Sage.

Riley, M.W., Foner, A. and Riley, J.W. Jr. (1999) The aging and society paradigm, in V.L. Bengston and K.W. Schaie (eds) *Handbook of Theories of Aging*. New York, NY: Springer.

Rix, S. (1999) The politics of old age in the United States, in A. Walker and G. Naegle (eds) (1999) *The Politics of Old Age in Europe*. Buckingham: Open University Press.

Robert, S. (1998) Community level socio-economic status effect on adult health, *Journal of Health and Social Behavior*, 39: 18–37.

Robertson, A. (1991) The politics of Alzheimer's disease, in M. Minkler and C. Estes (eds) *Critical Perspectives on Aging*. Amityville, NY: Baywood Publishing.

Robertson, A. (1999) Beyond apocalyptic demography: toward a moral economy of interdependence, in M. Minkler and C.L. Estes (eds) *Critical Gerontology: Perspectives from Political and Moral Economy*. Amityville, NY: Baywood Publishing.

Robnett, B. (1996) African American women in the civil rights movement, 1954–1965: gender, leadership and micromobilization, *American Journal of Sociology*, 101 (6): 1661–93.

Robnett, B. (1997) *How Long? How Long? African-American Women in the Struggle for Civil Rights*. New York, NY: Oxford University Press.

Rodriguez, L. (1994) Barrio women: between the urban and feminist movement, *Latin American Perspectives*, 21 (3): 32–48.

Rose, A.M. (1967) *The Power Structure*. New York, NY: Oxford University Press.

Rosow, I. (1967) *Social Integration of the Aged.* New York, NY: Free Press.

Rosow, I. (1974) *Socialization of Old Age.* Berkeley, CA: University of California Press.

Roszak, T. (1998) *America the Wise: The Longevity Revolution and the True Wealth of Nations.* New York, NY: Houghton Mifflin.

Rowe, J.W. and Kahn, R.L. (1987) Human aging: usual and successful, *Science,* 237 (4811): 143–9.

Rowe, J.W. and Kahn, R.L. (1998) *Successful Aging.* New York, NY: Pantheon Random House.

Royal Commission on the Distribution of Income and Wealth (1978) *Lower Incomes.* Report No. 6. London: HMSO.

Rubin, G. (1984) The traffic in women, in A.M. Jaggar and P.S. Rothenberg (eds) *Feminist Frameworks: Alternative Accounts of the Relations between Women and Men,* 2nd edn. New York, NY: McGraw-Hill.

Ruth, J. and Coleman, P. (1996) Personality and aging, in J. Birren and K.W. Schaie (eds) *Handbook of the Psychology of Aging,* 4th edn. New York, NY: Academic Press.

Sainsbury, D. (1996) *Gender, Equality, and Welfare States.* New York, NY: Cambridge University Press.

Sardar, Z. and Van Loon, B. (1997) *Introducing Cultural Studies.* New York, NY: Totem.

Sarvasy, W. and Siim, B. (1994) Gender, transitions to democracy, and citizenship, *Social Politics: International Studies in Gender, State and Society,* 1(3): 249–55.

Sassoon, A.S. (1987) *Women and the State: The Shifting Boundaries of Public and Private.* London: Hutchinson.

Sassoon, A.S. (1991) Equality and difference: the emergence of a new concept of citizenship, in D. McLellan and S. Sayers (eds) *Socialism and Democracy.* Basingstoke: Macmillan.

Sassoon, A.S. (2001) The space for politics: globalisation, hegemony and passive revolution, *New Political Economy,* 6(1): 5–13.

Sawchuck, K. (1995) From gloom to boom: age, identity and target marketing, in M. Featherstone and A. Wernick (eds) *Images of Ageing.* London: Routledge.

Schneider, G. and Shackelford, J. (2001) Economics standards and lists: proposed antidotes for feminist economists, *Feminist Economics,* 7(2): 77–89.

Scholte, J.A. (2000) *Globalization: A Critical Introduction.* London: Palgrave.

Schultz, J.H. (2001) Public policy ambiguity, in N. Morrow-Howell, J. Hinterlong and M. Sherraden (eds) *Productive Aging: Concepts and Challenges.* Baltimore, MD: Johns Hopkins University Press.

Sen, A. (2000) Freedom's market, *Observer,* 25 June.

Sen, G. (1980) The sexual division of labor and the working-class family: towards a conceptual synthesis of class relations and the subordination of women, *Review of Radical Political Economics,* 12 (2): 76–86.

Shaw, M. (2002) *Theory of the Global State.* Cambridge: Cambridge University Press.

Sheehey, G. (1976) *Passages.* New York, NY: HarperCollins.

Sheehey, G. (1996) *New Passages.* New York, NY: HarperCollins.

Sicker, M. (1994) The paradox of productive aging, *Aging International*, 12(2): 12–14.

Silverstein, M., Burholt, V., Wenger, C. and Bengtson, V.L. (1998) Parent–child relations among very old parents in Wales and the United States, *Journal of Aging Studies*, 12(4): 387–409.

Smith, D. (1990) *The Conceptual Practices of Power: A Feminist Sociology of Knowledge*. Boston, MA: Northeastern University Press.

Spence, D. (1992) Narrative soothing and clinical wisdom, in T. Sarbin (ed.) *Narrative Psychology*. New York, NY: Praeger.

Starr, P. (1982) *The Social Transformation of American Medicine*. New York, NY: Basic Books.

Steans, J. (2002) Global governance: a feminist perspective, in D. Held and A. McGrew, *Governing Globalization: Power, Authority and Global Governance*. Cambridge: Polity Press.

Stearns, P. (1977) *Old Age in European Society*. London: Croom Helm.

Stevens, R. (1983) Comparisons in health care: Britain as a contrast to the USA, in D. Mechanic (ed.) *Handbook of Health, Health Care and the Health Professions*. New York, NY: Free Press.

Stiglitz, J. (2002) *Globalization and its Discontents*. London: Allen Lane.

Stone, D. (2000) Why we need a care movement, *The Nation*, 13 March: 13–15.

Strange, S. (1986) *Casino Capitalism*. Oxford: Blackwell.

Strauss, R. (1957) The nature and status of medical sociology, *American Sociological Review*, 22: 200–4.

Street, D. (1996) Maintaining the status quo: the impact of old-age interest groups on the Medicate Catastrophic Care Act of 1988, in J. Quadagno and D. Street (eds) *Aging for Twenty-First Century*. New York, NY: St. Martin's Press.

Street, D. (1999) Special interests or citizens' rights? 'Senior power', social security and Medicare, in M. Minkler and C.L. Estes, *Critical Gerontology: Perspectives from Moral and Political Economy*. New York, NY: Baywood Publishing.

Street, D. and Quadagno, J. (1993) The state, the elderly, and the intergenerational contract: towards a new political economy of aging, in K. Schaie and W.A. Anchenbaum, *Societal Impact and Aging*. New York, NY: Springer Publishing.

Tabb, W.K. (1999) Labor and the imperialism of finance, *Monthly Review: An Independent Socialist Magazine*, 51(5): 1–13.

Tarabusi, C.C. and Vickery, G. (1998) Globalization in the pharmaceutical industry, Parts I and II, *International Journal of Health Services*, 28: 67–105; 281–303.

Taylor, C. (1989) *Sources of the Self*. Cambridge: Cambridge University Press.

Taylor, V. (1999) Guest Editor's introduction – special issue on gender and social movements – Part 2, *Gender and Society*, 13 (1): 5–7.

Terry, P. (1997) *Counselling the Elderly and their Carers*. London: Macmillan.

Therborn, G. (1978) *What Does the Ruling Class Do When It Rules?: State Apparatuses and State Power under Feudalism, Capitalism and Socialism*. Thetford: Lowe and Brydore.

Therborn, G. (1980) *The Ideology of Power and the Power of Ideology*. London and New York, NY: NLB, distributed in the United States by Schocken Books.

Thomas, W.I. (1970) *The Unadjusted Girl*. Santa Fe, NM: Gannor.

Thompson, E.P. (1963) *The Making of the English Working Class*. New York, NY: Vintage.

Thomson, D. (1989) The Welfare State and Generation Conflict: winners and losers, in P. Johnson, D. Conrad and D. Thomson (eds) *Workers versus Pensioners: Intergenerational Justice in an Ageing World*. Manchester: Manchester University Press in association with the Centre for Economic Policy Research.

Timmins, N. (1996) *The Five Giants: A Biography of the Welfare State*. London: Fontana.

Titmuss, R. (1993) *The Welfare State in Britain Since 1945*. London: Sage Publications.

Tobin, S. (1989) The effects of institutionalisation, in K. Markides and C. Cooper, *Aging, Stress and Health*. New York, NY: Wiley.

Tornstam, L. (1994) Gerotranscendence – a theoretical and empirical exploration, in L.E. Thomas (ed.) *Aging and the Religious Dimension*. Westport, CT: Greenwood.

Tornstam, L. (1996) Gerotranscendence: a theory about maturing into old age, *Aging and Identity*, 1(1): 37–50.

Torres, S. (2001) Understanding of successful aging in the context of migration, *Ageing and Society*, 21(3): 333–56.

Torres-Gil, F. (1993) Interest group politics: generational changes in the politics of aging, in V.L. Bengston and W.A. Achenbaum, *The Changing Contract across Generations*. New York, NY: Adeline de Gruyter.

Townsend, P. (1957) *The Family Life of Old People*. London: Routledge and Kegan Paul.

Townsend, P. (1962) *The Last Refuge*. London: Routledge and Kegan Paul.

Townsend, P. (1981) The structured dependency of the elderly: creation of social policy in the twentieth century, *Ageing and Society*, 1 (1): 5–28.

Townsend, P. (1986) Ageism and social policy, in C. Phillipson and A. Walker (eds) *Ageing and Social Policy*. Aldershot: Gower.

Townsend, P. and Wedderburn, D. (1965) *The Aged in the Welfare State*. London: Bell.

Tulle-Winton, E. (2000) Old bodies, in M. Tyler (ed.) *The Body, Culture and Society: An Introduction*. Buckingham: Open University Press.

Turner, B. (1995) Ageing and identity: some reflections on the somatisation of self, in M. Featherstone and H. Wernick (eds) *Images of Ageing*. London: Routledge.

Turner, M.J., Shields, T. and Sharp, D. (2001) Changes and continuities in the determinants of older adults' voter turnout 1952–1996, *The Gerontologist*, 41(6): 805–18.

Twaddle, A.D. (1982) From medical sociology to the sociology of health, in T. Bottomore, S. Nowak and M. Sokolowska (eds) *Sociology: The State of the Art*. Beverly Hills, CA: Sage International Sociological Association.

Twine, F. (1994) *Citizenship and Social Rights: The Interdependence of Self and Society*. London: Sage Publications.

Urry, J. (2000) *Sociology Beyond Societies*. London: Routledge.

USA Bureau of the Census (1996) *Population Projections of the USA by Age, Race, Sex and Hispanic Origin: 1995–2050*, Series P25–1130. Table F, and *65+ in the USA*, Series P23–190, Table 2–1. Washington, DC: USA Government Printing Office.

USA Bureau of the Census (1997) *Statistical Abstract of the United States 1997*. Washington, DC: USA Government Printing Office.

Usita, P.M. (2001) Selective optimization with compensation among intermarried immigrant women in mid and late life. Program abstracts, 54th Annual Scientific Meeting of the Gerontological Society of America, Chicago, October.

Vaillant, G. (1993) *The Wisdom of the Ego*. Cambridge, MA: Harvard University Press.

Vaillant, G. and Mukamal, K. (2001) Successful aging, *American Journal of Psychiatry*, 158(6): 839–47.

Vincent, J. (1995) *Inequality and Old Age*. London: UCL Press.

Vincent, J. (1999) *Politics, Power and Old Age*. Buckingham: Open University Press.

Vincent, J., Patterson, G. and Wale, K. (2001) *Politics and Old Age*. Aldershot: Ashgate Books.

Wade, R. (2001) Winners and losers, *The Economist*, 28 April: 93–7.

Waitzkin, H. and Waterman, B. (1974) *The Exploitation of Illness in Capitalist Society*. Indianapolis, IN: Bobbs-Merrill.

Walker, A. (1980) The social creation of poverty and dependency in old age, *Journal of Social Policy*, 9: 49–75.

Walker, A. (1981) Towards a political economy of old age, *Ageing and Society*, 1 (1): 73–94.

Walker, A. (1986) The politics of ageing in Britain, in C. Phillipson, M. Bernard and P. Strang (eds) *Dependency and Interdependency in Later Life – Theoretical Perspectives and Policy Alternatives*. London: Croom Helm.

Walker, A. (1991) Thatcherism and the new politics of old age, in J. Myles and J. Quadango (eds) *States, Labour Markets and the Future of Old age Policy*. Philadelphia, PA: Temple University Press.

Walker, A. (1996) *The New Generational Contract*. London: UCL Press.

Walker, A. (1998) Speaking for themselves: the new politics of old age in Europe, *Education and Aging*, 13 (1): 5–12.

Walker, A. (1999) Political participation and representation of older people in Europe, in A. Walker and G. Naegele (1999) *The Politics of Old Age in Europe*. Buckingham: Open University Press.

Walker, A. and Maltby, T. (1997) *Ageing Europe*. Buckingham: Open University Press.

Walker, A. and Naegele, G. (eds) (1999) *The Politics of Old Age in Europe*. Buckingham: Open University Press.

Wallace, S. (1990) Race versus class in health care of African-American elderly, *Social Problems*, 37 (4): 101–19.

Wallace, S. (1991) The political economy of health care for elderly blacks, in M. Minkler and C.L. Estes (eds) *Critical Perspectives on Aging*. Amityville, NY: Baywood Publishing.

Wallace, S., Enriquez-Haass, V. and Markides, K. (1998) The consequences of color-blind health policy for older racial and ethnic minorities, *Stanford Law and Policy Review*, 9 (2): 329–46.

Wallace, S.P. and Villa, V. (1997) Caught in hostile cross-fire: public policy and minority elderly in the United States, in K. Markides and M. Miranda (eds) *Minorities, Aging, and Health*. Thousand Oaks, CA: Sage.

Wallace, S.P. and Williamson, J.B. (1992) The senior movement in historical perspective, in S.P. Wallace and J.B. Williamson, *The Senior Movement*. New York, NY: G.K. Hall.

Werbner, P. (2002) *Imagined Diasporas among Manchester Muslims*. Oxford: James Currey.

Westerhof, G.J., Dittmann-Kohli, F. and Thissen, T. (2001) Beyond life satisfaction: qualitative and quantitative approaches to judgments about the quality of life, *Social Indicators Research*, 56: 179–203.

Whitfield, D. (2001) 222.centre.public.org.uk/briefings/pfi, p. 33.

WHO (World Health Organisation) (2000) Health Life Expectancy Rankings, Press Release. Geneva: WHO.

Wiegersma, N. (1991) Peasant patriarchy and the subversion of the collective in Vienam, *Review of Radical Political Economics*, 23 (3 & 4): 174–97.

Williams, A. (1988) The importance of quality of life in policy decisions, in S. Walker and R. Rosser (eds) *Quality of Life: Assessment and Application*. Boston, MA: MIT Press.

Williams, A. (1997) Intergenerational equity: an exploration of the 'fair innings' argument, *Health Economics*, 6: 117.

Williams, B. (2002) *Truth and Truthfulness: An Essay in Genealogy*. Princeton, NJ: Princeton University Press.

Williams, F. (1996) Racism and the discipline of social policy: a critique of welfare theory, in D. Taylor (ed.) *Critical Social Policy: A Reader*. Thousand Oaks, CA: Sage Publications.

Wilson, G. (1991) Models of ageing and their relation to policy information and service provision, *Policy and Politics*, 19(1): 37–47.

Woodhouse, P. and Pengelly, P. (1991) *Anxiety and the Dynamics of Collaboration*. Aberdeen: Aberdeen University Press.

Woodward, K. (1991) *Aging and its Discontents: Freud and Other Fictions*. Bloomington, IN: Indiana University Press.

Woodward, K. (1995) Tribute to the older woman, in M. Featherstone and A. Wernick (eds) *Images of Ageing*. London: Routledge.

Woolfe, R. and Biggs, S. (1998) Counselling and psychotherapy with older people: special issue, *Journal of Social Work Practice*, 12(2): 133–226.

World Bank (1994) *Averting the Old Age Crisis*. Oxford: Oxford University Press.

Yeates, N. (2001) *Globalisation and Social Policy*. London: Sage Publications.

Index

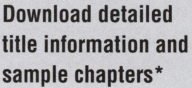